E t h . . . n
E d . . .

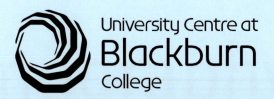
University Centre at
Blackburn
College
Telephone: 01254 292165
Please return this book on or before the last date shown

Research Methods in Education

Each book in this series maps the territory of a key research approach or topic in order to help readers progress from beginner to advanced researcher.

Each book aims to provide a definitive, market-leading overview and to present a blend of theory and practice with a critical edge. All titles in the series are written for Master's-level students anywhere and are intended to be useful to the many diverse constituencies interested in research on education and related areas.

Titles in the series:

Atkins and Wallace	*Qualitative Research in Education*
Hamilton and Corbett-Whittier	*Using Case Study in Education Research*
McAteer	*Action Research in Education*
Mills and Morton	*Ethnography in Education*

Access the additional resources here: http://www.sagepub.co.uk/beraseries.sp

BRITISH EDUCATIONAL RESEARCH ASSOCIATION

Los Angeles | London | New Delhi
Singapore | Washington DC

Ethnography in Education

David Mills & Missy Morton

Los Angeles | London | New Delhi
Singapore | Washington DC

Los Angeles | London | New Delhi
Singapore | Washington DC

SAGE Publications Ltd
1 Oliver's Yard
55 City Road
London EC1Y 1SP

SAGE Publications Inc.
2455 Teller Road
Thousand Oaks, California 91320

SAGE Publications India Pvt Ltd
B 1/I 1 Mohan Cooperative Industrial Area
Mathura Road
New Delhi 110 044

SAGE Publications Asia-Pacific Pte Ltd
3 Church Street
#10-04 Samsung Hub
Singapore 049483

Editor: Marianne Lagrange
Assistant editor: Kathryn Bromwich
Production editor: Nicola Marshall
Copyeditor: Neil Dowden
Proofreader: Emily Ayers
Indexer: Author
Marketing manager: Catherine Slinn
Cover design: Wendy Scott
Typeset by: C&M Digitals (P) Ltd, Chennai, India
Printed in India at Replika Press Pvt Ltd

First published 2013

British Educational Research Association, 9–11 Endsleigh Gardens, London, WCIH OED

Library of Congress Control Number: 2012930229

British Library Cataloguing in Publication data

A catalogue record for this book is available from the British Library

ISBN 978-1-4462-0326-2
ISBN 978-1-4462-0327-9 (pbk)

CONTENTS

ACKNOWLEDGEMENTS

This book began life as a conversation about the demands and rewards of teaching ethnographic methods within Education. As we compared notes, we realised that we had rather different approaches to ethnographic research, and that these were grounded in our own training and apprenticeship.

Teachers of research methods take for granted their local academic cultures and disciplinary world-views. Whilst both of us are committed to the value of ethnographic approaches for studying education, we agreed that our students would benefit from a book that helped them understand, appreciate and respect these epistemological differences.

In 2011 a series of devastating earthquakes hit Christchurch in New Zealand, causing huge disruptions to university life. Amidst the many aftershocks and slow reconstruction, Missy was unable to contribute to the writing of this book as she had originally intended. Instead she drew on her work with professional educators in New Zealand to offer the two teaching case studies discussed in the Conclusion. The book remains inspired by our original conversation and our commitment to methodological empathy between academic cultures and ethnographic traditions.

We wish to thank students and colleagues at the Department of Education in Oxford and the School of Educational Studies and Leadership in New Zealand. Particular thanks go to Patrick Alexander, Richard Ratcliffe, Nick Hopwood, Ingrid Lunt, Bernadette Macartney, Annie Guerin, Alis Oancea and Amy Stambach.

This book has been stimulated by friendly disagreements with Geoffrey Walford, Sara Delamont and Paul Atkinson, and we are grateful for their forbearance!

ABOUT THE AUTHORS

Dr David Mills is a University Lecturer in the Department of Education, University of Oxford. He also holds a Fellowship at Kellogg College. Trained in Anthropology, he is the author of *Difficult Folk: A political history of Social Anthropology* (Berghahn, 2008).

Dr Missy Morton is Associate Professor and Head of School of Educational Studies and Leadership, College of Education, University of Canterbury. Her research and teaching areas include qualitative research and Disability Studies in Education. She is particularly interested in using ethnography to understand curriculum, pedagogy and assessment.

INTRODUCTION:

SCHOOLING THE IMAGINATION

What is in this chapter?

- An introduction to ethnographic writing and its many strengths
- A brief explanation of why we have written this book
- A discussion of ethnography for/in/of/and education
- Some advice on how best to learn and develop ethnographic skills
- A vision for empathy as an ethnographic principle
- A guide to the structure of this book

Ethnography: being, seeing, writing

Being, seeing, writing. Simple participles that belie the complexity of their meanings. This book introduces the interwoven practices of methodological being, 'ways of seeing' (Berger 1972) and genres of writing that mark out the best ethnographic work in education. Whether encountering ethnography for the first time, using ethnographic methods in your own research, or exploring the diversity of approaches that trade under the 'Ethnography' label, this book is for you. It interprets 'education' in a broad sense to include learning in both formal and informal settings, and offer an up-to-date and comprehensive overview of ethnographic research practices in Education. We show how different intellectual fields and traditions understand and use ethnography, and demonstrate its evolving strengths and contributions.

We see an ethnographic sensibility as offering the researcher and the reader unique insights into the educational worlds in which we all now live and into which we invest our hopes, desires and aspirations. These are worlds in which pedagogic policies, institutional discourses and individual ideals are increasingly mobile and dynamic. Previous educational certainties – state versus private, academic versus vocational, policy versus practice – are being replaced by complexity, ambiguity and fluidity. Ethnography provides a way of following these changes, and of communicating the stories that matter.

We live in self-reflexive times. We can no longer pretend that our research personae are separate from the places and contexts we seek to understand. Methods play a role in making the worlds we inhabit. Our insights get appropriated, reworked and transformed: they go places and become part of the messy realities of social life. Scholarly knowledge is never innocent or pure – it always comes with baggage. This is not necessarily a problem. Most ethnographers have thought about the way they shape the story they tell, and paid close attention to the way in which they, and their ideas, become part of the social world they study. This is particularly visible in the marked transformations in the genre over the last two or three decades, and in the way today's ethnographic narratives are crafted.

Education is a peculiar thing. Most people have had deep and lasting encounters with formal schooling and the way it disciplines the imagination and shapes bodies and emotions. But even if we can tell heartfelt tales of our own schooling, this doesn't make us all ethnographers. The ethnographer's challenge is to weave the immediacy and rawness of educational experiences into a context from which analytical patterns and insights can be discerned. The ethnographer uses literary genres – stories, vignettes and portraits – as part of this process. These stories are ethnographic narratives rather than raw retellings. They convey the vitality of those experiences within a framing that allows the reader to make connections and comparisons. If education is always risky, always unsettling, then ethnography is the perfect method to capture its dynamism and power.

No matter how intense these lived experiences, they can only be communicated through writing. This is the paradox that sustains the ethnographic project. We go as far as to suggest that there is no other method in which writing is such an integral aspect to the method. As Clifford Geertz, one of America's most celebrated anthropologists, once quipped, 'I think of myself as a writer who happens to be doing his writing in

Anthropology' (1991, 246). A century ago the term *ethnography* – literally writing the people – was the term adopted by anthropologists in the British Empire to describe a revolutionary new way of doing research, working with and living amongst one's 'informants'. Soon afterwards the term also became popular in American Sociology to describe fine-grained empirical studies of urban communities, a tradition that started at the University of Chicago. Ethnographic methods matured and developed within these national traditions of Anthropology and Sociology that developed during the twentieth century in Europe and North America.

Today ethnography comes in a variety of flavours. No longer solely the preserve of its original 'home' disciplines, it has developed distinctive brews across and beyond the social sciences. Even within Education, scholars mean rather different things when they use the term. Some see it as a deeply humanistic endeavour, creating knowledge through the everyday exchanges and dialogues of social life. Others define it in a more scientific way, seeing it as offering a rigorous and empiricist research method. Others take a more explicitly activist stance, defining ethnography in political terms, using it to imagine research that is less hierarchical and exploitative. Some see ethnography's strength as its focus on people and lived experiences in schools and classrooms, whilst others use ethnographic approaches to study educational texts, policies, discourses, ideas and ideologies. The method has gone 'viral' beyond the university, and many companies now employ 'ethnographers' to do research or to inform their design processes. Popular representations and caricatures of ethnographic practice increasingly crop up in TV reality shows and everyday cultures, to the extent that one could feasibly claim that 'we're all ethnographers now'. This book conveys this rich smorgasbord of ethnographic traditions and understandings.

Three ethnographic principles

We want to encourage the reader to experiment with different types of ethnographic practice and writing. But we also stake out our own epistemological positions. Three broad principles orient our approach to ethnography. The first is that we view ethnography as a way of being, seeing, thinking and writing. For us, it is not just another 'tool' or method for social research, but rather a way of thinking about social research that brings together a range of methods under a shared disposition. Far from 'switching off' at the end of the day or after an interview, some scholars feel that the ethnographic 'habit' defines their whole persona.

So what is an ethnographic habit or disposition? Our second principle is that ethnographic work should aim to be an 'uncomfortable science' (Firth 1951), an approach to research that is a little unconventional, a little exposed. The first colonial anthropologists who left their shady verandahs and cosy library armchairs to live and work with people would have felt this discomfort. For many ethnographers, the key protagonist of this vision was Bronislaw Malinowski. His stylishly written account of a complex exchange ritual in the South Pacific Trobriand Islands, entitled 'Argonauts of the Western Pacific' (1922), was written during an enforced extended sojourn during the First World War. His choice to put up a tent in the middle of a local village symbolised for him the best way to capture 'the imponderabilia of everyday life'. An avowed self-publicist, his catchily titled monographs popularised the ethnographic method. Much later on, the posthumous publication of his diary (Malinowski 1967) revealed his loneliness, neuroses and prejudices.

His struggles with his own inner worlds highlight the emotional dislocation that accompanies any social research that strives towards subjective understanding. There is a German philosophical tradition that asks whether and how one can best understand (*verstehen*) the subjective experience of others. At around the same time the sociologist Max Weber was writing about this aspiration to communicate meaning: he and Malinowski were near contemporaries. A century later, the question remains. Is it possible to be deeply and fully immersed in a situation and at the same time to stand back and make sense of it? As an influential feminist philosopher of science notes, 'ethnography is not so much a specific procedure in anthropology as it is a method of being at risk in the face of the practices and discourses into which one inquires' (Haraway 1999, 190). For us, being 'at risk' means being exposed to the profound complexities of the social and educational worlds of which ethnographic researchers are a part. It involves questioning the things others take for granted, making the familiar strange, not jumping to conclusions. But don't we all aspire to these virtues? In an age where emotional intelligence and self-insight are marketable social attributes, delineating what makes for a distinctively *ethnographic* approach to being reflective (or what is now called reflexivity) is tricky.

This leads us to our third principle – that ethnography demands empathy. If ethnography is an approach to scholarship that puts one emotionally at risk, then it also involves empathy, understood as the ability to understand and be attentive to the feelings of another on their terms. This does not mean condoning or seeking to justify political positions that one finds disagreeable or even irrational. It simply involves recognising that this tension exists. Creating ethnographic knowledge through empathetic dialogue, exchange and collaboration is hard work. It brings emotional and intellectual risks but can also be accompanied by profound insights. We return to our understanding of ethnographic empathy in the chapters that follow. It underscores our argument that ethnography is an embodied practice that uses all our senses and emotional sensibilities.

The remainder of this introduction begins this task of helping students navigate their way in a complex and changing scholarly landscape. We reveal more about our own initiation into this field, reflect on the best way to learn ethnographic skills, and think further about the relationship between ethnography and education.

Ethnography 'in', 'of', 'and' or 'for' Education?

Who remembers their first day of school? One's first encounters – and the tastes and smells that went with it – tend to be etched on most people's memory. David's first day of ethnographic research in a Ugandan secondary school was no different, as this ethnographic vignette seeks to capture:

> Across Uganda the first Monday of each February ... pupils who have received the results of the nation-wide Primary Leaving Exam (PLE) arrive at secondary schools in freshly-starched bewilderment. The school year at Kikomera Senior Secondary School (SSS), a school in a small town 50 miles north of Kampala, may have already begun, but it is an apprehensive first day for the new Standard One pupils, and their new English teacher – me. I've had more than my fair share of first days, but am still nervous, for lesson plans and homework marking have been timetabled to clash with double ethnographic diary-writing. The new students might well have arrived to enrol with the requisite 12 exercise books plus hoe; but I clutch my wittily perceptive letter of permission from the District Education Officer to the Headmaster. 'He would like to teach in your school to familiarise himself with the cultural set up – please timetable him.' (Mills 1999a, 3)

This vignette, taken from an article based on first fieldwork experiences, seeks to capture the influence of first impressions of a Ugandan school. It situates the ethnographer and the reader within the research, whilst also introducing the school that acts as the case study for the account. Drawing together a range of different fieldnotes and materials, this passage was rewritten and condensed many times in the months that followed field research. The passage sought to leaven strangeness with familiarity, to find a way of changing scale. The ambition was to find a way to knot together experiences of national policies, district governance and everyday educational practices within the school. The aim was taut, analytically vivid and readable insights that mark out good ethnographic writing. The role of the writer is to help the reader quickly locate and understand his role in the school and in the text, but also to convey the expectations and implications of the 'high-stakes' academic assessment system that dominates Ugandan education. There is also a hint of the material expectations placed upon students. This later develops into a discussion of school fees and teacher salaries. There is much left unsaid in this short passage. Yet there is also a glimpse of the 'ethnographic imagination' at work, one guided and informed by more than a year spent living and working at the school, teaching, attending staff-meetings and hanging out with other teachers.

Ethnographic vignettes, interspersed with analysis and theory, are one way for ethnographers to write about education. But there are other ethnographies of education, and other possible relationships. A feminist researcher interested in gender production in the playground is going to adopt different research methods, and have different findings, from a teacher-practitioner ethnographer interested in the identities of trainee teachers. These will differ again from a critical ethnographic account of audit culture and higher education policy. Not all ethnographers will want or need to present a holistic picture of a school or university, or wish to link what happens within an institution to larger social processes. Linguistic anthropologists might be interested primarily in classroom talk and language turn-taking, or perhaps an analysis of discourse in the special-needs classroom. Some will be highly critical of educational processes, whilst others will be seeking to improve them. Ethnographies of French schools may have little relevance for studying universities in Uganda. Each has its place. Rather than try and encompass the whole diverse field of 'ethnography and education', the onus is on the researcher is to develop a sense of different histories of ethnographic practice, and to map their own vision of the key literature and central debates in relation to the topic under investigation.

Education is a generative site for ethnographic research. It is also a place in which ethnography can be put to work, as the last chapter of this book demonstrates. Drawing on a range of examples we encourage you to think about how you might use ethnographic methods and insights in your own everyday teaching or professional practice. Every ethnography *of* education also has insights *for* educators. Most ethnographers are also teachers, and so are able to put their insights to use *in* education and in their teaching practices. The final chapter demonstrates how ethnographers put their skills and research insights to work in a variety of different ways within educational settings.

About the authors

This book is a product of our own experiences of encountering and learning about ethnography. We both 'discovered' ethnographic writing as undergraduates, carried out ethnographic research for our doctorate, and remain passionate about the method and its potential. But we still puzzle over how best to teach and communicate ethnographic practice. Through our own writing, we have developed our own ethnographic imagination, and see it as informing our approach to research. We have gone on to teach ethnographic methods and to supervise research students who use these methods to investigate educational questions.

Writing a textbook makes one think about the books that formed one's own thinking. Reflecting on our own training, we began to appreciate the different national and disciplinary methodological traditions within which ethnography is sustained and communicated. For Missy, studying qualitative research in Education in the US, her entrée into ethnographic work was via the sociological training of Robert Bogdan and Sari Knopp Biklen (1992, 2007). Brought up in the Chicago sociological tradition, her training involved reading a wide range of ethnographic monographs and carrying out a range of structured ethnographic observations. This was coupled with detailed feedback on her fieldnotes and analytical memos, as well as careful discussion of initial attempts at analysis. This careful attention to one's daily ethnographic chores is often overlooked. One contribution of this volume is to draw attention to these techniques and skills.

For David, studying Anthropology in the UK, there was relatively little formal methods training. The Malinowskian founding myth meant that the ethnographic method was largely taken for granted. In retrospect, this became a potentially noxious pedagogic brew of intellectual confidence and methodological vagueness. The focus of his teachers was on communicating disciplinary and regional traditions (Fardon 1990) of ethnographic writing, on absorbing the exemplars of anthropological elders, and on anticipating the vagaries and uncertainties of fieldwork. With his fellow students, he was more concerned about the implications of postmodern and postcolonial theory for the very survival of the anthropological project. These debates seemed to profoundly question the nature of anthropological authority and the very possibility of reliable ethnographic representation (Clifford and Marcus 1986; Clifford

1988). The academic foundations of anthropology seemed increasingly insecure, and many students developed severe cases of ethnographic angst and writer's block. They wondered what accidents of history and privilege gave them the right to represent and make truth claims about social worlds very different from their own. The debates have moved on. Most ethnographers now acknowledge that the politics of representation are complex and unavoidable, and tackling them is an integral step on one's methodological journey.

Each pedagogy, if one can call them that, had its strengths and weaknesses. This book is an opportunity to learn from those experiences and to provide the guidebook we might have wished for on our own ethnographic journey. As a student, one only dimly understands the politics and practicalities of knowledge production. Why were there such different disciplinary embodiments and understandings of the ethnographic method? Why do teachers either shy away from teaching (and even talking about) methods, or talk about them endlessly? More than a decade later, the theoretical and methodological literature on ethnographic research has burgeoned, but the disagreements persist. Some feel that too much attention to method is a distraction, some that we need to pay more attention. This book will guide you through these debates, suggesting that these differences and conflicts offer highly productive entrées into the issues that matter. It points you to the very best ethnographic writing and contemporary resources, as well as offering key critical tools.

Can I be taught ethnography?

How does one learn the skills of ethnographic research? Can one even be taught such skills? Some anthropological ethnographers continue to argue that methods courses and textbooks risk imposing a one-size-fits-all approach, downplaying the contingencies, uncertainties and anxieties that stimulate the ethnographic imagination. Instead, they would say, one learns by example, through reading, listening and writing. An influential advocate of methodological reform, George Marcus (2009, 3) suggests that anthropology is 'less a matter of training in method' than of participating in a 'culture of craftsmanship'. Rather than focus on training, Marcus calls for 'method' to be rethought at an epistemological level, and for us to pay more attention to changing our 'metamethods', namely 'the norms of professional culture that shape the actual form of research' (ibid., 4).

It is an appealing if somewhat elitist vision. Not every budding ethnographer can benefit from the heady atmospheres of departments grounded in sociological and anthropological research traditions. Not every student can absorb the wisdom of the elders through intellectual apprenticeships. Those studying and teaching in Education departments have to make the case for ethnography amidst competing intellectual paradigms. When these rivals coolly insist that quantitative 'evidence', 'generalisability' and statistical 'significance' are key, becoming an ethnographer can feel like a retreat into unscientific generalisations and subjectivity. How does one respond to what feels like the unanswerable question: 'Is your work representative?'

A response is required. In the UK, a close-knit community of educational ethnographers have advocated a robust and explicit empiricism. The best-selling textbook by Martyn Hammersley and Paul Atkinson, now in its third edition (1983, 1995, 2007), has done a great deal to promote this version of ethnography. Whilst acknowledging the iterative, uncertain nature of ethnography, they nonetheless adopt a didactic approach to social research, foregrounding rigour, process and accountability. In his provocatively titled *What's Wrong with Ethnography?*, Hammersley makes the case that the goals of ethnographic analysis need rethinking (1992, 28). In Chapter 2 we discuss Hammersley and Atkinson's influential manifesto further. Vexed by the way that anthropological monographs seem to ignore questions of method, they insist on the importance of thinking about research design at every stage of a project.

A problem facing any methods text is that books have beginnings and ends. Their linear structure neatly lulls the unsuspecting reader into thinking that research potentially could proceed in a similarly straightforward fashion. One starts with a research question, develops a research design and then proceeds to 'collect' and analyse one's 'data'. But what if your experience of ethnographic fieldwork not only forces reflection, but leads you to rethink the very research question and design? Can one ever be prescriptive about a method that depends so much on how the researcher responds to the world in which they find themselves?

The answer to whether one can be taught ethnography depends on how one understands teaching. We seek to find a middle way between the extremes of a 'sink or swim' pedagogy and methodological prescriptivism. We draw on our own experiences of learning and unlearning to make the case for developing one's ethnographic imagination and an empathy for these different traditions. To help our readers on this journey, we do this through extensive readings, case studies and practical exercises.

Ethnography takes time. And time can sometimes feel like a precious asset in today's educational settings and fast-changing world. Classically, anthropological fieldwork involved spending a year or more in one place. Even if this isn't always possible, this book is intended to provide something of an introduction to the intellectual 'ambience' that characterises research training in anthropology, the discipline that has arguably done most to champion ethnography, and a field whose intellectual currency remains the full-length monograph. One 'short cut' is to spend time reading some of these classic texts, and we feel strongly that students should read and critically assess a range of educational ethnographic monographs. To help you, this book offers annotated further readings and resources at the end of each chapter, including introductory methods texts and region-focused texts that you might not otherwise encounter.

What sort of ethnographer are you?

How much influence do you have over the epistemological assumptions that inform your work? If you are a student, it may be less than you think. Academic departments are often grounded in a shared intellectual tradition and set of methodological expectations. You may not fully realise what these assumptions are. Even if you do, it is hard to reject the advice of others or doggedly insist that you can plough your own furrow. It is equally challenging to argue for a form of activist ethnography in a department that has historically been suspicious of action research. Or to pursue participatory research in a department that is used to observational approaches. Working in a field involves being 'disciplined' within that field's intellectual tradition. The key to working creatively within these constraints is to understand as much as possible about the tradition in which you find yourself, and why seniors, supervisors and colleagues in your 'epistemic community' (Knorr-Cetina 1999) take and defend the views they do.

Much like moving house, arriving in a new academic department as a student involves getting to know the neighbours. You will want to make sense of this new intellectual 'home'. A good way of doing this is by finding out more about the institutional and intellectual history of the place. If there is an ethnographic tradition, what part has it played in the history of the department? Who have been its key protagonists? Which work is repeatedly re-read and cited? Who are its key influences and what have they published? This 'locality work' is particularly important for those studying within a multidisciplinary field like Education. Look out too for points of disagreement: not everyone will have the same views about writing in the first person, or using ethnographic portraits. It may soon become clear that there is not one 'approved' way to do ethnographic research. Providing one can justify one's approach, there may indeed be space to innovate and be creative in your approach and writing.

Can one be too explicit about method? If anthropologists have taken their method for granted, is it equally possible to spend too much time accounting for one's methodological choices? Textbooks, even this one, risk encouraging what the influential Harvard psychologist Gordon Allport disparaged as 'methodolatry', the replacement of 'big questions' by 'neat little studies'. More recently, Denzin and Lincoln defined methodolatry as 'a preoccupation with selecting and defending methods to the exclusion of the actual substance of the story being told' (Denzin and Lincoln 2005, 48).

It is important not to put the methodological cart before the interpretive horse. Academics specialise in specialisation. It is all too easy to become overly focused on getting one's chosen method 'just right'. At worst, your method becomes more important than the question you seek to understand. This can lead to 'methods' becoming a field of disciplinary expertise in itself, with its own journals and debates, semi-detached from substantive concerns. Does this matter? A potential risk is that it promotes methodologically accountable but ultimately unimaginative research. Remember to think about method as a reflective space in which to reflect on your research dilemmas, not as a set of rules or directions to be followed. This is all the more important when the object of ethnographic study is difficult to define. As Law comments in *After Method*, 'while standard methods are often extremely good at what they do, they are badly adapted to the study of the ephemeral, the indefinite and the irregular' (2004, 3). One could not get a better description of the stuff worthy of ethnographic pursuit. It is a reminder that the ethnographic imagination is hard to standardise.

What's special about this book?

This book sits on a library bookshelf or catalogue surrounded by others with similar names and themes. But what if didactic ethnographic methods textbooks are part of the problem, rather than part of the solution? Can they ever communicate what the best anthropological ethnographies so convincingly achieve, namely the power of writing to connect the representation of social experience with scholarly analysis? Many of these books argue the case for 'their' way of doing ethnographic research, privileging one version of its history or methodological approach. As Neve and Unnithan-Kumar note, 'there is never just one answer to an ethnographic exploration, never only one way of interpreting ethnographic data, and never just one way of being an anthropologist' (2006, 19). We tend to agree.

Does it matter that there may be as many ways of being ethnographic as there are ethnographers? We suggest not. Perhaps there can never be one 'right' way when the method is partly defined by the embodied practice of the ethnographer themselves. It is a way of thinking about social research that brings together a range of methods under a shared disposition towards the world. Ethnographers can do more to help readers understand 'their' version by demonstrating its links to particular disciplinary traditions and approaches. *Ethnography in Education* will introduce you to the range of such approaches – and their epistemologies – used to study Education, as well as the core differences that divide scholars. As anthropological debates about fieldwork practice and method are little known in many Education departments, we make a point of highlighting the early – and ongoing – contribution of anthropological ideas to ethnographic debates.

Ethnographic researchers employ a range of methods, from textual analysis to basic quantitative approaches. It is not just 'deep hanging out' (Geertz 1998). Nor is it 'just' the study of culture. They may well decide to count things, to carry out interviews, to analyse documents, even to conduct surveys. Today they are as likely to study social networks, transnational political movements, intergovernmental policies, or new knowledge assemblages – from genes to financial markets. Despite the mythology of the fearless 'lone ethnographer' (see Galman 2007), they are unlikely to work alone. They actively create shared knowledge with their research participants and collaborate in multidisciplinary teams. In a 'knowledge economy' full of symbolic analysts, some seek to do analytical work with their participants. Others are committed activists and see research as a political act. There is almost no limit to the possibilities that the method opens up.

In Education, the best ethnographies conjure up vivid and lively descriptions of classroom and school dynamics. They bring places and people alive for the readers in other places and times. Yet much of what determines the shape of learning lies far outside the classroom. There are a whole range of ethnographic writing genres that tend not to be discussed in textbooks, and the act of writing is something we return to again and again.

For all the common interests, there are also marked differences amongst scholars in their understandings of ethnography. Where do these disagreements lie? There are three big unspoken disagreements, each of which has implications for the design and practice of ethnographic research. The first is how ethnographers understand the relationship between observation and participation. Some traditions prioritise detached systematic observation; others feel embodied participation is key. The second disagreement is over how one conceptualises the ethnographic 'field' and one's relationship to it. Is the field a bounded physical site, a set of social relationships, or a conceptual and metaphorical space? The final difference is in how scholars relate to the method at an embodied, emotional level. Some, especially anthropological ethnographers, feel so attached to ethnographic ways of seeing and being that these become an existential part of their academic (and even non-academic) identity. Others are much less emotionally attached to the method, and are more pragmatic, treating ethnography as another tool in their methodological tool-box. As these divisions cut to the heart of ethnographic research design, we discuss them at length in Chapters 2 and 3.

Where does this book stand? Whilst wary of romanticising the ethnographic persona, there is an intellectual coherence to seeing ethnographic techniques, writing and analysis as intimately connected. Paul Willis writes about the importance of cultivating an 'ethnographic imagination', a view we share. Writing is the key to bringing this imagination to life, to making analytical sense of experience. We return repeatedly to the importance of imaginative and accessible writing – in a range of genres – for communicating ethnographic insights.

Ethnographic empathy

Imagine being invited to a party where you know no one. One has to feel brave to enter a room full of strangers and strike up a rewarding conversation. It is much more fun to share an in-joke with one's peers and friends. Ethnographers are no different, even if anthropology has long made a virtue of engaging with radically different ways of knowing and being. Difference emerges in unexpected moments. In Britain for example, middle-class researchers can find it hard to understand working-class attitudes to education, as Gillian Evans describes in her puzzlement over attitudes to what she saw as 'educational failure' in south London (2007). By the same token, it is easier to read and engage with work that shares one's intellectual tastes than to work at understanding very different disciplinary presuppositions. Even small communities of ethnographers can talk past each other.

In response, the book makes the case for what we call 'methodological empathy'. Even though Geertz famously questioned the possibility of 'inner correspondence of spirit with your informants' (Geertz 1974, 29), the ambition to gain subjective understanding or *verstehen* continues to motivate most ethnographic work, and remains an implicit aspect of participant-observation or 'insider' research.

But *verstehen* needs to be repatriated to the academy. Academics often spend too little time understanding each other. Universities are full of artefactual disputes and intellectual bunkers. Part of our purpose is to argue for greater methodological and epistemological empathy between ethnographers of different stripes.

Some, especially in an American tradition of cultural anthropology, have championed cultural relativism as a necessary methodological tool. A strong relativist position presumes the independent existence of moral worlds where very different standards apply. This is analytically questionable, and one can quickly get tied up in ethical knots. All ethical and moral positions are contingent, located in particular contexts. Less absolutist positions are more useful. These include what can be called 'methodological relativism', the art of what we call 'wilful ingenuousness and the momentary suspension of disbelief' (Mills 2003, 31) in understanding other ways of being in the world. This 'momentary' relativism can be invaluable at certain reflective moments of fieldwork, a useful counterweight to snap judgements and hurried reactions.

Ethnographers are unlikely to cultivate a relativism about their methodological choices. However, an empathetic approach to understanding the reasons for why other scholars make different epistemological presumptions and use contrasting toolkits is a vital aspect of scholarship. This idea of methodological empathy is one we develop in subsequent chapters.

How is this book organised?

The book begins and ends with a discussion of ethnographic writing. This emphasis on writing is deliberate. Whilst the book goes on to discuss 'performative ethnographies' and the role of visual media, it is primarily through writing that ethnographers think, organise and communicate ethnographic experience and analysis. The remaining chapters tackle aspects of ethnographic research that are the subject of ongoing debate, that deserve particular thought and care, or have been neglected in existing texts. These include developing an understanding of the ways ethnographers conceive of research design (Chapter 2), the different meanings they give to the 'field', fieldwork and their research relationship (Chapter 3), how they take fieldnotes and analyse them (Chapter 4), new spaces and ethnographic approaches (Chapter 5), how scholars bring together theory and ethnography in their analysis and writing (Chapter 6), and ways in which ethnographers are doing research differently (Chapter 7). Chapter 8 comes back to writing, exploring the range of writing practices that ethnographers engage in and innovative ways of taking ethnography to broader audiences. The Conclusion takes up the question of how to use your ethnographic experiences, and cultivate an ethnographic sensibility, in your own professional practice. Each chapter also offers an in-depth reading of one or more educational ethnographies to illustrate its themes.

There are some things this book does not do. It does not aspire to be a self-contained 'how-to' handbook. Nor does it discuss the practical aspects of the methods that one might use as part of one's ethnographic research. Where there are already excellent guides to research interviewing, participant-observation, life history or documentary analysis, there is little point in repeating their insights. The book offers annotated reviews of relevant further reading at the end of each chapter, intended to point you to the best of this work. There is also a huge range of resources available online and in the journals; again, these are highlighted and reviewed. Like the best guidebooks, the aim is to take the reader to interesting and stimulating places. It is then up to you what you do there.

There are several aspects of this book that are novel. One is the careful discussion of extracts of ethnographic writing, along with examples of exemplary educational ethnographies. More importantly, this book is designed to complement rather than repeat the insights offered in existing guidebooks to ethnographic research, focusing primarily on issues that many of these books tend to ignore. Third, the book offers a critical evaluation – and appreciation - of seemingly new ways of thinking about and conducting ethnographic research, especially those that require full use of all our senses. Finally, we aim to help the reader prepare for the ethical questions that accompany ethnographic practice. In every chapter we seek to provide practical research advice as well as vignettes and case studies.

Conclusion: schooling the ethnographic imagination

During two years spent carrying out research in Uganda, David became increasingly curious about the moral hierarchies that the students and teachers in a rural school created around education. As he wrote in an article published shortly afterwards: 'Why is Kikomera SSS described – somewhat dismissively – by its teachers as a "Third World" school, despite contemporary national discourses and state practices viewing education as the key path to "development" and "modernization"'? (Mills 1999a, 14). Was it a well-developed sense of irony or incisive sociological insight that led the teachers to label the well-resourced urban schools as 'First World'? What were the consequences for students and teachers at Kikomera? Was it ever possible to feel successful or rewarded in such contexts? Education creates moral worlds that at once liberate and constrain.

Across the world, education is now all about the struggle to make one's aspirations and desires real. Ethnography is the ideal way to access and describe these possibilities and the institutional structures that get built around them. But schooling one's ethnographic imagination takes time. Along the way there is much to read, lots to learn and many mistakes to make.

Don't be too ambitious. Remember that whilst writing is a powerful form of communication, it can never fully encompass experience. In ever more complex systems and social worlds, we have to strive to find new and creative ways to capture this experience, even where words fail us. As John Berger noted, 'it is seeing which establishes our place in the surrounding world; we explain that world with words, but words can never undo the fact that we are surrounded by it' (1972, 7). The book returns repeatedly to questions of how to read and how to write. There is no easy shortcut to developing one's own ethnographic voice.

It is best to think of your own research experiences and attempts at ethnographic writing as a stage on this journey into a fascinating intellectual tradition. It is a journey best carried out with fellow travellers, as sources of feedback, critique and support. *Ethnography in Education* is much more than a 'how-to' textbook. It is a guidebook for a journey through different ethnographic traditions, and the intense loyalties they generate around 'their' methods and approaches. The chapters are full of insights into the rich diversity of ethnographic practices, leavened with methodological empathy and political sensitivity. This book, with all its resources, is intended to accompany you en route. If this book helps to school, discipline and focus your 'ethnographic imagination' (Willis 2000), it will have served its purpose.

Exercises

- Find out more about the research training that your own supervisors or teachers received, and how they now view and remember this training. They might be willing to be interviewed about this topic. This would be an excellent way to learn interviewing skills, and would help you understand the disciplinary socialisation they received as new researchers.

- Write a short (1000-word) portrait of your own personal educational journey to this point. Try to be as frank and honest as possible. Pay particular attention to critical events and significant moments, describing how these have shaped your intellectual likes and dislikes. Compare these with colleagues. Then explore the following questions:

  o Why and how do your accounts differ?

  o How much have you emphasised the role of family, friends and institutions?

  o How have you portrayed your own agency in this story?

  o How does it feel to be critically honest about one's desire and hopes?

  o To what extent does the account seek to theorise these experiences?

By doing this, you will quickly see how ethnographic writing can be very personal, and why people's own experiences are integral to the ethnographies they produce.

Readings and resources

Each chapter in this volume provides an annotated bibliography for further reading and thematic exploration. To complement the introductory chapter, we offer a more extended set of general readings and resources. We begin with four recently published introductions to ethnographic work, all of which combine a fresh and innovative approach with thoughtful reflections. We go on to suggest core reference texts and a range of web-based resources.

Galman, S. C. (2007). *Shane the Lone Ethnographer*. Lanham, Md., AltaMira Press.

Whimsical, amusing and instructive, this is the first (and only?) introduction to ethnography written in the style of a cowboy comic. Sally Galman is an anthropologist based in a School of Education, and her witty drawings of Shane's first ethnographic adventure perfectly capture the highs and lows of social research. Behind the jokey style, there is lots of sensible advice for those doing ethnographic research in educational settings for the first time. Whilst written for a US context, it is the perfect leaven to the more dour methods texts in the field of Education. Occasionally a little didactic, but mostly a great read.

Madden, R. (2010). *Being ethnographic: A Guide to the Theory and Practice of Ethnography*. Los Angeles; London, Sage.

A thoughtful and articulate explication of ethnography from an Australian anthropologist who admits to never having 'made much of the distinction between qualitative sociology and anthropology'. As a result, Madden has written one of the few guides that combines an attention to both 'thinking about' and doing ethnography. Attentive to ethnography's different histories, Madden is at home discussing ethnographic classics and contemporary debates, and the book leavens practical research advice with reflective asides about his own research on the Aboriginal community in his home town. His aim is to 'articulate "doing" and "thinking" into a logical whole', an approach that Madden calls 'being ethnographic'. It is an appealing and coherent vision, and is perhaps the best single-volume introduction to ethnography. The book is complemented by an up-to-date list of selected readings.

Murchison, J. M. (2010). *Ethnography Essentials: Designing, Conducting, and Presenting Your Research*. San Francisco, Jossey-Bass.

A comprehensive, accessible and straightforward beginner's guide to ethnographic research, Murchison draws on his Tanzanian anthropological research experience to guide the reader through each stage. Written in clear and didactic style, particularly useful are chapters on writing research proposals, on ethnographic maps, tables and charts, and on analysing cultural artifacts. Each chapter has learning objectives and discussion questions. The chapter sub-headings (such as 'What do I need to write down?' and 'Shall I write it down immediately?') are helpfully reassuring and sensible, if a bit 'teacherly' at some points.

O'Reilly, K. (2011). *Ethnographic Methods*. London; New York, Routledge.

This is the second edition of a measured introduction by a qualitative sociologist who has done research with the British expatriate community in Spain. Written for undergraduates, it is gently paced and encouraging, with lots of guidance on participatory research, on ethnographic interviews, focus groups and using visual materials. It also offers thoughtful readings of key theorists and a history of anthropology. She recognises that 'qualitative research is as often art as science' and admits 'I cannot tell you what to do but only what choices there are and how others have resolved various problems' (p. 4). A thoughtful and sympathetic guide, somewhat less didactic than Murchison.

Recommended reference texts

Anderson-Levitt, K. M., (ed) (2011). *Anthropologies of education: A Global Guide to Ethnographic Studies of Learning and Schooling*. Oxford, Berghahn.

This is less of an introductory handbook than a chapter-by-chapter review of different national histories of ethnographic research of Education. It usefully highlights European debates and other traditions beyond the Anglophone world of the US and the UK. A good way to situate one's work in relation to these national debates.

Atkinson, P., Delamont, S., Coffey, A., Lofland, J. and Lofland, L. (eds) (2007). *Handbook of Ethnography*. London, Sage.

If you are in need of a compendious bible and reference source on all matters ethnographic, then look no further. This authoritative five-hundred page handbook has thirty-three well-written chapters that weave together accounts of the different US and UK ethnographic traditions, reviews of ethnographic research in a range of substantive areas (including education) and advice on the practicalities of ethnographic research and analysis. Each chapter comes with a fulsome, if not exhaustive, bibliography. Atkinson and Delamont are also the editors of *Representing Ethnography*, an even more voluminous four-volume Sage benchmark publication that brings together a comprehensive collection of influential writing in the field.

Levinson, B. A. and Pollock, M. (eds) (2011). *A Companion to the Antbropology of Education*. Oxford: Wiley-Blackwell.

This reader offers an excellent cutting-edge introduction to the range of different approaches taken by ethnographers and anthropologists working on education, with a particular focus on the vibrant US scholarly community. Rather than take the field for granted, the editors ask the contributors one central question: where and what and when is 'education' to anthropologists? The contributions offer many – and sometimes divergent – answers.

All of the thirty-two specially written chapters address this question in some way, whether through a discussion of the history of the field, through an attention to language, or to politics, or to experiences or hands-on interventions. This reader highlights the many different stories one can tell about the nature of the field in the US, its theoretical and applied traditions, its boundaries and its seeming marginalisation within the broader discipline.

Levinson, B. A. et al. (eds) (2000). *Schooling the Symbolic Animal: Social and Cultural Dimensions of Education*. Lanham, Md.; Oxford, Rowman & Littlefield.

This is a judicious and stimulating sourcebook for those new to the anthropological study of education, and brings together a century of writing and two dozen influential anthropologists and sociologists. The 'Foundations' section ranges widely, and includes pieces from Emile Durkheim, Margaret Mead, Raymond Williams and Clifford Geertz. Subsequent sections have a more North American focus and specifically attend to ethnography and education, with contributions from scholars such as Deborah Reed-Danahy, Dorothy Holland, Margaret Eisenhart, Jan Nespor and Sherry Ortner. The contributions are best read as 'tasters' of these scholars' work, as the extracts can do little more than introduce the issues. Hopefully they will encourage you to root out the original monographs.

O'Reilly, K. (2009). *Key Concepts in Ethnography*. London, Sage.

This contribution to Sage's 'Key Concepts' series complements O'Reilly's textbook and offers pithy two–three page discussions of forty or so key terms in the ethnographic lexicon. Each points to a useful set of further readings, and is also fully cross-referenced. With concepts ranging from 'Covert' to 'Coding', from 'Generalisation' to 'Going native', and from 'Rapport' to 'Realism', the book usefully bridges a range of different ethnographic traditions and epistemological positions.

Web resources and journals

Whilst many disciplinary journals publish ethnographic research on education, two scholarly communities, each with their own journals, are dedicated to the sub-field. The journal *Ethnography and Education* was launched by a group of British sociological ethnographers in 2006.

Under the editorship of Bob Jeffrey and Geoff Troman, the journal sought to distil the legacy of three decades of dialogue and publications by ethnographers broadly sympathetic to symbolic interactionism. Since the first conference at St Hilda's in Oxford in 1978 on ethnographic methodology brought together an invited group of thirty researchers, this scholarly community has developed its own distinctive identity. As the website www.ethnographyandeducation.org makes clear, the community is 'committed to the development of ethnography in education as a vital research methodology that prioritises the perspectives of people's lives'. It has a growing set of resources and an active JISCMail list.

Anthropology and Education Quarterly, edited from the US, is the house journal of the Council of Anthropology and Education (CAE), a section of the American Anthropological Association. CAE's website www.aaanet.org/sections/cae/ has a range of resources, including links to its list-serv, publications and details of conferences and funding, together with an excellent and comprehensive archive of book reviews published in the journal.

Despite their international aspirations, each journal reflects the particular national character of their own field. Many anthropology journals publish ethnographic studies of education, as does the *British Journal of the Sociology of Education* (BJSE). The journal founded by Paul Willis, simply titled *Ethnography*, opens up a stimulating interdisciplinary space for ethnographic work.

There are a growing number of print journals dedicated to the discussion of qualitative methods, including *Qualitative Research*, *Qualitative Inquiry* and *International Journal of Qualitative Studies in Education*, which regularly publish ethnographic contributions, often with frank methodological insights and reflections. The 'mainstream' educational journals tend to discourage more experimental ethnographic writing.

Finally, and perhaps most useful for students, are the range of online journals, forums, blogs and resources dedicated to thinking about ethnographic methods and offering up-to-date reflections and discussions. Shielded from the scholarly conventions of print publication, online journals are open and honest about the privations that accompany learning to be an ethnographer. Particularly recommended is the graduate journal www.anthropologymatters.com and the sociology journal www.socresonline.org.uk. The US journal *Cultural Anthropology* has assembled an impressive set of web resources around its print journal.

Beyond the journals, there is a growing range of open resources for educational ethnographers available online. Some of the best blogs and forums include Savage Minds and the Open Anthropology Co-operative. Many individual academics and researchers post initial thoughts and reflections, and even fieldnotes, online, and it is worth looking at some of these to get a sense of the messiness of work in progress. A few minutes' searching will reveal a wealth of individual blogs that relate to your own areas of interest.

Additional online resources can be found at: www.sagepub.co.uk/beraseries.sp

CHAPTER 1

READING ETHNOGRAPHY, WRITING ETHNOGRAPHY

What is in this chapter?

- A short history of ethnographic writing and its key protagonists
- An introduction to influential educational ethnographies
- Advice and guidance on reading ethnographic texts
- A reading template to structure your own reading
- A discussion of recent debates around ethnographic representation

Introduction

We begin with a puzzle. If, as we argued in our Introduction, ethnography is simultaneously about being, seeing and writing, how does one combine these together? More than a research method, more than a genre of writing, it is an approach to crafting knowledge that makes heavy demands on the researcher. It takes time, sensitivity and an acceptance that, as a budding ethnographer, you become a central part of the research. The word itself contains the etymological clues you need to understand this commitment, *'ethnos'* and *'graph'* – writing the people. Ethnography is an approach that structures both your research and writing. Or rather, it disavows the possibility of dividing the two: writing becomes integral to the ethnographic method. As Madden puts it, 'writing is a method' (2010, 25). Rather than being the final act of the qualitative research drama, writing is the stage on which the ethnographic encounter unfolds. As Delamont and Atkinson remind us, 'the discipline of ethnography must include an awareness of how it is written … it is time for us to realise that ethnographic work is inescapably rhetorical' (Delamont and Atkinson 1995, 49). Ethnographers are always writing: writing is integral to the method. If you like keeping a diary, or taking notes, you'll relish the challenge of learning how to turn fieldnotes and diaries and into more polished pieces of writing, a topic we return to in Chapter 4.

As students, we were both encouraged to read as many ethnographic monographs as we could. These single-authored book-length accounts of a particular ethnographic setting or topic were not always immediately accessible. They required patience and time as they unfolded the shared significance and meanings behind particular linguistic concepts, symbols or rituals. But the rewards were manifold. We still have strong memories of the worlds that were evoked within them, from spirit possession amongst Sudanese women to dope-smoking American teenagers, from the legitimisation of male violence in Uganda to the anomie of disenchanted British school-kids.

The only way to grasp the full potential and strength of ethnographic writing is to read ethnographies. The best writers are always the most diligent readers. By reading voraciously and widely you will begin to understand how ethnographic writing and argument 'works', the truths it conveys, and the forms of rhetoric and style it relies on. Reading ethnographies helps you understand the disciplinary debates to which this writing contributes, and develop your own ethnographic 'being' or sensibility. In this chapter, we start with some examples of the connections that ethnographers make in their writing, in order to illustrate the particular combination of description and analysis that characterises the genre. We want you to think about whether these rhetorical and argumentative connections work for you.

The tricky task facing every ethnographer is working out how, both in your writing and your research, to maintain a balance between familiarity and strangeness. The ambition is to help one's readers be surprised and puzzled by the situations being described, but also help them make connections between these lived experiences and the understandings they bring to them. This stylistic balancing act is particularly tricky when you are doing research in one's own school or college, but it is one that all ethnographic writing has to deal with. If, as we have suggested in our Introduction, ethnography is an 'uncomfortable' science, this book explores how to sustain a generative sense of critical discomfort and distance.

How is this chapter structured?

To help you on your way this chapter starts with 'Making ethnographic connections', a short history of educational ethnography, highlighting path-breaking work and influential texts. We go on in 'How shall I read?' to offer advice on how to read critically, and provide a reading template for you to use, whether on your own or with others. It gives you some tools and tips on what to look out for, but also serves as a reminder to keep writing. Reading whilst keeping your own project at the back of your mind, you will soon find that your notes begin to develop an ana-lytical tone, as you make connections and links. Finally, in a section entitled 'Ethnographies are not what they used to be', we introduce you to the heated debates about ethnographic writing and representation that stirred up so much controversy in the late 1980s. The self-criticism led some to abandon the ethnographic project, but also provoked experimental new ways of representing, engaging with and portraying social worlds. Rather than be intimidated by these critiques, we wel-come the creativity that this has emerged, highlighting a couple of recent examples.

Making ethnographic connections

When does ethnography begin? The label hardly existed before the 1920s, but some anthropologists have suggested that the Greek historian Herodotus should be our first role model, with his interest in depicting strange customs and exotic social mores. If thoughtful and perceptive travel writers have existed since classical times, the modern age brought with it European explorers' and adventurers' accounts of 'uncharted' ter-ritories and 'unknown' worlds. This new genre relied for its authority on the sense of immediacy and 'being there' that the narrator created in the text. Colonial rule brought a host of new contributions from amateur collectors, missionaries and administrators, all of whom shaped the rise of the anthropological sciences. Come the twentieth century, the first professional ethnographers embarked on an unmapped literary journey towards a genre of 'writing culture' that was scientifically authoritative but also rhetorically convincing.

Bronislaw Malinowski – a Polish émigré of immense self-belief – did more than anyone else to crack this conundrum. Trapped in the South Pacific by the declaration of hostilities in the First World War, he embarked on an extensive period of research that involved living in the community which he was studying. His famous first book, jauntily titled *Argonauts of the Western Pacific* (1922), is an ethnographic account of the complex symbolic 'Kula-ring' trading network between a set of Pacific Islands. Its style is partly explained by Malinowski's huge admiration of Joseph Conrad and his writing. After a few pages explaining his scientific approach, Malinowski leavens his writing with this vignette:

> Imagine yourself suddenly set down surrounded by all your gear, alone on a tropical beach close to a native village, while the launch or dinghy which has brought you sails away out of sight. Since you take up your abode in the compound of some neighbouring white man, trader, or missionary, you have nothing to do, but to start at once on your ethnographic work. Imagine further that you are a beginner, without previous experience, with nothing to guide you and no one to help you. For the white man is temporarily absent, or else unable or unwilling to waste any time of his own on you. This exactly describes my first initiation into fieldwork on the south coast of New Guinea. I will remember the long visits I paid to the village during the first weeks; the feeling of hopelessness and despair after many obstinate but futile attempts had entirely failed to bring me into real touch with the natives, or supply me with any material. I had periods of despondency, when I buried myself in the reading of novels, as a man might take to drink in a fit of tropical depression and boredom. (1922, 14)

This one paragraph has come to represent, more than any other, the founding moment of the ethnographic genre and the discipline of social anthropology. Encouraged to put ourselves in his shoes, our trust in his depiction of this social world is bolstered by his own brutally honest self-dissection. There was no doubt that he was there, and we're not sure if we want to be there too. Despite the paradise South Sea setting, he lets us know of his deep frustrations and the deprivations. The posthumous publication of his diaries made clear just how much he tormented himself. Most of the book is written in an objectivist tone, but the rhetorical power of such vignettes is what remains with the readers. To use a phrase popularised by Clifford Geertz, that most literary of ethnographers, ethnographic writing is all about conveying 'being there' (Geertz 2000).

At around the same time, Margaret Mead, perhaps the first ethnographer of education, was pursuing a rather different fieldwork project on Samoa. Drawing inspiration from Freud rather than Conrad, her search to make sense of her own upbringing led her to ask about informal educational cultures: 'Are the disturbances which vex our adolescents due to the nature of adolescence itself or to the civilization? Under different conditions does adolescence present a different picture?' (Mead 1928, 3). Mead's playful writing and cross-cultural populism appealed to her growing American readership, and she draws a number of lessons from her ethnographic vignettes of Samoa about American adolescence. Accused by some anthropologists of adopting an over-simplistic 'an x is simply a y' approach to comparing cultures (di Leonardo 1998), the sweep of her analysis, and her willingness to make audacious statements about American mores, guaranteed her an illustrious career. She became the grande dame of American cultural anthropology and a sixties counter-culture icon. She was not unique in pointing to what she saw as the malign effects of modern 'Western' education on other societies, but she did it with a rhetorical flourish:

> All the irritating, detailed routine of housekeeping, which in our civilization is accused of warping the souls and souring the tempers of grown women, is here performed by children under fourteen years of age. A fire or a pipe to be kindled, a call for a drink, a lamp to be lit, the baby's cry, the errand of the capricious adult – these haunt them from morning until night. With the introduction of several months a year of government schools these children are being taken out of their homes for most of the day. This brings about a complete disorganization of the native households ... (Mead 1928, 28)

We turn now from 1920s Samoa to 1970s Birmingham, and a vignette of a different sort. For many ethnographers of education, Paul Willis's *Learning to Labour* is the defining modern classic, and remains much discussed and much cited, partly because of Willis's sophisticated theoretical discussion of the relationship between education and social-class formation. However the book begins with an initial forty pages entitled simply 'Ethnography'. This section is full of vivid tableaus that immediately invoke the ambience of an inner-city secondary school and the tension between working-class 'lads' and the more diligent 'ear'oles'. Take this brusque dialogue, as the researcher realises that 'having a laugh' is a key motivation of the 'lads', and explains their dismissive attitude to school and formal qualifications:

> 'Why not be like the ear'oles, why not try and get some CSEs?'

> 'They don't get any fun, do they?'

'Cos they'm prats like, one kid he's got on his report now, he's got 5 As and one B.'

'… I mean what will they [the ear'oles] remember of their school life? What will they look back on? Sitting in a classroom, sweating their bollocks off, you know, while we've been … I mean look at the things we [the Lads] can look back on … Some of the things we've done on teachers, it will be a laugh when we look back on it.' (Willis, 1977, 14)

Whilst the first forty pages of *Learning to Labour* may feel as if it somehow offers a 'raw' and unedited ethnographic account to which debates in Althusserian theory can then be applied, this is somewhat of a rhetorical trick. Ethnographic writing is a craft, but often highly strategic. Vignettes and imageries are deployed for a purpose, as the next extract shows:

In the corridors there is foot-dragging walk, an overfriendly hello or sudden silence as the deputy passes. Derisive or insane laughter erupts which might or might not be about someone who has just passed. It is as demeaning to stop as it is to carry on. There is a way of standing collectively down the sides of the corridor to form an Indian gauntlet run – though this can never be proved: 'We're just waiting for Spanksy, sir.'

After vividly evoking this submerged tension, the tone immediately shifts:

Of course individual situations differ, and different kinds of teaching style are more or less able to control or suppress this expressive opposition, But the school conformists – or the 'ear'oles' for the lads – have a visibly different orientation. It is not so much that they support teachers, rather they support the idea of teachers. Having invested something of their own identities in the formal aims of education and support the school institution – in a certain sense having forgone their own right to have a 'laff' – they demand that teachers should at least respect the same authority. There are none like the faithful for reminding the shepherd of his duty.

Note how quickly Willis's writing, even in the 'Ethnography' section of the book, moves to a theoretical register. We go from being jostled in the corridor outside the classroom to far-reaching statements about educational authority. He makes a generalisation about the behaviour of the ear'oles compared with the lads, musing on the nature of authority and student identity, before signing off with a quasi-religious metaphor.

This ability to shift gear, to jolt the reader, and to combine 'thick description' and sharp analysis, is a mark of some of the best ethnographic writing. As Willis puts it, 'theoretical imaginings of the social sciences are always best shaped in close tension with observational data' (Willis 2000, xi).

It is an argumentative and analytical style that seeks to stay close to the ethnographic data whilst using the vividness of experience as a springboard from which to open up much broader debates. As a genre it relies on telling juxtapositions, jarring the reader into seeing how one can bring together the very different concerns of those being written about and those being written for. Willis himself writes vividly about this process, suggesting that we should see the 'ethnographic as conditioning, grounding and setting the range of imaginative meanings within social thought … ethnography is the eye of the needle through which the threads of imagination must pass' (2000, xii). The biblical metaphor conveys something of the existential struggle that many ethnographers go through. Relatively few anthropological commentators are honest about this struggle. As Gay y Blasco and Wardle point out, 'Ethnography is a curiously double-edged sword: the difficulty of doing justice to lived social experience is ever present, but the need to organise ethnographic material convincingly is also pressing' (2007, 101).

Gripping vignettes and vivid portraits are not enough in themselves: their role is to locate and legitimate the ethnographic arguments being developed. Given the power of ethnographic rhetoric, this approach is sometimes accused of being merely journalistic anecdote. Perhaps this is not surprising, given the genre's origins in travel writing and exploration narratives. The skill is to ensure that academic debates inform the choice of the particular case or vignette being described. The aim is to ensure that the chosen vignette fairly represents and illuminates the larger theoretical issues at stake.

One final illustration of this juxtaposition comes from twenty-first-century Beijing, a study exploring the schooling of 'migrant' children in the capital (Woronov 2004). Using ideas about power drawn from the French theorist Michel Foucault, Woronov asks questions about the reproduction of Chinese patriotism and loyalty, and how Beijing's role as moral centre of the Chinese state is communicated within the classroom, Terry Woronov vividly conveys her ethnographic research with a kindergarten class. In this extract they are being taught about the city's landmarks:

Then the final question: 'What can we do at Tiananmen Square?' More puzzlement from the students. With a sigh, Bai provided the answer: 'At

Tiananmen, we can see Chairman Mao.' He paused then asked loudly: 'Do we love Chairman Mao?' The children roared back: 'Yes! We love him!' 'Who was Chairman Mao?' Bai continued after a pause, and the room fell silent in response. At about that time the other classes let out for recess and, the text completed, Bai let his kindergarteners out as well. (Woronov 2004, 290)

The author's descriptive prose helps us imagine the puzzled expressions on the children's faces and the mood in the classroom, together with the frustration of the teacher at their lack of knowledge of recent Chinese history. She immediately uses this to inform her larger analytical purpose, which is to explore the connection between space and power in Beijing, and the way in which these children are made to feel marginalised and unwanted in comparison to pupils in schools for the city's residents. The account allows her to connect global ambitions with intimate feelings and subjectivities.

Learning through discomfort

Miner's famous 'Body rituals amongst the Nacirema' has been used to gently tease every new generation of 'American' anthropology students. Who is this strange tribe that they have never heard of before? The article also serves to illustrate the ways in which ethnography can make the familiar strange, as the following extract shows, gently mocking our morning dental hygiene routines:

> The daily body ritual performed by everyone includes a mouth-rite. Despite the fact that these people are so punctilious about care of the mouth, this rite involves a practice which strikes the uninitiated stranger as revolting. It was reported to me that the ritual consists of inserting a small bundle of hog hairs into the mouth, along with certain magical powders, and then moving the bundle in a highly formalized series of gestures. (Miner 1953, 7)

The difficulty of making things strange in order to see them afresh would seem to be a particular problem for educational ethnographers working in classroom settings. After all, we've all (or nearly all) spent many years in class, for better or worse. The famous sociologist Howard Becker described his frustration at talking to 'a couple of teams of research people who have sat around in classrooms trying to observe and it is like pulling teeth to get them to see or write anything beyond what "everyone" knows' (Becker 1971, 10). In their 1995 book *Fighting Familiarity*,

Delamont and Atkinson come up with tactics for sustaining a sense of strangeness, through working in new and unfamiliar settings or repeatedly returning to gender issues.

We confess to being less worried about this need for strangeness. One does have to see things in a new light, and not take things for granted. But that is true for all social research. And the very act of adopting an ethnographic persona brings its own risks and discomforts. Having to repeatedly explain what an ethnographer does is hard enough in itself, and negotiating informed consent can be ethically discomforting, especially if your research participants are also your friends. Participating as a researcher in a school environment can make one feel all too exposed and disoriented. The writer's task is to communicate this experience in a way that conveys these tensions and ambivalences to the reader too. For the reader to understand the connections your writing is seeking to make, they need to feel something of the confusion and discomfort you will have experienced. Don't be scared to be honest about this aspect of your work. These emotional and moral conundrums are part of everyday life, and describing them allow you to demonstrate the value of the 'partial knowledges' you seek to create.

Some writers choose to instil a level of epistemological discomfort in their readers, as a way to highlight the power relations woven into ethnographic representations. Pictures, poems and vignettes can all be used very productively. Rather than write oneself out of the text, ethnographers find ways to remind the reader that they too are participating in the creation of knowledge.

What educational ethnographies should you read?

We feel that it is vitally important that students read and critically assess a range of educational ethnographies (written by both anthropologists and sociologists) with a particular focus on book-length 'monographs', both classics and recent work in the field. Don't neglect fictional accounts either. To help you, we provide an extensive set of suggested readings at the end of each chapter that illustrate some of the themes and issues being discussed. There is no one right set of readings. What matters will partly be determined by the educational world you inhabit or are interested in understanding. You also have to balance work that is theoretically astute and rhetorically convincing with scholarship that may be of less significance but closer to your own research interests.

Most ethnographers of education have been trained in the US, primarily within an anthropological tradition. The breadth of this work is conveyed in two recent readers (Levinson et al. 2000, Levinson and Pollock 2011), regular reviews of the field (e.g. Foley (2002), Yon (2003), Levinson et al. (1996)), and the diversity of work published and reviewed in *Anthropology and Education Quarterly*.

The early history of educational ethnography is also the history of anthropological attempts to 'apply' ethnographic insights to policy and practical issues. Margaret Mead went on to write about the crisis that she felt faced the American educational system. Her 1951 *The School in American Culture* helped make Mead the public face of the discipline, even as her populism alienated some of her academic colleagues.

The next generation of educational ethnographies sought to bring alive different cultural worlds of informal learning for the non-specialist – from the Amish (Hostetler and Huntington 1971) to the Kwakiutl Eskimos (Wolcott 1967), and from the Menomini American Indians (Spindler and Spindler 1971) to the Ngoni in Malawi (Read 1959). Harry Wolcott went on to write accessible methods texts (Wolcott 1994, 2008), as well as his influential *The Man in the Principal's Office* (1973), an intimate account of a US primary-school principal and his life. Alan Peshkin wrote his first book on schools in Nigeria, and then accounts of an evangelical academic and an elite private school (Peshkin 1972, 1986, 2001). Unlike the vignettes with which we began this chapter, many of these books are less driven by theoretical concerns than with a belief that careful ethnographic description allows cross-cultural comparison.

Within the UK, ethnographic research in schools was the brainchild of Max Gluckman, charismatic founder of the influential 'Manchester School' of Anthropology. As part of his ambition for an anthropology of modern communities, he saw ethnographies of education as a way of engaging teachers. His vision came to pass with a Ministry of Education keen to find out how the new grammar schools were faring research. This funded the doctoral work of Colin Lacey (1970), Audrey Lambart (1976) and David Hargreaves (1967), three innovative ethnographic studies of schooling and classroom dynamics in Manchester in the 1960s.

By the late 1960s, boom times for Sociology, relations between anthropologists and sociologists in the joint department at Manchester were growing increasingly tense. As doctoral students, Lacey and Hargreaves were more inspired by the work of Irving Goffman than in anthropological debates. They sought to reconcile Marxist theory with symbolic interactionsim in order to understand educational inequality. This led them to jobs in Sociology, and to champion a new field of 'micro-ethnographic' observational studies of classrooms.

Their work was highly influential for succeeding generations of sociological ethnographers in the UK (Stubbs and Delamont 1976; Burgess
1983) and set a precedent for detailed 'close-up' empirical fieldwork of
classrooms and schools that is still followed today. Whilst *Learning to
Labour* may still be one of the best-known educational ethnographies,
it was frowned upon by educational ethnographers for its lack of
engagement with the ethnographic detail and its cavalier approach to
empirical analysis (Delamont and Atkinson 1995; Walford 1998).

The next generation of British educational ethnographers, trained
within a raft of new Sociology departments, owed little allegiance to
anthropological approaches. One of the few direct links between
this anthropological past and the emergent British field of educational ethnography was Colin Lacey's supervision of Stephen Ball at
Sussex, leading to the publication of *Beachside Comprehensive* (Ball
1981). Committed to critically addressing policy questions through
empirical research, this new community of educational ethnographers saw the classroom as a site for observation rather than participation. The journal *Ethnography and Education* sustains this
tradition, though it rarely engages with anthropological debates.
The contributions to Anderson-Levitt (2011) discuss different
national traditions of educational anthropology and ethnography,
underscoring the limited and sometimes parochial concerns of both
American and European debates.

If the 'classics' are a good place to start, they also need to be read
alongside exemplars of contemporary educational ethnographies, prefer-
ably full-length works. Amy Stambach's work on schooling in Tanzania
questions the analytical boundaries erected around both schools and the
study of schooling, insisting that 'schools are often pivotal social institutions around which the configuration of society as a whole is imagined,
contested and transformed' (2000, 3). Stambach has gone on to write
about the influence of US evangelists on East African education (2010).
Terri Woronov's work in China and Veronique Benei's work in India
bring together debates around embodied nationalism and schooling, as
does Sam Kaplan's research on the Turkish 'pedagogical state' (2006) and
Cati Coe's work in Ghana (2005). Reflecting on Chinese families' emotional and social investments in education, and the way the state mobil-
ises and manages these ambitions, Andrew Kipnis develops a notion of
governing 'educational desire' (2011), whilst Vanessa Fong explores the
experiences of the Chinese student diaspora (2011). In the UK Gillian
Evans's ethnography explores the resilience of working-class localities in
London and their attitudes to formal education (2007). One can think too

of many other exemplary recent works (Abu El-Haj 2006; Benei 2008, Garcia 2005, Lukose 2009; Bartlett and Garcia 2011; Fong 2011; Fournier 2012) that demonstrate ethnographers' ability to make unexpected connections across the social sciences, and at pursuing scholarship that unsettles easy categorisation. Their research demonstrates the value of situating studies of schooling alongside broader debates around nationhood and social power.

How shall I read? In praise of reading templates

It is one thing knowing what to read. The next is knowing how to read. What should you look out for? The best ethnographies convey an intensity of purpose and knowledge, often based on long-term engagement with a topic or issue, sometimes over a number of years. They also have the ability to combine a close-grained analysis of telling details with the larger argument being made. Yet this can make them hard to disentangle and assess. And without knowing much about the authors you are reading and their research experiences, how does one develop the ability to discern better from worse accounts? In this section we introduce some of the questions that need to be asked of ethnographic texts.

The first thing to think about is the purpose of the text – what's it for? How, if at all, does the text set itself a research question, puzzle or problem? Is its focus an educational site, a learning 'culture', a set of pedagogic relationships, a mesh of policy networks, a set of statistics, or all of these? How was the knowledge generated, and how is this presented and structured? Who was it written for? Who is reading it? Does it set its own parameters, or is the emphasis on the researcher's experience or ethnographic methods? What has been included and what left out, and how is this justified? We flesh out these questions in the template below.

Quickly you'll want to know more about the author and why they have written this text. Develop a familiarity with their biography, perhaps through some background research online. This helps to understand their own academic socialisation, their interests and the disciplinary community they see themselves as part of. It also helps assess the analytical claims they make. Try to think about how this text relates to other work they may have done and to a sense of their larger academic project. Reflexivity is a buzz-word, but ethnographers vary greatly in their ability to acknowledge how their personal biographies, experiences and politics shape their research interests. The reader has to look out for how they 'locate' themselves in their text. Admissions about mistakes, moments of humour and examples of reciprocity will all help situate the writer.

Many ethnographers write for other ethnographers. Only then do they try to communicate to the larger intellectual community. Every ethnography needs to signal which conversation they are joining and why. But each author will be joining a scholarly conversation with its own unspoken assumptions and shared knowledges. Hence the importance of attending carefully to how other academic writing is drawn upon and discussed, whether in an initial literature review or throughout a text. Are they engaging major social theorists or fellow educationists, scholars across sociology or just those in a specific sub-field? In each case the positioning and rhetoric will be different.

There are certain code words that one has to learn to recognise. As we show in Chapter 2, ethnographers of a more anthropological stripe shy away from terms such as 'data', 'objectivity' and 'neutrality'. Some educational ethnographers are at ease talking about and trying to represent 'culture'; others are aware that this word comes bundled with too many meanings and assumptions to do useful analytical work. Instead they seek to 'unpack' the term or to attend to the power relations within. This leads to framings of cultural politics and the processes through which 'cultures' are negotiated and contested. Some will be very explicit about their methodological approach and assumptions, whilst others will hardly mention method.

A key contention of many ethnographers is that research monographs are the only way to do justice to the length and intensity of their fieldwork, and to provide the reader with the background knowledge they need to engage with the more theoretical arguments being made. One can read such monographs in two different ways, both for their regional or substantive knowledge and for their engagement with existing theoretical and ethnographic literature.

Whether reading a book or an article, the challenge remains: developing a critical appreciation of its contributions and its weaknesses. One way of developing one's critical reading skills is to read with a set of intellectual questions in mind. In the reading template we provide a fuller set of questions that you might find useful to guide your own note-taking and thinking, drawing on a similar template developed by Fortun (2009). The aim is to remind you that reading and writing are intertwined. Your notes will quickly begin to reflect your concerns and interests as much as those of the text you are reading. They may become your first fieldnotes and analytical reflections.

Reading ethnographies … some suggestions

1 What is the text about?
What educational phenomenon/policy/change/process is being addressed?
What are the research themes, questions or issues driving the writing?
How are these questions and empirical themes generated, and why are they seen to matter?
2 Space
How does the text define or create an ethnographic research space or landscape? Is it one school, a school's community, a regional economy, a policy, a transnational imaginary? How does it cross or link spaces? How much is this space created by the ethnographer themselves?
Does this ethnographic landscape dwell on the empirical, or seek to combine theory and context, time and space, the empirical and the analytical?
Does the ethnography connect different empirical and conceptual scales?
How are new virtual social spaces incorporated?
Is there an attempt at holism, or is the focus on tracing one object or idea through space?
3 Time
How is time framed? Does it have a historical trajectory? Is memory important?
How much historical context is provided, and how important is that?
Are key historical events at the heart of the text? The opening of a school, or the launch of a policy?
4 People and other social agents
Who or what are the significant actors, participants or relationships in the account?
If people, how are they chosen and why? What explanation is given for these decisions?
How is human agency, and that of non-humans, presented? Are they at the centre of the narrative?
How is children's agency presented and evoked?
How are the different actors related and connected?
5 Power and its disguises
How, if at all, is power shown to operate within the educational and social system/s described by the text?
What sort of theory of power is implicit (or explicit)?
And how are people and social agents written into, or out of, this theory of power?

Does an attention to gender, age and other forms of social hierarchy and stratification inform the text?

Are social practices and structures invoked and described? Is there a focus on resistance?

Is there an attention to the politics of representation, and the power of the text itself?

What ethical issues are raised by the research? How are these resolved? If none are raised, why not?

6 Evidence

What sorts of evidence and 'data' are mobilised? Interviews? Documents? Fieldnotes?

How much are we told about this evidence and how it was collected?

Is there missing evidence that would have been useful to have?

How does the text make use of other sensory evidence (e.g. visual evidence) or bodily experiences?

How important is this for the analytical argument being made?

How is the ethnographic 'evidence' analysed?

7 Rhetoric and authority

Is a narrative genre adopted? What other genres are used? How well do they work? How important is trust?

How does it represent existing ethnographic literature in their work?

Does the text challenge this work? How important are the views of other writers and authors?

Are the analytical arguments convincing? How do they relate to the empirical presentation?

Is there an implied audience? Does it make a contribution to policy and popular debates? How effective is this?

Ethnographies are not what they used to be: debates about writing

For the last three decades anthropological debates about ethnographic writing have led to a great deal of disciplinary angst and a whole raft of creative new approaches. One of the easiest ways to understand these debates is to read *Writing Culture*, a collection of essays edited by a literary studies scholar and an anthropologist (Clifford and Marcus 1986). Influenced by debates in feminism, postmodern philosophy and literary theory, its contributors set out to show how ethnography was 'always caught up in the invention, not the representation, of cultures' (1986, 2). For many, the text marked an epistemological watershed, even if it was hardly the first text to raise such questions. But it captured an anxious zeitgest, and Clifford's introduction became a manifesto for rethinking ethnographic writing. It still rewards reading today. When first published, it was seen to threaten the very existence of the ethnographic project, and led to heated divisions within and between departments. American sociology departments were similarly riven by debates about postmodernism (Denzin and Lincoln 2005).

It was not the first time that ethnographic endeavours had been subject to questioning. The Vietnam War pushed many American academics to think hard about whether their work was complicit with American geo-political agendas, and these debates led to the first anthropological code of ethics being published in 1971, as discussed in Chapter 3. Talal Asad's edited *Anthropology and the Colonial Encounter* (1973) also tackled the question of whether British anthropology really had been a 'handmaiden' to colonialism, but did not focus on the power of ethnographic writing per se.

Feminist anthropologists were the first to appreciate the importance of reworking a scientific and ethnographic genres. As early as the 1960s, several had written more dialogical and biographical accounts of their fieldwork (such as Powdermaker 1966). The publication of Malinowski's diaries similarly raised questions about the gap between ethnographic rhetoric and experience. And since the early 1970s Clifford Geertz had been seeking to develop a more interpretive approach to anthropology. Famously he defined culture 'an ensemble of texts, themselves ensembles, which the anthropologist strains to read over the shoulders of those to whom they properly belong' (Geertz 1973: 452). All the ethnographer could do was make interpretations of interpretations. Meanwhile, the Birmingham school of Cultural Studies was also hard at work rethinking culture in a more political vein, albeit from a perspective that sought to rethink Marx's theoretical legacies.

These different intellectual histories have tended to be collapsed together in discussions around *Writing Culture* (Clifford and Marcus 1986). This volume marked a growing recognition that one could no longer talk about culture as something objectively 'out there', possessed by a people or an institution. As the renowned anthropologist Eric Wolf noted, 'by endowing nations, societies or cultures with the qualities of internally homogenous and externally distinctive and bounded objects we create a model of the world as a global pool hall in which the entities spin off each other like so many hard and round billiard balls' (quoted in Leonardo, 1998, 56). Not only were ethnographers guilty of 'othering' their subjects through their research, but their writing also risked 'billiard-ball representations of otherness'.

There are many different ways of retelling this complex and fluid history, and trying to periodise it is unhelpful. However by the 1990s, most agreed that 'culture' had become an increasingly inadequate way for ethnographers to talk about the complex production and reproduction of social power relations in everyday life. British 'social' anthropologists had never deployed culture as an explanatory term, and instead had focused on social relations and social structures. Whilst this left them less vulnerable to charges of culturalist thinking, the residual 'rhetoric of holism' that informed their work (Thornton 1988) was still open to critique for the assumption that the ethnographer could separate themselves from the larger power-laden social relations that enabled them to carry out their work. As Clifford had noted, 'Ethnography is actively situated between powerful systems of meaning. It poses its questions at the boundaries of civilisations, cultures, classes, races and genders' (Clifford and Marcus 1986, 2). These boundaries could no longer be taken for granted.

Debates about the politics of representation continue across the academy, and have led many ethnographers to be far more aware and reflective about their writing. If ethnographic truths are, as Clifford put it 'inherently partial – committed and incomplete' (Clifford and Marcus 1986, 3) then it becomes incumbent on ethnographers to position themselves in their texts, to explain why they focus on some things rather than others, and why acting as a 'modest witness' (Haraway 1999) might be more appropriate than striving for full objectivity. No longer would anthropologists aspire to write ethnographies of the X or the Y, with chapters devoted to economics, kinship and ritual. Initially these debates passed unnoticed by educational ethnographers, but they have implications for all forms of ethnographic writing, whether one's ethnographic gaze is defined by the classroom or the city.

Along with the angst, much good has come from these debates. A whole range of new writing genres have emerged, attentive to questions of genre, authorial credibility and representational power. Ethnographers have written autobiographies, experimental dialogues, collaborative accounts with their 'informants', as well as auto-ethnographies and ethnographic portraits. Many of these experiments are driven by a commitment to making ethnographic writing more accessible, more engaged and more collaborative. We discuss these new approaches further in Chapter 5.

Educational ethnographers have been less troubled by these questions, partly because of the pressing empirical and policy concerns that drove many of those who came into the field. This is beginning to change, and in his contribution to the edited collection-cum-manifesto 'How to do

Educational Ethnography' (Walford 2008), the sociologist Dennis Beach brings questions of textual representation to the fore.

Conclusion

Do students need to get into these debates about power and representation, or about different genres of ethnographic writing and analysis, when they face so much pressure to write their thesis? Can these matters be left to one's supervisor? There are several reasons why these debates matter. The first is that one needs to learn the disciplines and traditions of a community in order to become an active member and participant within it. It is only by understanding this tradition that one can work within it. The second is that good social researchers always reflect on the role they play in creating the knowledge they seek to document. Some would even argue that 'methods, their rules, and even more methods' practices, not only describe but also help to produce the reality that they understand' (Law 2004, 6). Even if you disagree, and feel strongly that there is an independent 'reality' out there separate from the languages and practices through which we seek to describe it, you still need to decide how you are going to write about that world ethnographically. And that, of course, brings us back to reading.

Exercises

- Use the reading template to review a recent educational ethnography. How useful do you find it for developing a critical appreciation of the work?

- Try and write a catchy but communicative title for an educational ethnography you would like to produce. Compare these with some recently published titles. How important is the title for catching the reader's attention? What are the key code-words used by the authors?

Further reading

The best possible preparation for ethnographic writing is to read as many monographs as possible, especially in your substantive area.

Some will be overly theoretical, some overly descriptive. Develop your own taste, your own likes and dislikes. How do you feel about confessional or experimental accounts? How interested are you in theoretical debates? How much methodological detail do you need? Most importantly, are you convinced by the rhetorical role of vivid ethnographic description? This will help you decide on your own approach to writing, and to your research. To help you along the way, there are books about reading (Gay y Blasco and Wardle 2007) and accessible ethnographic writing (Waterston and Vesperi 2009), readers that offer 'tastes' of a range of ethnographic styles (e.g. Taylor 2002), as well as a range of experimental, autobiographical and 'auto-ethnographic' texts (e.g. Jeffrey and Dyson 2008, Shostak and Nisa 1988, Shostak 2000):

Gay y Blasco, P. and Wardle, H. (2007). *How to Read Ethnography*. London, Routledge.

Unusually for anthropologists, the authors combine a practical guide to reading ethnographies with a thought-provoking set of arguments about ethnographic practice. The chapters range across discussions of comparison, context, meaning and argument. Each is complemented by crisp summary points and excerpts of ethnographic writing, together with activities and exercises, intended to illustrate and provoke further thinking. The ethnographies range from Levi-Strauss and Edmund Leach to recent work by Keith Hart and one of the authors. An accessible but deceptively sophisticated pedagogical text, and a handy companion on any ethnographic journey.

Jeffrey, C. and Dyson, J. (2008). *Telling Young Lives: Portraits in Global Youth*. Philadelphia, Penn., Temple University Press.

An innovative and highly readable set of ethnographic portraits demonstrating the potential for communicating ethnographic research to non-academic audiences. The individual accounts are designed to encapsulate social and political worlds and foreground a strong attention to issues of social justice.

Shostak, M. and Nisa (1988). *Nisa, the Life and Words of a !Kung Woman*. New York, Vintage Books.

One of the best known of a string of accessible ethnographic biographies, presenting the life of a Botswana !Kung woman. Others of note include *Getting to know Wai-wai* (Campbell 1995). Such works are not without their critics, but they do demonstrate the power of illuminating ethnographic narratives.

Taylor, S. (2002). *Ethnographic Research: A Reader*. London, Sage.

Put together initially as an Open University set text, the ten chapters illustrate a range of approaches to ethnographic writing. The volume includes several extracts from ethnographies of young people and schooling, including Valerie Hey's *The Company She Keeps: An Ethnography of Girls' Friendship* (1997), based on research in south London, and Claire Alexander's *The Art of Being Blac*k (1996).

Waterston, A. and Vesperi, M. D. (2009). *Anthropology off the Shelf: Anthropologists on Writing*. Chichester, Wiley-Blackwell.

A passionate defence of accessible and engaging writing by eighteen leading North American anthropologists. Contributors explore how they navigate the formal constraints of disciplinary canons and academic careers while finding ways to reach out to people through the power of good storytelling.

Additional online resources can be found at: www.sagepub.co.uk/beraseries.sp

CHAPTER 2

ETHNOGRAPHY BY DESIGN, ETHNOGRAPHY BY ACCIDENT

What is in this chapter?

- An introduction to the notion of ethnographic research design
- Two different 'recipes' for research design and their advocates
- A discussion of the importance of planning, questioning and failure
- A defence of participant-observation
- An explanation of why ethnographic research is never without impact

---

Introduction

Culinary metaphors have long dominated writing about methods. It is not hard to see why. If research is akin to cooking, then the ingredients and utensils matter, but the recipe is key. Research design is the recipe that brings together one's empirical ingredients with a set of methodological utensils. It is the conceptual blueprint that aligns research question, methods, modes of analysis and approach to writing.

But just as cooks have very different styles in the kitchen, there are many ways of thinking about research design. For some commentators, being clear from the start about one's design (whatever it might be) illustrates one's credibility, trustworthiness and ability as a scholarly cook. But not all ethnographers like following recipes, or at least admitting that they follow them. The meaning that research design takes in your research will depend on your own philosophical tastes and the culinary expectations placed upon you by your supervisor, your institution and your field. Even a 'wait and see' approach is implicitly an approach to design. More important than the precise design you adopt is the acknowledgement that you will always be coming to a research question with a set of interests, skills, competencies and theoretical hunches. In short, there is always a design.

One of our aims for this book is to help new researchers develop an awareness of the range of ethnographic approaches taken in the study of education. Our ambition is to cultivate a degree of 'methodological empathy' through an appreciation of different understandings of research design.

How is this chapter structured?

In 'Two traditions of ethnographic design' we start this process of sketching out different approaches to studying education, with two sections provocatively titled 'Relying on the recipes' and 'Tasting as you go along'. Each tradition has its protagonists and its defenders. Explaining these different histories, we highlight the strengths and weaknesses of both. What of our own preferences? We argue for a middle way. Rather than seeing your research design as a blueprint to be carefully followed, or abandoning all pretence at design and simply celebrating 'mess', we think design has to be an ongoing concern, a constant weaving back and forth between a conceptual framing and the intellectual problem at issue. Your research questions and research design can and should change over the course of a project. This is why setbacks are so important. Failure is often at the heart of ethnography. The seeming 'failure' of your initial research recipe and proposal can be a transformative moment, enabling you to refocus and rethink your questions and purpose in the light of your experiences, relationships and the situation in which you find yourself.

The way you conceptualise your relationship with your research participants and practices is integral to your research design, to the questions you wish to ask and to the knowledge you will create. Indeed, your understanding of the ethnographic 'field' can equally define your design. So in the second part of this chapter, 'Participation, observation, or both?', we explore the different views that educational ethnographers hold on this. Rather than worry about losing your objectivity by 'going native', our own feeling is that some form of active participation is the best way to observe and record the issues you seek to comprehend. It is not easy, but can be very rewarding. Being honest about the way we become 'entangled' with our research and our participants is key. We return to questions of reciprocity in Chapter 3.

Finally, in our 'Conclusion: rethinking design', we mention some recent ethnographic experiments that begin to rethink research design. We hope that this will encourage you to be creative in thinking about these research relationships, and risk trying different approaches to collaboration and sharing learning.

Two traditions of ethnographic design

We all know cooks who never seemed to use recipes or look at books. In the same way, ethnographers tend to cluster in two camps, those who talk of research 'design' and 'analysis' and those that won't. Relatively few social anthropologists refer explicitly to their 'data': it is equally rare to find educational sociologists that don't. In what follows we capture something of the thinking within each group, explain why these differences matter, and how to make the best of both approaches.

Relying on the recipes

In 1988 Atkinson and Delamont made the ambitious claim that 'the most successful textbooks on ethnographic fieldwork published in Britain are by authors whose empirical research includes educational settings' (1988, 235). They attributed the success of works such as *Ethnography: Principles in practice* (Hammersley and Atkinson 1983, now in its third edition) to its 'deliberative and systematic' approach, and to the way in which it combined reflexivity with preparation, as this quotation reveals:

> Certainly we must recognise that, much less than other forms of social research, the course of ethnography cannot be pre-determined. But this neither eliminates the need for pre-fieldwork preparation nor means that the researcher's behaviour in the field need to be haphazard, merely adjusting to the events by taking 'the line of least resistance'. Indeed, we should argue that research design should be a reflexive process operating throughout every stage of a project. (Hammersley and Atkinson 1983, 28)

It was a view shared and nurtured by a close-knit group of British sociologists of education that began their careers in the 1970s. These included Martyn Hammersley, Paul Atkinson, Sara Delamont, Geoff Esland and Peter Woods. Influenced by the critical sociological insights into education offered by Michael Young in his 1971 *Knowledge and Control*, they cut their academic teeth by writing teaching materials for a highly successful Open University course, 'Schooling and Society'. Later recruits included Geoffrey Walford, Bob Jeffrey and Dennis Beach. Through regular conferences held in Oxford from the late 1970s, this group created a tight-knit scholarly community and worked towards a shared set of methodological principles. Their work has ensured that ethnographic approaches are alive and well in Education departments in the UK, and in cognate fields, as Walford demonstrates in his short history of the annual St Hilda's conferences that brought this community together (2011). The journal *Ethnography and Education*, launched in 2006, offers scholarly legitimacy and publishing opportunities.

Whilst many of these scholars have sustained their academic careers writing about methods, they would distance themselves from what Delamont and Atkinson portray as the 'paradigm mentality' (1995) they see within the US academy. Safely on the other side of the Atlantic, their work has tended to caricature US sociology and anthropology departments as fractured by methodological identity politics, with rival camps advocating different approaches and ever more specialised tools.

Recognising the impossibility of living by just one set of instructions or methodological approach (Brewer 2000), Delamont and Atkinson instead champion what we call methodological 'explicitness'. Insisting that a range of methods can and should be used by ethnographers, they see the researcher as responsible for defending the methods and the design they have chosen to use, and explaining why their choices are well suited to the task at hand. As they put it 'Research design should be a reflexive process operating throughout every stage of a project' (Hammersley and Atkinson 1983, 28). However their use of the language of reflexivity is tactical, and they use it to distance themselves from the traditions of action research that have found favour within Education, seeing them as overtly political and insufficiently objective.

This attention to methodological detail is perhaps a consequence of the time many have faced defending the validity of ethnographic approaches in interdisciplinary schools of Education. With a determination to make the method as robust and accountable as possible, the writing has repeatedly clarified the nature of ethnography's empirical depth and rigour. Eschewing what some would see as anthropology's 'fashion for theory' (Atkinson et al. 2003), the focus has instead been on calling theory to account. *Ethnography and Education*'s aims reveal this community's theoretical predilections, prioritising the 'experiences and perspectives of those involved', a commitment to 'generating data', a focus on 'understanding their cultures', and on highlighting the 'agency of educational actors'.

As is so often the case with language use, much is communicated in these few phrases. Their symbolism may not be immediately obvious to those new to qualitative research. Nor would their presumptions be shared by all ethnographers. So what are these differences, and why do they matter? Some historical clues will help here. Growing away from their anthropological 'ancestors', British ethnographers of education have been inspired by the up-close and empirical 'symbolic interactionist' tradition of research developed by the American sociologists Herbert Blumer and Erving Goffman. Blumer emphasised the importance of attending to individual actions and their meanings associated. Goffman had famously focused on understanding the 'presentation of self in everyday life', with a careful attention to the smallest details of social action, behaviour, dress and presentation, including that of the researcher themselves. His pioneering *micro-sociology*, as he called it, led to the pathbreaking *Asylums: Essays on the Social Situation of Mental Patients and Other Inmates* (1961). Whilst schools were hardly asylums, Goffman's focus on 'total institutions' had resonances for school-based researchers, and his approach seemed perfectly suited to those, like Colin Lacey (1970) and David Hargreaves (1967), seeking to understand social dynamics amongst pupils within a formal classroom setting. Classroom observations were already an uncontroversial and everyday aspect of school life, and a model easily adopted to this ethnographic paradigm.

This tradition of 'micro-ethnographic' work, as it became known, foregrounded close-grained active empirical research, with theoretical ideas being 'interrogated' and 'developed' through the 'generating of data'. To this day, this empiricist commitment continues. It has led to a shared commitment amongst educational ethnographers to carefully collecting, recording and analysing 'data' that pertain to the specific research questions being asked. This care and modesty has lead to a suspicion of theoretical fashions and ungrounded speculations.

Hammersley has been the most vocal apologist for this understanding of ethnography. In his many articles he has repeatedly underscored the importance of striving for objectivity and rigour:

> I argue that researchers should be committed primarily to the pursuit of knowledge, and should be as neutral as they can towards other values and interests in their work, in an attempt to maximise the chances of producing sound knowledge of the social world. (Hammersley 2000, 12)

Accompanying this dedication to scientific rigour is a belief in the possibility of dispassionate scholarly inquiry, and in the Mertonian ideals of

social research, even if the actual circumstances of knowledge production never quite live up to the ideal. In its search for 'sound knowledge',
it is an approach that is comfortable with attempting to establish 'objective' truths. It is a philosophical position that leaves Hammersley and his
colleagues suspicious of 'advocacy' research, of mixing politics and
scholarship, of postmodernism and other 'isms'. Combining a determined
empiricism with a wariness of theoretical fashions, the resulting brew is
measured, sensible and very English.

Tasting as you go along

If you've only ever come across one ethnography, the chances are that
it will be *Learning to Labour* by Paul Willis. Written while he was a
researcher at the now famous Centre for Contemporary Cultural Studies
in Birmingham, its explanation of why working-class kids rebel against
the middle-class expectations that schools place on them has come to
represent the best – and for some, the worst – of the ethnographic
endeavour. As one might guess, his subsequent self-portrayal as a rebellious academic 'vandal' does not endear him to scholars keen to establish
the credibility of educational ethnography, and his work has come in for
strong criticism (e.g. Delamont and Atkinson 1995, Walford 2008).

> Imagine that I am a bit of an academic vandal, in the nicest possible and
> disciplined way. I take, develop or invent ideas (while immersed in the data)
> and throw them, in a 'what if' kind of way, at the ethnographic data – the
> real world of the nitty-gritty, the messiness of everyday life – to see what
> analytic points bounce out on the other side, pick them up again, refine
> them and throw them again. (Willis 2000, x–xi)

Willis remained unrepentant, and has gone on to launch the journal
Ethnography that now attracts high-quality work from a range of fields.
Trained within a cultural studies tradition inspired by the political writing
of Raymond Williams and the teaching of Richard Hoggart, he also had
acquired an interest in aesthetics and literary style after studying English
as an undergraduate with F.R. Leavis in Cambridge. Despite little exposure
to anthropology, his vision and writing style paralleled those favoured by
many anthropologists, even if talk of ethnography made him unpopular
amongst his radical colleagues in Cultural Studies at Birmingham (Mills
and Gibb 2000). His vision of an 'experimental, profane theoretical
methodology', and his desire to 'refrain from precise or neat definitions of concepts' (Willis 2000, viii) eloquently articulate an approach to
ethnographic design very different from that developed by some educational sociologists. Questioning the social scientific ambition to

aspire to 'objectivity', he instead feels that the best we can hope for are 'sensitising' concepts.

In his own reflections on his training, Willis highlighted the importance of what Hoggart called 'the destructive element', and the willingness to be thoroughly befuddled:

> If you know exactly what you want or what you're going to prove, then you go to the field for a few exemplifications and you write what you always knew. But if you are willing to get disoriented and confused, which can feel, well, disorienting and confusing, it's not necessarily a bad thing, out of it can come real gems. (Willis in Mills and Gibb 2000, 394)

This is not to say that Willis abhors method. In his writing he makes much of the vital importance of attending to everyday experience as both the 'bread and butter of ethnography', and as the 'grounds whereupon and the stake for how grander theories must test and justify themselves' (Willis 2000, xii). For him, ethnography is all about being 'so moved with curiosity about a social puzzle that you are seized to go and look for yourself'. But it is also about coping with confusion and the unpredictable effects of throwing 'concepts at things'.

If Willis can defend this eclectic, experimental and 'tasting as you go' approach to ethnographic research, why don't others? Whilst not wishing to caricature, it is fair to say that most social anthropologists shy away from using words such as 'objectivity', 'validity' and 'generalisability'. They are even uncomfortable talking about 'data', as quickly becomes evident in any comparison of anthropological and educational ethical codes. Yet they don't announce their disagreements very loudly. When they write about ethnographic practice, many social and cultural anthropologists end up discussing (and implicitly defending) their discipline rather than its methods. There is an implicit assumption of an intimate and necessary connection between 'their' method and 'their' disciplinary identity (Mills 2008). Despite eminent contributions made by sociological ethnographers, many social anthropologists can't quite imagine how one could do 'real' ethnographic research without wanting to be 'one of us'. The ethnographic method gets taken for granted, and hardly worthy of comment. Hardly worthy, that is, until others seek to redefine or adopt the term. At that point anthropologists can become rather territorial, which might explain why cross-disciplinary collaborations with ethnographic researchers working in sociology or education departments are unusual.

Willis is not a lone voice, however. His rebellious manifesto calls to mind the epistemological anarchism of Paul Feyerabend – best known for his *Against Method* (1975) – whose work questioned the very possibility of a singular scientific method. This methodological eclecticism has taken up by other scholars in Cultural Studies and those working in Science and Technology Studies (STS). Both fields bring together a range of disciplinary approaches and welcome methodological experimentation. Influential ethnographers here include Bruno Latour and Steve Wolgar, whose pioneering *Laboratory Life* (1979) offered a vision for new forms of ethnographic practice and ethnographic reflexivity. Their colleague and fellow advocate of Actor Network Theory, John Law, has distilled his thinking into a book called simply *Making a Mess with Social Research* (Law 2004). More accessible and practical for new researchers is Kristen Luker's *Salsa Dancing into the Social Sciences* (2008), a gently irreverent attack on 'canonical' approaches to social research.

Anthropologists have tended towards impressionism in their approach to research design. One recent volume on innovative approaches to fieldwork offers a new set of metaphors: 'For research design to work, without becoming formulaic, students must engage with it as play … One moves through a research design process ready, quick on one's feet, attuned to what many would discount as noise … Certitude about what one is doing should not be the goal' (Fortun 2009, 180).

Keep planning, keep questioning

In the first part of this chapter we have simplified methodological cooking into two contrasting techniques, visible within different schools of anthropological research on education. Amidst the choices, how does one find a middle way between following ethnographic recipes and tasting as you go along? Each has its strengths and its drawbacks. The first school, for all its commitment to getting 'up close and empirical', does not acknowledge the rich possibilities created by participant-observation, a theme we discuss below. Its practitioners tend not to worry about awkward questions posed by postmodernism and feminism about the role of the researcher (and the method) in shaping knowledge. Meanwhile the latter set of cooks sometimes spend too much time worrying, and forget to tell us exactly how they did their research, who they talked to, how and why. Anthropologists can dwell at length on the politics and poetics of writing, but are often short on the messy pragmatic details of why they made the choices they made, and how they developed the conjectures and hunches they developed.

In their different ways, both schools are striving for accountable research. The first seeks to develop robust methods that meet the expectations of an interdisciplinary scholarly community like Education, whilst the second is more concerned about being accountable to the community being researched. Each is important, each needs attention. Once you have developed your own sense of positioning, developing a level of 'methodological empathy' to that of others is important.

So how should students and those starting out on ethnographic projects approach the question of research design? Apart from the 'arrival' trope that tends to characterise many ethnographies, there is little focus in most textbooks on the first tentative attempts of 'doing' ethnographic research; this tends to get left to the unpublished diaries, the confessional biographies and the research exposes. But it is only through the experience of trying out fieldwork that you can begin to understand ethnographic research design and its generative serendipity. If the best way to learn about fieldwork is to do fieldwork, the second-best-but-also-very-important way is to read about other people's first experiences.

We feel that you need to learn from both schools of thinking. To convince scholars in Education, your research proposal needs to articulate a clear rationale and design for your research. More important still, you'll need to be able to articulate a research question. You are unlikely to be surrounded by researchers who are happy to dilate about abstract social theory. They will want to know what you want to look at and why it matters. Malinowski memorably described the 'foreshadowed problems' that all ethnographers bring to their research. You too will already have some hunches and ideas about the questions you want to explore. But these problems need to be brought into the limelight, spelt out and written down. Try doing this in 500 words, then 300 words, then 100 words, then 50 words and then 30. If you can set out the core ideas, issues and questions you want to explore in one pithy and convincing sentence or two, you are well on your way. The aim is to be coherent without being prescriptive, to be focused without being narrow. The ability to articulate a generative research question in a concise way is an invaluable skill, and one that comes with practice.

An image might help here. Think of a tiny flower bud, wrapped up and protected against the winter cold. Contained within the bud are all the key organs of the flower, albeit in embryonic form. As the warmth returns, the bud can begin to unfold and develop. If the research question is framed in a way that allows the ideas to organically grow, then the core elements of the generative ethnographic bud can blossom and flourish.

Once you've written this question, and an accompanying rationale, keep it to hand. You will return regularly to it, and may need to subtly reframe and rewrite it again and again. There are lots of reasons for doing so. One is to watch closely how your question relates to your fieldwork as it unfolds and develops. It will help you ground your thinking, but also allow you to track how your thinking is changing. It is only by having the question to hand that you can actively decide that it needs to be reframed or developed. It may be that its emphasis needs to change or develop, or that an additional aspect needs to be included. Your remit is to be open to new possibilities whilst making sure your ethnographic inquiries stay focused.

This core rationale can also play other roles. From it should emerge a set of sub-questions, and from them a set of potential themes and structures to pursue during fieldwork. This might include ideas to explore in interviews, or things to look out for as a participant-observer. A research project focused on, for example, gender identities in a girl's *madrasah* might look to understand the values, aspirations and expectations of parents and teachers as well as the girls. But it would also seek to try and understand the girls' lives through the way they dress, decorate their rooms, play together or organise visits. The research design would lead to a set of themes for the researcher to 'look out for' and stay attentive to. Whilst this list might well change and evolve, the very process of thinking through possibilities is worthwhile.

When David set out to do his doctoral research on masculinity and AIDS in an area of Uganda still recovering from the civil war of the 1980s, he had little idea that he would end up writing about students and gender politics in a rural secondary school (Mills and Ssewakiryanga 2002, 2004). His initial research question asked about the relationship between masculinity, AIDS and local power structures. But he soon realised the difficulties that faced a *muzungu* outsider in addressing the complex politics and social stigmas that surrounded AIDS. Meanwhile he was teaching, getting to know the students and spending time in school. He began to realise that the students' understandings of 'love' and 'money' were rather different from his, and that they saw the emotional and financial aspects of their relationships as deeply intertwined. This led him to begin to ask a rather different set of research questions about the materiality of intimacy, and to redesign the project as a whole.

Here the cooking metaphors in this chapter might need rethinking. Rather than tasting as you go along, or trying to follow the recipe, what if the very layout of your kitchen begins to shift? You might no longer know where to find your utensils, or have to find a new set of ingredients and try to cook something different. Your agency, and control over the research process may be less secure than you think.

Many ethnographers have similar experiences, and indeed what Willis calls disorientation has become something of an ethnographic rite of passage. In her account of the collapse of her ethnographic research project on bioprospecting in West Africa after a year in the field, Kristin Peterson (2009) describes how it was a 'career-defining failure'. It forced her to take a very different tack, and ultimately helped her define a far more fruitful contribution. Again, one's notion of the field is key in defining how one understands 'data', and even if one wants to use this term. An attention to the field helps you understand when you are being directed away from your original goals, or when being redirected may indeed be the right thing.

Participation, observation or both?

One of the most troublesome terms in the ethnographic lexicon is 'participant-observation'. Much ethnographic ink has been spilt in pursuit of this apparent contradiction, and the term immediately invokes strong feelings. The sharpest divisions between different methodological schools emerges in their understanding of this notion. Shaped by what Blumer called the 'cardinal principles of empirical science' (1969, 21), Hammersley and Atkinson, along with other educational ethnographers, are suspicious of participation. Whilst they recognise a spectrum going from complete participation (which they define as covert research) to complete observation, their inclination is clear: the 'researcher' role must come first. They feel that participation takes up too much 'sheer time and energy' (2007, 84), and cite the example of one pair of researchers who 'stopped pretending that they were becoming Brazilian villagers and turned to systematic research activity'.

Influenced by Goffman's thinking about social roles, Hammersley and Atkinson spend time reflecting on how to depict oneself in the field. Their book has sections entitled 'Impression management', 'Field roles' and 'Managing marginality', all of which focus on how to portray a research persona. Participation, if necessary at all, is a means to an observational end, rather than integral to the research strategy in itself. For them, the most common danger in ethnographic research is 'going native' – losing one's detachment and scholarly identity, as the following quote demonstrates:

> Even if successfully maintained, the strategy of complete participation will normally prove rather limiting. The participant will, by definition, be implicated in existing social practices and expectations in a far more rigid manner than the known researcher. The research activity will therefore be hedged round by these pre-existing social routines and realities. It will therefore normally prove hard for the fieldworker to arrange his or her

actions in order to optimize data collection possibilities. (Hammersley and Atkinson 1983, 84).

Anthropologists take an almost directly opposed view. Rather than feeling 'hedged round', anthropologists thrive on feeling entangled and involved in the worlds in which they are describing. Yes, this can mean 'culture shock', but confronting and participating in moral and political constellations different from one's own can make the issues at stake much clearer. My anger at what I saw as the misogyny of many of the male students I met at Makerere led me to think much further about Euro-American attitudes to gender and female equality, and why Ugandans articulated a very different understanding of male–female relationships. An empathetic ethnographic sensibility means taking the time to listen, discuss and appreciate. It cultivates a form of methodological relativism that allows new insights to emerge, even if this can be confusing and dislocating:

> The challenge is to become part of a foreign milieu, to submit to the outside, to get drowned in and carried away by it, while staying alert to the gradual emergence of a theme to which chance encounters, fugitive events, anecdotal observations give rise. (Rabinow et al. 2008, 116)

For many anthropological ethnographers, the ideal was once to spend long periods of time 'in the field', or make repeated visits. As we will show in the chapters that follow, this is now changing with the rise of multi-sited fieldwork. Beyond anthropology, attitudes towards participation vary depending on the local research traditions. The issue is less the amount of time one spends than the quality and focus of the research relationships one develops.

In his *Identities and Social Change in Britain Since 1940* the sociologist Mike Savage offers an intriguing account of the post-war rise of sociological methods. He describes how early researchers sought to build rapport on the doorsteps of urban Britain, while struggling to silence and deny their own moral and class prejudices about the people they were interviewing. The interviewees increasingly realised they were being 'classified' into social classes by the researchers. He suggests that the researchers 'could not but create new kinds of social relations through their own research practices' (2008, 9).

This leads Savage to make the provocative claim that survey methods themselves changed the way in which modern nations imagine themselves, and individuals increasingly thought of themselves through the categories of class, identity and ethnicity. Anthropologists' endless focus on culture has had a similar impact. Our academic terms and language are taken up by those whom we write about. We not only communicate a vision of social relations through our fieldwork practices, but also offer a language through which others can understand these relationships.

Savage's point is that science is not innocent or neutral. We can never fully detach ourselves from the worlds in which we work, or see our methods as mere technical tools. Rather, we participate fully in a social setting and attend to the consequences than pretend that we are disembodied observers with no impact or influence. Methods and ideas go places and do things, and our ideas go with them. The challenge we face is to understand how our methods might shape the worlds in which we work, and are in turn shaped by the social changes around them.

Conclusion: rethinking design

Taking an ethnographic approach to your research is never the easy option. It presents ethical and emotional demands, along with difficult questions about design. However, it does help with the thorny question of what 'theory' to choose. Ethnographers' attention to the everyday, the insignificant and the nascent is itself a theoretical commitment and a reminder that research is not just about developing abstract concepts and disembodied theory. An attention to the mundane and 'taken for granted' aspects of life is core to ethnographic sensibility. The focus is on what Ferguson (2011, 198) calls 'changing the question', 'moving away from the notion of an object of study altogether' and translating theoretical objects into 'specific activities engaged in by specific people'. Paul Rabinow et al. go further and seek to reclaim the meaning of design, arguing that the term 'expresses the primacy of inquiry and data over theory which all four of us affirm as an essential feature of anthropological knowledge production' (Rabinow et al. 2008, 112).

They foreground artistry, creativity and responsiveness, suggesting that 'today's students need to cultivate the art of finding the design of research in the course of inquiry, to let the field or the particular story of theme that is emerging take over the design' (ibid., 116).

Not everyone would agree with this inchoate definition, as we show in the chapters that follow. Today, traditions of ethnographic design remain divided by familial lines of intellectual descent and disciplinary loyalty. Some branches of this family tree may not even survive. Yet, as a student, you may have little choice but to conform to the practices and beliefs of your supervisor and the local cultures and traditions of your 'home' department. But you'll also want to find your bearings in a broader methodological landscape, if only because you'll probably want to leave 'home' at some point and look for work elsewhere.

In Britain, educational and sociological ethnographers continue to find ways to promote rigour and accountability, even if bemoaning the lack of dialogue with anthropology (e.g. Delamont 2012) about such matters. Meanwhile, anthropological ethnographers are shrugging off postmodern angst, bucking methodological tradition, and experimenting with new forms and genres. Some work outside the discipline, as part of interdisciplinary teams, or champion public anthropology. Others combine scholarship and advocacy, and call for more explicitly activist research. We live in an age where many of those with whom we work are 'knowledge workers' in their own right, with their own analytical explanations and insights. Ethnographers will not be able to simply observe, but will increasingly require participation, dialogue and collaboration. Through involving those who we are researching as participants, design visions can be explored, refined and improved. Ethnography's future is likely to be participatory *and* accountable.

Exercises

- Distilling a research problem, concern or question into one potent, pellucid and illuminating sentence is the hardest part of ethnographic writing. The process is invaluable. Write 500 words on your research topic and central questions. Reduce it down to 300 words. Reduce it again to 100 words, then 50 words and finally 30 words. If you can set out the core ideas, issues and questions you want to explore in one pithy and convincing sentence or two, you are well on your way. Keep a record of these different distillations. Repeat regularly.

- Develop a one-page set of detailed themes and topics that you plan to observe and attend to in your research. Think about, and list, all the people who might be relevant, or the types of conceptual objects, settings, interactions or relationships that need closer attention. Drawing on Fortun (2009) try and map the social and political forces acting on them, and consider how you might differentiate these different groups. The topics should include fieldwork pointers, ideas to be explored in dialogue and interviews, or interactions to look out for as a participant-observer. Keep returning to these to revise and update.

Further reading

One of the barriers faced by both student researchers and teachers of ethnographic methods is navigating a huge range of different methods textbooks. Each has slightly different interpretations and approaches, with its own adherents. They divide between more prescriptive 'recipe-rich' accounts of the research process (e.g. Bogdan and Biklen 2007; Hammersley and Atkinson 2007) and those that are more anecdotal, drawing on personal experience (e.g. Wolcott 2008, Luker 2008). Whilst now more than a decade old, Mason (2002) is a good compromise, as is Pole and Morrison's account of educational ethnography (2003). A more 'postmodern' experimental vision is offered by the comprehensive assemblages of Denzin and Lincoln, such as *Strategies of Qualitative Enquiry* (2008). Each text has its own vision and makes its own contribution, but not all foreground an attention to design. You may find it helpful to dip into a mixture of approaches. Neyland's book on organisational ethnography (2007) makes a good case for a focus on 'sensibilities' rather than principles. There are many books on particular qualitative methods, but Walford et al. (2008) brings together some practical advice from sociologists of education whose work broadly aligns with the values set out in Hammersley and Atkinson (1983).

Bogdan, R. and Biklen, S. K. (2007). *Qualitative Research for Education: An Introduction to Theory and Methods*. Boston, Mass.; London, Pearson Allyn & Bacon.

A compendious research handbook written by two educational researchers trained in the 'Chicago School tradition' of social research and ethnography. First published in 1982, it questions the presumptions of 'conventional' social science, and draws on the grounded theory tradition to highlight writing techniques such as 'analytical memos'.

Denzin, N. K. and Lincoln, Y. S. (2011). *The SAGE Handbook of Qualitative Research*. Thousand Oaks, Calif.; London, Sage.

The latest iteration of a compendious methods handbook that promotes work within an interpretive and postmodern sociological tradition.

Hammersley, M. and Atkinson, P. (1983). *Ethnography: Principles in Practice*. London, Tavistock.

A best-seller and the ur-text for many educational ethnographers, now in its third edition. Hammersley and Atkinson set out a vision of an ethnographic practice that is 'deliberative and systematic', steering a middle path between reflexivity and rigour. Organised with chapters on research design, access, field relations, oral accounts, documents, organising data, analysis, writing and ethics, its format has influenced many other textbooks. The chapter on the processes of analysis exemplifies their philosophical commitment to generating robust ethnographic knowledge. Less visible is their disavowal of engaged and explicitly political forms of ethnographic practice, and their consequent wariness of participation and participant-observation. Written in a slightly detached, third-person style, the book relies heavily on examples and quotations, and is also fortified with a range of different research examples, many from education. Few of these examples are developed at any length, leading to a slightly disjointed style. Whilst not for the absolute beginner, this is a guide for returning to at each stage of research.

Hammersley, M. (1992). *What's Wrong with Ethnography? Methodological Explorations.* London, Routledge.

This provocatively titled book is initially hard to fathom. Is it a critique or a defence? It turns out to be both. Elaborating on some of the themes addressed in *Ethnography: Principles in Practice*, Hammersley makes the case for 'subtle realism', for some forms of empirical generalisation, and rehearses debates in the philosophy of knowledge in order to question the quantitative/qualitative divide. Is there a risk of tilting at windmills?

Luker, K. (2008). *Salsa Dancing into the Social Sciences: Research in an Age of Info-glut.* Cambridge, Mass.; London, Harvard University Press.

A refreshingly iconoclastic and fun set of reflections on how not to be a CSS (canonical social scientist) and instead to 'salsa-dance' one's way towards theoretical generalisations and insights. Informed by an impressive research career as a feminist sociology of law, Luker's book combines humility with intellectual sophistication. Touches only tangentially on ethnography, and makes the case for using fuzzy logic for the analysis of 'data'.

Mason, J. (2002). *Qualitative Researching.* London, Sage.

There are many books like this holistic account of each stage of a qualitative research process, but reading one or two helpfully situates ethnographic debates in a larger field. The test for ethnographers is to read such texts and yet not feel pressurised to adopt the linear chronology they appear to espouse. Mason's book is well written and sensible.

Neyland, D. (2007). *Organisational Ethnography*. London, Sage.

This is an articulate vision for thinking about research design as a set of ethnographic 'sensibilities' rather than a prescriptive list of principles. Drawing on research conducted in corporations and large organisations, it points to the growing interest in ethnographic research within business studies. Unlike some books, it combines practical advice with thoughtful theory.

Pole, C. and Morrison, M. (2003). *Ethnography for Education*. Buckingham, Open University Press.

Whilst its title is very promising, this is a somewhat conventional socio-logical account of ethnographic practice, but its focus on educational contexts and literature makes it a useful resource for those working in education. It helpfully works through the practicalities of the research tasks.

Walford, G. (ed.) (2008) *How to do Educational Ethnography*. London, Tufnell Press.

A short if slightly irresolute volume, with half a dozen chapters by experienced ethnographers distilling experience and offering helpful practical advice. These are followed by two that are far more concerned with debates in social theory and the politics of representation. The practicalities – fieldnotes, interviewing, access, videoing – are helpfully addressed in chapters by Sara Delamont, Martin Forsey and W. Douglas Baker. The final two chapters take a different tack. Drawing on his work with Willis, Matts Trondmann defends the importance of theory, whilst Dennis Beach raises important questions about representation. The result of a collaboration through the Oxford Ethnography and Education conferences, the book hints at unresolved epistemological tensions between the different contributors.

Additional online resources can be found at: www.sagepub.co.uk/beraseries.sp

CHAPTER 3

INTO THE EDUCATIONAL 'FIELD': RELATIONSHIPS, RECIPROCITIES AND RESPONSIBILITIES

What is in this chapter?

- The problem of defining an ethnographic 'field'
- Reflections on how fieldwork is changing
- Advice on ethnographic reciprocity and responsibility

Introduction

Spend any time with an anthropologist, and soon the conversation will turn to 'fieldwork'. The metaphor conjures up the image of a researcher hard at work in the open air, tilling their intellectual soil. But a moment of thought reminds one that research is defined as much by lived relationships as by physical geography. Ethnographers of education do not take off their ethnographic uniform at the end of the school day, and the quality of 'fieldwork' depends on how they relate to their participants and informants. For ethnographers, research relationships are first and foremost social relationships, with all the concomitant responsibilities and demands this brings. It is beholden on the researcher to think about how best to nurture and negotiate these relationships – both with humans and non-human others – in ways that will enable ethnographic analysis.

How is this chapter structured?

In this chapter, we help you conceptualise your 'field' and your research role within it, as well as pointing to the limits of the metaphor itself. We start with history. There is a whole range of different approaches to ethnographic 'fieldwork': the term itself has come in for intense scrutiny in recent years. We describe how the 'field' came to lose first its political innocence and then its self-evident status. The first section, 'Making ethnographic fields', asks you to think about how these histories of practice might influence your own understanding of your research site/s and relationships, and how these define you.

Drawing on a range of ethnographic examples, we show how educational spaces and pedagogic relationships are not just accidents of geography, or inert containers for social life: they are created and nurtured by people (including researchers) in myriad ways. Even if your research is spatially bounded – whether by relationships in a school staffroom or the networks that facilitate international educational policy flows – you will repeatedly foreground certain spaces and relationships whilst disavowing others. Being aware of these choices is key.

In 'Ethnography on the move', we go on to explore recent thinking about spaces and places, and the way we inhabit an increasingly interconnected world. We introduce the concept of mobile or 'multi-sited' ethnographies as one way to making sense of contemporary educational practices, and the implication of this approach for one's research and writing. We also think about other ways in which, as writers and researchers, we make connections between spaces and scales.

In the third section, entitled 'Ethnography as reciprocity?,' we discuss the social relationships that not only enable but are also integral to ethnographic research. We reflect on the forms of reciprocity that may be appropriate for the educational world you are exploring. These relationships are not just with other people, but may well be with other social agents. Each case brings its own responsibilities. You are likely to have a range of skills and knowledges that you could offer, but reciprocity is rarely calculable in material terms. It may be that in offering to teach, write policy documents or help people negotiate alien bureaucratic worlds, you can play an invaluable role. Reciprocity and participation may be two sides of the same coin – the things you offer are also ways of learning. It may go further still, and lead you to take on the mantle of advocate or activist. We return to these debates in Chapter 7.

In the final section, 'Ethnographic ethics, ethnographic politics', we consider the ethical and political dilemmas that accompany the ethnographic journey. Difficult questions about academic accountability and the politics of representation are sharpened by the way many ethics committees frown upon the protean and flexible aspects of ethnographic research. Anthropologists and other ethnographers have responded by writing about the consequences of these review boards for research. Whilst there are no simple answers, they benefit from careful thought. We end with questions and dilemmas to help think through these issues, along with ideas for further reading.

Making ethnographic fields

Once upon a time, ethnographic 'fieldwork' was primarily conducted outdoors. In North America, the first empirical research was carried out amongst native American communities, whilst European researchers worked in Africa and Asia, facilitated by the *'pax imperium'* and the largesse of colonial research institutes and grants (Tilley 2011). Anthropological field knowledge was no longer just a question of 'notes and queries' but about the time spent in one's research site. Despite the magisterial armchair scholarship of the French sociologists Emile Durkheim and Marcel Mauss, Malinowski's research manifesto meant leaving the verandah behind, and led to modernist classics such as Evans-Pritchard's *The Nuer* (1940), accounts that prided themselves on their 'ethnographic holism' (Thornton 1988) and that foregrounded participation in people's lives as the best way to observe. The establishment of US anthropology also depended on adopting the rhetoric of science, though influential figures such as Franz Boas also pointed to the risk of the discipline being used as a cover for government espionage (see Stocking 1960 for an account of this early history).

But even then there were other approaches, such as the ethnographic aspects of the work carried out at the so-called 'Chicago School' of sociology. Under the influence of W. I. Thomas and Robert Park, generations of students and scholars sought to make sense of the social dynamics of the new metropolis. Given the size of the Chicago department and its influence on the history of Sociology, a whole range of approaches to studying urban communities were pioneered, including observation studies, life histories and documentary analysis (Bulmer 1984).

Away from Chicago's urban grime, anthropological ethnographers represented 'their' people or community in book-length accounts, with
chapters grandiosely titled 'Economy', 'Religion' and 'Kinship'. Spurred
on by the legitimacy offered by 'functionalist' theories of society, the aim
was to understand and describe social formations as functional 'going
concerns' within one comprehensive monograph. Amongst the more
sophisticated writers, this was a knowing conceit, but their works
acquired canonical status, and the discipline acquired a cult status.
Amidst the post-war UK university boom and US Cold War funding for
Area Studies, field-based anthropological research flourished. An
extended period of 'ethnographic' fieldwork became enshrined as a disciplinary rite of passage, and a shibboleth of anthropological rigour. The
length of time spent in the field became a proxy for the quality of one's
research (Marcus 2007; Okely 2007).

During the 1960s, politically astute ethnographers once again began
to be troubled by the colonial histories, research institutes and postcolonial power relations that continued to facilitate their access to these
'fields'. For some anti-colonial critics, anthropology, and by association
ethnography, was irreversibly tainted by its colonialist origins. US government agencies had already drawn extensively on anthropological expertise in the Second World War (Price 2008), but now came rumours of
CIA plots to research counter-insurgency movements, the most famous
of which was 'Project Camelot' (Mills 2003). Growing dissent and tension
came to a head during the Vietnam War, and marked the publication of
the first anthropological code of ethics, which led to an increasing interest
in carrying out ethnographic research 'at home' and a concern with
'studying up' (Nader 1974).

If the anthropological 'field' had lost its innocence, it took longer for
the discipline to work through the epistemological implications of this
debate. Initiated by the rise of postmodern theory and poststructuralist
debates around textual power, the 'field' as a site of ethnographic work
received particular scrutiny in the work of Marcus and Clifford. As Clifford
put it, 'Fieldwork is a complex historical, political, intersubjective set of
experiences which escapes the metaphors of participation, observation,
initiation, rapport, induction, learning and so forth, often deployed to
account for it' (1990, 53). It is no surprise that it is so hard to describe.

Whilst seeking to hang on to empirical research practice, some scholars have sought to rethink the field, suggesting that an ethnography of a
single site could never really capture the multiple and multi-stranded
networks that shape the contemporary moment. Gupta and Ferguson's
work (1997) has been particularly helpful. They questioned what they
called the 'spatial metaphysics' (Malkki 1989) of the British fieldwork

tradition and its fetishisation of the 'local'. Instead they called for a more pluralistic approach to writing about the multiple and multi-stranded networks of contemporary social life. Their work called not for the abandonment of fieldwork, but rather for its reconstruction, as 'one element in a multi-stranded methodology', a shift from 'bounded fields' to 'shifting locations' (Gupta and Ferguson 1997, 37). This to what Gupta and Ferguson call 'location-work' echoes debates within feminism around the importance of 'situated knowledges' (Haraway 1988). The cultural studies ethnographer Paul Willis made similar points, warning that the ethnographic field 'still carries with it a whole set of imperial baggage and social relationships as well as the notion that you can describe a whole world' (1996, 186).

More recently still, attention has turned to the involvement of ethnographers in creating these fields. As Raymond Madden neatly frames it, 'ethnographers are place makers ... ethnography turns someone's everyday place into another very particular sort of place' (Madden 2010, 38). Whilst you may not agree that 'ethnographic fields do not exist beyond the imaginings of the ethnographer' (Madden 2010, 38), there is no doubt that 'fieldwork' now becomes as much a state of mind as a set of research practices.

Echoing Madden's argument, Cook et al. (2009) go one further, and suggest that we ought instead to think of our ethnographic research as 'unsited' – proposing that 'in exchange for acknowledging that fields are always constructed out of a too-rich reality, we would gain the freedom to determine their boundaries explicitly, in relation to our research questions' (Cook et al. 2009). Another solution may be to discard the agricultural imagery altogether, and to talk instead about sites or zones of engagement. The terms change, but the commitment to 'being at risk' remains.

Shielded by disciplinary boundaries and a realist commitment to empirical research, educational ethnographers have focused less on these epistemological debates. Their research sites have often seemed practical and self-evident: the classroom, the curriculum, the playground and the staffroom. Their focus has been the pragmatic aspects of research: how best to define one's case, to negotiate access and to conduct interviews (Walford et al. 2008).

Whether pragmatist or theorist, the task facing ethnographers of all stripes remains the same: delimiting one's 'case', object or field of study, and gaining access to the social actors that matter. Let us assume, for example, that you are interested in making ethnographic sense of the informal power hierarchies found in school playgrounds and how the concept of 'bullying' gets deployed within a school. The first decision is to find out what one can reasonably (and ethically) research. Questions of research ethics frame every aspect of the research process, as we discuss below. The researcher has to consider the sensitivity of the topic, and how they deal with questions of confidentiality, especially if they uncover cases of abuse. All research now has to get ethical clearance, and the onus is on ethnographers to explain the particular way they sustain informed consent over extended periods of time.

The next question is how to divide up one's precious research time. Should one try and develop a relationship with the kids who seem to wield influence, or with those left on the margins? Should one do interviews with dinner ladies, teachers and parents, or engage students through participatory research activities? Is what is happening in the classroom, and in children's families, relevant for understanding playground cultures? Is the history of playground bullying in the school, or the school's anti-bullying policy, also relevant? Or the way bullying gets talked about in films and on TV? What about the way that neighbouring schools, the local authority or school board deal with the issue? What about school and government policies? Many ethnographers would start by questioning the very connotations of a term like 'bullying', and whether it had come to be taken for granted within the school.

The illustration is a reminder that even before field research begins, the ethnographer may have a series of implicit 'hunches' and presuppositions that will shape the genre of participation and the focus of observation. In the next chapter we discuss the way that 'analytical memos' can be used to reflect on one's fieldnotes. But there is no reason why this process of articulating one's hunches should not start earlier. Some writers recommend that novice researchers try drawing diagrammatic visualisations of the relationships and forms of power that potentially define their field, using mind-maps, lists and sketches to help them identify key issues. Several of these practical exercises are included at the end of this chapter.

Ethnography on the move

In a world of global 'always-on' connectivity, ideas, imageries, policies, symbols and meanings circulate increasingly fast. It may be very difficult to keep the ethnographic 'object' still for long enough to study and make sense of it. Perhaps you are interested in studying international student mobility, a global network of boarding schools, or the way transnational organisations such as the OECD promote a tool such as

PISA for promoting educational standards within national education systems. In each case, the field becomes increasingly amorphous. Yet we also argue that ethnographers create understandings through nurturing social relationships, a process that takes time for trust to develop. Can one be an ethnographer on the move? Does the networked society present ethnography with an impossible contradiction?

One response is to carry out ethnographic research in more than one place or locale. If the artefacts and meanings one seeks to understand don't stand still, why should we as researchers? If educational policies and practices travel transnationally, aided and abetted by governments and non-governmental agencies, can schools ever now be understood or explored as self-contained bounded entities? In their *Globalizing the Research Imagination* (Kenway and Fahey 2009) two educationalists interview ethnographers from anthropology, sociology and geography whose work has set out to redefine the research imaginary and the way research is taught. Whilst not all the contributors are ethnographers, all are profoundly aware of the demands placed on students to develop a conceptual tool-kit that allows them to think across boundaries and borders. As Fazal Rizvi puts it:

> It is impossible to look at a place or a culture without seeing it as inter-related to other places and cultures, to history and to the cultural politics of interdisciplinarity ... And that really is the shift I would like to see in students, away from a static, positivist bounded view of places and cultures, to a perspective that is defined in terms of their relationship and connections to the rest of the world. (2009, 113)

Whilst some remain sceptical about what Willis (in Mills and Gibb 2000) called 'trickle-down' ethnographies, ethnographers cannot ignore questions of scale. National debates get intertwined with local agendas, whilst at the same time global issues can only be understood in a more intimate frame. The question becomes one of how to understand and represent these connections and relationships.

Ever attuned to methodological trends, Marcus gave this attention an influential label: 'multi-sited ethnography'. He suggested a shift from 'a conventional single-site location ... to multiple sites of observation and participation', allowing the researcher to follow the 'circulation of cultural meanings, objects, and identities in diffuse time-space' (1995, 96). This methodological vision resonated with the growing emphasis among experimental ethnographers such as Bruno Latour on understanding and following the networks and connections that shaped the social. The 'field' was no longer simply a geographical place but became rather a conceptual space that allowed abstract connections and rewarded close theorisation. Ethnography increasingly began to be understood as something intersubjective, co-constructed and mediated.

Bruno Latour has been a particularly creative and influential ethnographer, and his ethnographic studies of everyday scientific practice with Steve Woolgar have led him to champion 'actor-network theory', and an approach that seeks to treat human and non-human agents as equally important shapers of social worlds. They are perhaps best known for their *Laboratory Life: The Social Construction of Scientific Facts* (1979), an ethnography of a neuro-endocrinology laboratory that highlights the importance ascribed to the production of academic papers. Given its focus on the creation of scientific knowledge, one could indeed see it as an educational ethnography. Latour's work, increasingly ambitious and theoretical, has shaped anthropological theory and practice perhaps more than any other recent scholar. The field of Science and Technology Studies, of which he has been an influential pioneer, and its attention to knowledge generation, has much to offer ethnographers of education.

The idea of multi-sited ethnography has now become commonplace within anthropology, even if fewer educational ethnographers have explored its potential. And despite its increasing popularity, mobile, multi-agential ethnography does not resolve the ethnographer's dilemma. If anything, being 'on the move' makes ethnographic practice even more complicated. It multiplies the demands of access, of developing trust and sustaining empathy. Instead of just negotiating access to one research 'site', the ethnographer has to make sense of the relationships across a range of social spaces and entities, requiring ever more attention to what has become known as the 'politics of location'. Location work is hard work.

On the other hand, educational practices were never static and place-bound. Location-work allows one to change scale, to juxtapose experiences and insights from a range of settings, and to zoom in and out between localities. It is a technique that emphasises disjunction and fragmentation, rather than coherence.

David's research experience in Uganda is instructive. Whilst he initially planned to work just within one rural secondary school, he became more and more interested in the way a national conversation about 'gender' shaped relations amongst students. Each day the school's teachers would sit in the staff room dissecting and debating a well-thumbed copy of yesterday's national paper, a paper that was often full of debates about feminism and gender equality. He realised that he couldn't limit his analytical focus to the school itself. He began to document and analyse media representations, the government's equality policies and even Ugandan discussions of an international women's conference being held in Beijing that year (Mills and Ssewakiryanga 2002). These were sites in which discourses around gender were being produced and circulated. He also taught and carried out research within Makerere University, trying to understand the rather different refractions of feminism amongst students on a Women's Studies course. Realising Ugandan journalists based in London provided another perspective on these debates in their weekly columns in the same paper on life in Britain, he went on to spend time with the Ugandan diaspora in the UK. Each context carried its own expectations and demands, and each affected the other.

Anthropologists of education are increasingly exploring educational connections across time and space. Stambach's *Faith in Schools* (2010) follows American evangelicals from US universities to Tanzanian and Ugandan schools. Her ethnographic vignettes depict debates in American anthropology classrooms and East African primary schools as US evangelical students carry out their own particular types of 'fieldwork' as part of their summer service. She pays particular attention to the role that anthropological and ethnographic work play in informing missionary practice, and how missionaries 'compared their faith-based, service-learning mission work to participant-observation methods of anthropology' (ibid., 5). But this is not just a set of vivid descriptions of American students teaching the creation story in Tanzania. She juxtaposes these with critical reflections on the 'faith' many educators have in secular education models, as her larger aim is to look at education as a 'pivotal site in which multiple and crosscutting 'schools of faith' inform and transform the state' (ibid., 7). It is an ethnographic analysis that has serious theoretical ambitions.

As increasing numbers of researchers realise the potential of 'multi-sited' ethnography, a critical and experimental literature around this topic is growing. Edited collections by Mark-Anthony Falzon (2009) and James Faubion and George Marcus (2009) demonstrate the range of approaches and opinions that exist. Like any method, multi-sited (or unsited) research offers new solutions and presents new problems.

Ethnography as reciprocity?

The anthropologist Clifford Geertz once memorably described ethnography as 'deep hanging out', at once affirming and teasing the disciplinary attachment to 'being there'. But this metaphor, perhaps even more than the similar rich imagery of 'thick description' (Geertz 1973), meant being in, and negotiating, a complex skein of social networks and relationships. Hanging out is never something to be done alone. Yet it is surprising how little attention there has been to research relationships within methods textbooks. Even the best contemporary guides (e.g. Madden 2010) focus primarily on how best to 'be' around people rather than on relationships with them, and dwell little on the forms of empathy and involvement this might imply.

If ethnographic relationships are always also social relationships, then there can be no easy how-to formula to guide one through the tangled thicket of social life. Empathy is a useful resource but so too is a certain judiciousness and judgement, along with the ability to read social situations, bodily deportments and emotional regimes. Anthropologists have sometimes characterised themselves as child-like in their lack of 'local knowledge', but this would seem disingenuous. An academic training should give one the ability both to 'code switch' and to quickly pick up an awareness of local social expectations and etiquettes. Becoming best buddies with just those people who seek to befriend is never a wise tactic in life, nor should it be in social research.

Many sociological commentators highlight the risks of 'going native' and of losing one's detachment. It is a position informed by work within ethnomethodology and the importance it ascribes to attending to 'members' experiences' while losing one's objectivity as a researcher. Such caution is not always helpful. It presumes that objectivity is best found by maintaining social distance, and that the researcher should not get too close. The spectre of relativism also lurks: that one might become uncritical and unreflexive. Yet whilst full-blown moral relativism is ethically indefensible, there is a space for a degree of 'methodological relativism' (Mills 2003) in ethnographic research, and for not immediately jumping to conclusions or positions. Meanwhile, anthropological ethnographers have highlighted the value of getting entangled, the limits of any insider/outsider dichotomy, and the benefits of being a 'native' ethnographer (Narayan 1993).

The value of getting entangled is best illustrated through examples of ethnographic work. Craig Jeffrey is a cultural geographer whose ethnographic writing seeks to capture the paradoxes surrounding education in rural north India. In *Timepass* (Jeffrey 2010) he documents how the extravagant promises made for higher education by Indian policy makers and development experts had turned sour. For many of his participants, continuing in higher education was primarily a way to avoid unemployment, whilst for some union activists it became a survival strategy and way to generate an income by working as a 'fixer' and go-between. In order to understand the politics of everyday corruption, Jeffrey had to tread carefully, getting to know the students and simply hanging out with them, chatting, joking and drinking tea.

Whilst open about the power inequities in ethnographic research, he is also thoughtful about how he developed rich and insightful relationships with his participants. It meant giving something of himself, his personal background and his history, as well as his own local knowledge:

> I believe that a constant attention to various forms of reciprocity is crucial to successful ethnographic fieldwork. Although my research felt highly extractive, it involved constant 'back and forth' with my informants as we debated striking contrasts and unexpected similarities between politics and society in the UK and India, and repeated efforts to share my emerging results via seminars and articles that I wrote in local newspapers. (Jeffrey 2010, 32)

He went on to acknowledge his mediating role, helping people make sense of the situations they find themselves in, and providing them with a comparative perspective on education in other parts of India and abroad, including in his home country, Scotland.

> But I did often feel part of an interpretative community of young people interested in social and political change. Many of my informants said that they valued our discussions as opportunities to vent frustration and reflect on their socio-political position. It also became clear that for many students I was a resource: a source of information on what was happening outside UP and a sounding board for students' own ideas about how north Indian society was changing. (ibid., 35)

These group conversations often developed at road-side drinks stalls, presenting Jeffrey with the tricky task of recording and sustaining these dialogues, but also ensuring endless opportunities to try out ideas in an iterative way.

Ethnographic ethics, ethnographic politics

In 2005 an American professor of anthropology published, under the pseudonym Rebeka Nathan, an accessible and pacy account of a year spent as a student in her own university. Entitled *My Freshman Year: What a Professor Learnt by Becoming a Student*, the ethnography offers intriguing insights into the lives of Midwest college students as they learnt the art of 'college management', juggling paid work, academic study and friendships. Particularly telling are her vignettes of dorm life, with its rituals of belonging and forced jollity. There are also some pithy comments on the marked racial divides on campus, on the experiences of black students and the lack of interest among American students in the international students on campus.

But none of this seemed to matter in the months that followed publication. Instead, Nathan was quickly 'outed' as Cathy Small, a professor at Northern Arizona University, by a reporter working for the *Chronicle for Higher Education*. A heated public debate ensued about the ethics of having become a covert student carrying out undercover research, even if this had been approved by the local institutional review board (ethics committee). Instead of generating informed debate about the purpose of college today for many young Americans, the book became known as a textbook case of 'unethical' ethnographic research. The online exchanges were acrid and angry.

Nathan may well have anticipated trouble. In her Afterword, entitled 'Ethics and ethnography', she confesses to 'coming out' to particular students on three occasions, including once to her dorm 'resident assistant' who was concerned that she was falling behind with her academic work. She admits to growing increasingly uneasy about her choice to adopt a student persona: 'I realised that my level of comfort and certainty was shifting with the depth and quality of my relationships … incidents, stories and conversations attached to real people and real encounters' (ibid., 164).

This lack of certainty came to a head when she began to write, and began to ask herself how students would feel if they discovered that their informal conversations had been published by a professor at their own university. Her solution was to discard much of what she had learnt: 'I have in my notes and my memory much richer and more intimate knowledge than I sometimes share directly in this book' (ibid., 165). But lines such as 'my commitment to not lie directly' are uneasy attempts at moral rationalisation. She never explores the possibility that being more open about her position in the university may also have led to rich and insightful relationships, and to generating knowledge that she could have used directly. She ends the book with her 'sheepish' admission to a former classmate that she is no longer a student but now 'back to being a professor'. The student's disbelief is palpable.

Contrast Nathan's approach to that of the sociologist Gaye Tuchman. Her 2009 ethnography of a 'mid-ranking' state university she calls *Wannabe U* is based on several years of observation, a lightly disguised portrait of her own institution, the University of Connecticut. She describes her portrayal of a 'conformist university' as one that would match many such institutions seeking to 'elbow their way up the rankings' (Nathan 2009).

Tuchman became interested in these transformations as she watched departments break into open warfare in their struggles over resources.

Her focus is on the institutional transformations wreaked by an administrative cadre (not to forget the trustees and state legislature) who lust after 'fame, funding and power' (ibid., 15). She is quick to make her own role clear. Once she decided to carry out this research, she gained ethical clearance, and was given permission to take notes but never to tape or take photos on campus.

She developed creative techniques to anonymise her informants, and is proud of the fact that one of them read and commented on a whole chapter without realising that he was the person being quoted. Having previously written an ethnography of journalistic practices, she borrowed techniques from journalism, such as always getting two people's accounts of any event in order to corroborate individual narratives. She was assiduous at taking notes at public meetings within the university, pointedly tapping loudly on her laptop to draw attention to herself, but also at attending closely to the way the university portrayed itself, in news media, in internal emails and newsletters. As she put it: 'I have followed a key rule: "Everything's data unless it will harm someone"' (ibid, 18). On the other hand, she decided not to interview current administrators, and this is the one significant weakness of the book, because their interpretations and justifications for their actions are rarely heard.

Both accounts illustrate the mutual entanglement of the ethical and political dimensions of ethnographic research, and the difficulty of separating and isolating the two (Mills 2003). Both grapple with the conundrums of doing research as an 'insider' within an education setting, and both try to find ways of dealing with the ethical and political consequences. There are also marked differences. Nathan's work largely ignores existing ethnographies of universities (e.g. Becker et al. 1968; Moffatt 1989), several of which address the ethical conundrums. Tuchman's work is much more politically and theoretically sophisticated, and from the start is not scared to ask the big questions about the changing role of the university in today's society, and the pressures created by the expectations of accountability and the pressures of competition. One cavil might be that Tuchman knew what she wanted to find, but on the other hand her own candour about this makes it easy for the reader to critically assess the evidence she presents. Both illustrate the importance of ethnographers taking seriously questions of personal research accountability. They demonstrate the lack of simple formulae or answers, and the importance of working through ethical questions in practice.

Nathan's ethnographic approach was not the first to stir up controversy. Laud Humphreys' *Tea-Room Trade* (1970) represents, for some, a textbook example of unethical ethnographic practice. He followed up his observations of sexual encounters between men in public toilets by taking down car number plates and then following people to their homes in order to invite them for interview.

The history of the emergence of the ethical codes that now govern social research is a complex one (Israel and Hay 2006), shaped by many such episodes. The scandals of mid-twentieth-century scientific arrogance – from Nazi experimentation to the American syphilis and gonorrhea experiments – prompted public outcry and demands that medical researchers should be held accountable. Whilst an initial set of principles emerged from the Nuremburg trials, they were developed by a series of conventions and protocols that sought to define a shared set of ethical underpinnings to research.

These principles – 'confidentiality', 'informed consent' and 'the avoidance of harm' and 'anonymity' – are now at the core of all research ethics. Adopted first in the US by institutions and scholarly associations, starting with Psychology in the 1950s and Anthropology in the aftermath of the Vietnam War, they are now universally recognised and applied. In the US this was driven by national legislation, and more recently in UK universities at the insistence of medical research charities. Whilst the precise wording and focus varies by discipline, the codes are used by institutions and research councils to vet all proposed social research.

Many ethnographers and qualitative researchers have been unhappy about the way such ethical principles get put to work (Dingwall 2006; Sin 2005; Hedgecoe 2008). They come freighted with a heavy load of assumptions about the nature of social research and the form that research encounters take. 'Informed consent' presumes that the very notion of research is fully understood, and that the encounter is bounded and defined. Some people may not want to give written consent, whilst many might find the unstructured and ongoing nature of ethnographic research difficult to comprehend. The objections of ethics committees to the uncertainties of ethnography are compounded by the rise of a defensive 'audit culture' within universities and demands for accountability and transparency (Strathern 2000).

A more epistemological objection to governance by ethical code is that these codes rely upon a process of value-bifurcation (Mills 2003). They carve out a field of personal behaviour that can be judged solely in ethical terms, ignoring questions of context, politics and power. Getting ethical clearance for one's ethnographic research project does not absolve one from difficult questions about representation, the benefits accrued from research or the larger political economy structuring knowledge production.

We thus question Hammersley's insistence that scholarship has to disregard the political, and his argument that researchers should 'try to minimise any distortion of their findings by their political convictions or practical interests' (Hammersley 2000, 12). This may not be possible or wise. Activists and advocates can make good scholars, though they need to be frank about their positions if they are to maintain their credibility and trust.

What to do? The onus of defining an ethical ethnographic research practice falls largely on the ethnographer. From 'gaining access' to reciprocity and the ongoing negotiation of consent, every aspect of ethnographic practice has an ethical dimension. The dilemmas, and one's responses, are unpredictable and always emergent, and so no set of guidelines or codes can adjudicate on precisely how often consent should be obtained or when the expectations of confidentiality have been fulfilled. As ethnographers, we also have to keep returning to questions of ethics, asking about the additional ethical responsibilities that come from participating as opposed to simply observing, thinking further about reflexivity and textual representation.

Perhaps the best one can do is to try and anticipate the sorts of dilemmas that one might face. One's very choice of a research topic carries with it ethical responsibilities and demands. New fields and sites of ethnographic practice, together with a growing diversity of ethnographic approaches, mean new dilemmas and opportunities. Whether working alone or in larger teams, the epistemological task is the same: remaining attentive and reflective to the way we are positioned and embodied within our research, and the way we represent our research to others.

Conclusion

Despite the innovations and rethinking of the nature of the field, ethnographic theorists are reluctant to abandon the concept altogether. We may not be sure what or where it is, but we hang on to the field as a way of thinking about research of productive strangeness. As Rabinow et al. see it:

> The challenge is to become part of a foreign milieu, to submit to the outside, to get drowned in and carried away by it, while staying alert to the gradual emergence of a theme to which chance encounters, fugitive events, anecdotal observations give rise. In short, the term design emphasises the significance of long term research, the need to be sensitive to the singularity of the field site, and the art of not letting one's research and thinking be dominated by well-established theories of what fieldwork is, of what a published monograph should look like. (2008, 116)

Perhaps it is best to think about the 'field' as an artefact of research – a thing to fully understand and comprehend only in retrospect. It is at once a space invoked and shaped, a lens through which to think about that space and a process of learning about that space.

Exercises

- Think about your research field as a set of social and moral relationships. List the significant relationships that you may need to develop. What are some of the ethical dilemmas that you may encounter as you seek to negotiate access? How might you deal with them?

- Imagine you are doing ethnographic research in a school on pupils' attitudes to bullying. You assure the students that their accounts of their experiences will remain confidential and be anonymised. The school then approaches you and asks you about what you know about a particularly painful and difficult case. You are aware that you have a legal duty to protect a child if they are 'at risk of significant harm'. What should you do?

Further reading

Many anthropologists have written autobiographical accounts of their fieldwork experiences, and often they make gripping reading. Malinowski's *A Diary in the Strict Sense of the Term* (1967) should still be required reading for all budding ethnographers, but the following texts offer more organised reflections on the 'field' and its travails. Robben and Sluka (2007) is the most comprehensive of the texts, but Blommaert and Jie (2010) offer a digested summary.

Blommaert, J. and Jie, D. (2010). *Ethnographic Fieldwork: A Beginner's Guide*. Bristol; Buffalo, NY, Multilingual Matters.

Short, quick and punchy: a good read. The narrative unfolds through the experiences of Dong Jie doing ethnographic research on schools for rural migrants in Beijing for his dissertation, with a particular focus on sociolinguistics.

Cerwonka, A. and Malkki, L. H. (2007). *Improvising Theory: Process and Temporality in Ethnographic Fieldwork*. Chicago; London, University of Chicago Press.

This book is built largely around the email correspondence between a doctoral student in politics and her anthropological mentor, vividly illuminating the process of methodological improvisation, ethical learning and theory building that accompanies any ethnographic fieldwork. An honest and unflinching account of the trials and hazards facing a novice researcher.

Falzon, M.-A. (ed.) (2009). *Multi-sited Ethnography: Theory, Praxis and Locality in Contemporary Research*. Farnham, Ashgate.

This edited collection critically assesses George Marcus's concept of multi-sited ethnography, with some chapters seeking to question the concept and defend the importance of being located, whilst others put the concept to work in their own research. Not for beginners, but helpfully signals the ways in which fieldwork practices are changing.

Faubion, J. D. and Marcus, G. E. (2009). *Fieldwork is Not What it Used to Be: Learning Anthropology's Method in a Time of Transition*. London, Cornell University Press.

A thoughtful and articulate set of reflections from a group of Rice-based anthropologists on doing (and teaching) fieldwork today. Sophisticated and nuanced accounts of ethnographic ethics, graduate pedagogies and research design.

Gardner, A. and Hoffman, D. M. (2006). *Dispatches from the Field: Neophyte Ethnographers in a Changing World*. Long Grove, Ill., Waveland Press.

A set of raw accounts of fieldwork written by American anthropology doctoral students whilst in the field in 2002–2003. Little is edited out, and their troubled reflections on guilt, hostility, and the expectations of reciprocity are illuminating. Will the vividness of these depictions continue in their subsequent scholarly writing?

Israel, M. and Hay, I. (2006). *Research Ethics for Social Scientists: Between Ethical Conduct and Regulatory Compliance*. London, Sage.

This is a useful potted history of the rise of ethics regulation coupled with thoughtful reflections on how to negotiate these regimes and sustain ethical mindfulness. There are no direct reflections on ethnographic practice. In their voluminous *Handbook of Social Research Ethics* (Mertens and Ginsberg 2009) they do include a specific chapter on ethnography.

Kvale, S. (2009). *InterViews: Learning the Craft of Qualitative Research Interviewing*. Los Angeles, Sage.

Whilst not a handbook on ethnographic research per se, this is one of the best guides to thinking – and rethinking – the politics and ethics of interviewing. Questions of power are never far away.

Robben, A. C. G. M. and Sluka, J. A. (2007). *Ethnographic Fieldwork: An Anthropological Reader*. Malden, Mass.; Oxford, Blackwell.

This is a well-chosen reader bringing together insights and reflections on ethnographic fieldwork by key anthropological thinkers from Malinowski to Rabinow. Whilst it inevitably sets up an ethnographic canon, the readings cover the gamut of theoretical debates, with a strong focus on the ethical, political and personal aspects of fieldwork. An excellent introduction to the anthropological tradition, even if none of the readings relates directly to formal education. Comes with a comprehensive list of suggested further readings.

Additional online resources can be found at: www.sagepub.co.uk/beraseries.sp

CHAPTER 4

BEING, SEEING, WRITING: THE ROLE OF FIELDNOTES

What is in this chapter?

- A discussion of different approaches to writing fieldnotes
- Advice on how to take your first fieldnotes
- A discussion of using fieldnotes in analysis and writing
- Reflections on archiving fieldnotes

Introduction

If there is still a mystique around the practices of ethnographic field-work, then 'fieldnotes' are partly responsible. They are still talked of in hushed terms by some anthropologists: rarely shared, carefully hoarded, a secret treasure to be returned to again and again throughout one's career. If it is the case that, as Delamont once put it, 'fieldwork is only as good as the fieldnotes', then the art of ethnographic note-taking needs careful attention, both by teachers and students.

This chapter aims to dispel some of the aura that has surrounded 'fieldnotes'. We show how fieldnotes enable ethnographic researchers to combine 'being', 'seeing' and 'writing'. Ethnographic fieldnotes, in their varied genres, allow the researcher a powerful way of 'being' in one's research, documenting sensory experiences, and recording one's changing understanding. They also provide an invaluable personal archive for the researcher, and for future researchers to come. At their best they provide ethnographers with a way to create a distance and a way of making sense of the raw and sometimes overwhelming aspects of being at risk in their research. As Jack Goody wisely noted, 'A significant attribute of writing is the ability to communicate not only with others, but with oneself' (Goody 1977).

Ethnographers of education use a variety of tools in their research: observations, participation, interviews, focus groups, documentary analysis, life histories, to name but a few. There are now numerous methods texts dedicated to each method, and they all have their own lists of things to remember and snippets of advice. Our focus in this chapter is on the writing that characterises and accompanies an ethnographer's use of such methods, particularly in Education.

How is this chapter structured?

The first section of the chapter, 'The many lives of fieldnotes', explores the diversity of ways in which people write when in the 'field' and purposes to which these texts can be put. We draw on examples of fieldnotes made by ethnographers of education, as well as pointing to places to find wise advice and guidance in this process.

Ethnographers of different stripes approach the tasks of observation, recording and sense-making in different ways. Along with the emotional and symbolic significance of fieldnotes, there are practicalities to attend to. 'Pencil to paper?' reflects on what gets put into the ethnographers' notebooks, what gets left out, and how fieldnotes emerge. Questions of tone, voice and narrative style loom large. It is also a chance to muse on tomorrow's writing technologies. As social media develop and writing technologies continue to change, fieldwork and fieldnotes increasingly take on virtual, hyperlinked and diverse forms. Social relationships are also mediated through these writing technologies, bringing new opportunities and threats.

The relationship between writing and thinking is intimate, interwoven and iterative. If ethnographers use writing to develop their thinking, then thinking also informs the writing and rewriting of fieldnotes. 'Putting fieldnotes to work' explores a range of approaches to framing, developing and extending fieldnotes and observations, and the way ethnographers segue from observation to analysis in their fieldnotes. Do notes 'speak for themselves', or does the researchers' theoretical perspective shape what gets noticed, prioritised and analysed? We introduce a range of approaches to writing fieldnotes that offer different answers to this question. We return to the inductive process in Chapter 6, where we also discuss the merits and otherwise of computer-assisted approaches to analysis.

Finally, the section entitled 'Creating the ethnographic archive', we ask about the afterlife of fieldnotes. To what extent are they simply a private resource for researchers, to be returned to over time? Do they become an archive for other researchers? Should they be deposited in an online archive and be shared? What of the politics that surround their subsequent use? These are questions that all ethnographers have to address when writing, and afterwards when storing and preserving their notes.

The many lives of fieldnotes

Scratch notes, rough notes, cryptic scribbles. Notes unread, unremembered, destroyed. In a revealing piece on anthropological attitudes to fieldnotes, entitled 'I Am a Fieldnote', Jean Jackson describes the fraught emotions and intellectual torments that surround their inscription and use. For one, 'they are like your first child'; for another, they 'reveal the kind of person you are'; and for a third, their 'dirt, blood and spit' offer a 'tangible sign of … legitimacy' (1990, 26–29). Despite this fetishised way in which many anthropologists view fieldnotes, more than one anthropologist in her study admits to never reading them again. The act of writing may be enough to ensure that the experiences are indelibly etched. One of the authors (David) found returning to the raw emotions of his Ugandan fieldnotes very difficult. He relied instead on memory, together with extensive interview notes and focus-group transcripts in much of his subsequent writing.

So what is a fieldnote? The very difficulty of coming to a conclusive definition reveals something about ethnographic sensibilities. The term offers a shared language and academic identity uniting very different writing practices and technologies. It raises the question both of what is worth 'noting', and of what counts as a note. Is a quick scribble on the back of a hand a 'proper' fieldnote? What about an SMS text or a Facebook update? And a diary or interview transcript?

Does it matter where fieldnotes are written? Do they have to be recorded in the field? Is scribbling a note even possible amidst the busyness of participating in a social world? And what then? At what point in the 'writing up' of notes and scribbles does the analytical process begin? Many opinions; few answers.

Despite being more than two decades old, Sanjek's edited volume *Fieldnotes* (1990) remains an invaluable introduction to the complexities of anthropological thinking about fieldnotes. Sanjek helpfully suggests a vocabulary for talking about fieldnotes. He starts by highlighting the importance of what Ottenberg calls 'headnotes', the field knowledge that is never written down, and might indeed be hard to record. He goes on to talk about 'scratch notes', the quick scribbles and surreptitious jottings, mnemonics written amidst the flow of events. The very term 'scratch notes' is a reminder that writing can get in the way of just 'being'. It may not always be appropriate to pull out a pen and paper (or even a mobile or iPad). Many methods books reproduce some hand-written scribbles or cryptic codes, both to exemplify such jottings and sometimes to demystify the genre.

So what are you going to jot, note, draw or scribble? It is not enough to take Malinowski's advice to his student Camilla Wedgewood to ensure that fieldnotes 'contain a chaotic account in which everything is written down as it is observed or told' (quoted in Lutkehaus 1990, 305). Any attempt at trying to encompass the whole realm of sensory experience is going to fail. But this should not be seen as a shortcoming: note-taking allows and encourages individual reflexivity and creativity. That one observer might notice one thing and not another is inevitable. All writing is partial. The very practice of observational note-taking draws one's attention to the tangential and unexpected. And why focus on notes? Drawings, scribbles and sketches can all be ways of capturing embodied experiences in ways that transcend text (Taussig 2011).

The history of observation within social research dates back to the beginning of the twentieth century. In Britain it was popularised by the launch of the Mass Observation movement in 1937 (Summerfield 1985). The brainchild of an iconoclastic anthropologist (Tom Harrison) and a campaigning journalist (Charles Madge), the idea was to bring anthropological techniques home in order to create a 'science of ourselves' that would add to 'the social consciousness of the time'. The aim was to counter what they saw as growing commercial control of the mass media and the rise of fascism by encouraging ordinary people to record their subjective experiences and observations of 'ordinary lives'. It was launched with great fanfare on 12 May 1937, the coronation of King George VI. The republican-minded Mass Observation founders wanted to know whether ordinary people really were exuding the levels of patriotic loyalty ascribed to them by the newspapers. Whilst the original 'movement' petered out after the Second World War, despite being resurrected subsequently, the

1000 or so regular contributors and diarists left a fascinating archive of observational detail and insight.

The French surrealist writer Georges Perec took observation to its logical extreme in his *An attempt at exhausting a place in Paris* (Perec 2010 [1974]). Sitting in a Parisian café for the whole of one weekend, he attempted to record everything that happens 'when nothing happens'. In this excerpt his mundane observations take on an aesthetic aura through the attention to rhythm and flow:

A 63 [a bus] passes by

Six sewer workers (hard hats and high boots) take rue des Canettes.

Two free taxis at the taxi stand

An 87 passes by

A blind man coming from rue des Canettes passes by in front of the café; he's a young man, with a rather confident way of walking.

An 86 passes by

Two men with pipes and black satchels

A man with a black satchel and no pipe

A woman in a wool jacket, smiling

A 96

A differently cryptic account comes from Sara Delamont's notebooks. An influential educational ethnographer, this snippet is from her fieldnotes taken whilst observing a Capoeira dance-class, an AfroBrazilian dance form:

8.32 S yells 'Stop'. Circles them, S dem GBACM, S rdea IL GBACM neg, rol, au cw Dems routine 6 times. Says 'Train with yr frnd. Play with begs'. Pairs. (Delamont 2008, 48)

Written only for her benefit, it illustrates the importance of snatched notes and scribbles to help prompt later recall and elaboration. As Clifford puts it, jottings are mnenomics that 'fix' observation. Delamont goes on to unpack her acronyms and the abbreviations, and to show how with each rewriting, she gives her fieldnotes context and meaning.

Robert Emerson offers a different example from a student's ethnographic fieldnotes. Their scribbled note of a seemingly insignificant event in the nursery day – 'delivery of three bags of sand' (Emerson et al. 1995, 23) – later prompted the student to write at greater length about the way in which the playgroup's strict rules around children keeping their shoes on were relaxed when they were in the sandpit. One final example comes from Michael Taussig's *I Swear I Saw This* (2011).

Anthropologists have long been protective about their fieldnotes. Whether a reflection of personal commitment to total confidentiality or a sign of professional insecurity, most remain closely guarded. Paul Stirling was a notable exception. Founder of the anthropology department at the University of Kent at Canterbury in 1970, he was an early advocate of both methods training and the possibilities offered by the computer age. His doctoral ethnography documented the changes being wrought in rural Anatolia by economic development and political modernisation, and was subsequently published online, along with all his Turkish fieldnotes.[1]

The following fieldnote, recorded in 1949, is but one excerpt. It describes a day spent visiting a village, with a brief mention of the village school. It illustrates his approach to record-keeping and his attention to Turkish idioms, such as the term *usta*, meaning craftspeople. This attention to linguistic terms and local language use is a key strength of ethnographic work. He also records that the school is referred to as a KE or *Koy Enstitusu* (village institute), with one teacher and one assistant. The village institutes were a major Turkish government initiative to train local teachers and return them to their villages. He later added keywords to his filing cards, which in this case included discipline, education, occupation and nationalism.

1 Muallim (town), 50 usta (cf. June figures of. 80–90) 20 families with no land, depend on ustalik {gl: construction work} School 1 KE ?-gretmen 1 Egitmen

144 children; building a large old house, very solidly built with plenty of room. Small children in the morning, big ones in the afternoon.

Houses – carved stone, fitted windows, streets, – a much more substantial village; lovely view of Erciyas. Houses more scattered round the edge. Muhtar's house built by his father (40 years ago)

---

[1]An extensive set of web resources, including fieldnotes and the final published book, are available at www.lucy.kent.ac.uk.

What this record reveals is that ethnographic fieldnotes can combine a high level of careful empirical detail with personal asides and impressions. The subjective and interpretive dimensions of this note (such as 'lovely view' and 'solidly built') help the writer reconstruct the fieldwork experience in their mind by attending to the emotional impressions garnered during fieldwork. As Emerson reminds us, 'writing is a way of seeing, … a lived experience is not only preserved but also is illuminated through writing about it' (Emerson et al. 1995, 63).

The rich humanity of these fieldnotes does not make it to Stirling's published monograph. Instead, *Turkish Village* (1965) adopts the distanced, scientific rhetoric of the time, providing a comprehensive overview of the social and economic aspects of village life. In his final chapter, Stirling turns to schooling, pointing to the way that the urban-trained teachers faced 'a social barrier' as they symbolised the 'hostile outside urban world which had trained them and sent them back as its apostles' (1965, 277). He goes on to develop an argument that education 'belonged not to the village but to the outside world, where the skills and the knowledge it taught might conceivably serve some purpose'. Intriguingly the germ of this argument is visible within the fieldnote where he refers to 'town trained teachers', an aspect he had perhaps begun to think about at an early stage. This attention to the tensions surrounding modernisation dominated much anthropological writing in the 1970s and 1980s, and Stirling was prescient in addressing it in the late 1940s.

Today published monographs value 'located knowledge'. They encourage their authors to reveal something of their personal biographies and fieldwork experiences. In her account of working-class lives in Bermondsey in south London, Evans reflects on the demands that formal education places on families, and the way that young mothers prioritise their families and relationships over homework and schoolwork. Evans is candid about her decision to send her daughter to a private school when her own economic status suddenly changes for the better. For her neighbours this change in status is marked less by the new school uniform than the new car parked outside.

Pencil to paper?

Most methods texts devote a great deal of space to the practice of observing and note taking. Everyone has different advice. Some, like the veteran educational ethnographer Harry Wolcott, offer chatty and anecdotal wisdom built on years of experience, arguing for starting with the 'broad sweep', and then gradually focusing in (2008). Others, such as

Hammersley and Atkinson, emphasise the importance of always writing in copious detail to ensure the 'preservation of concreteness' (2007, 145) and to limit the level of inference made by the ethnographer. Others still have developed an elaborate approach to documenting time allocation, such as in the field of childhood studies pioneered by Whiting and Whiting (1975).

In the second edition of their comprehensive guide for those beginning ethnographic research, *Participant Observation* (2011), Billie and Kathleen DeWalt insist that the best way to learn is to experience fieldwork at every opportunity, and to practise the skills of 'active looking, improving memory, informal interviewing, writing detailed fieldnotes and most importantly patience' (ibid., vii). Their emphasis on patience reflects their wise insight that 'this is a method in which control of the research situation is less in the hands of the investigator than in other methods' (ibid., 7). Despite suggesting that this lack of control makes the method hard to write about, they do an impressive job.

Mentored by the Peltos, two anthropologists who were deeply committed to teaching and writing about anthropological methods (e.g. Pelto and Pelto 1978), DeWalt and DeWalt offer endless practical suggestions on every aspect of observation, from the detailed social maps one should draw to top tips for improving one's memory. The work is leavened with extensive field-note excerpts, including student observations of the same supermarket check-out queue, each picking up on different issues and concerns. Trained as nutritional anthropologists, the authors' concerns about 'culture shock' and the riskiness of participation would not be shared by all ethnographers.

The best way to learn about writing fieldnotes is to write some. Carrying out an unstructured observation might seem easy. Yet even before one gets to writing, there are difficult questions to answer. What should be the key focus of your attention? Are images and impressions more important than factual details? What recurring patterns of behaviour, action or conversation are significant? Should one focus on the mundane or the puzzling? Does one attend only to what seems particularly relevant or interesting?

Note-taking provokes a whole set of related questions. Given that not everything can be recorded, how should one focus one's writing? Is the aim to describe a telling vignette, to capture the flow of events, or to offer a detached third-person account? What voice or tense should one use? Is there a risk of over-interpreting the feelings and emotions of others? Can one be confident that one understands these subjective understandings? Being a participant-observer is no easier, especially if writing forces one to break off from full involvement in the flow of events. On the other hand, note-taking can also serve to mark out one's ethnographic persona, a way of reminding others of one's double life.

The received ethnographic wisdom is that writing of any kind helps our fragile memories and nascent creativity perform the best they can. Going back over one's jottings to fill in telling details is one way to patch and augment one's memory. Ethnographers get no rest, and the privacy of one's own room, at the end of the day, is often the place for writing 'up' one's fieldnotes. This may involve re-writing illegible scribbles and random mental jottings, or be the first point at which fingers reach the keyboard. Some see this as a process of 'filling in the gaps' in an empirical record, others as the chance to actively construct understandings.

There is no right way to write a fieldnote, just as there is no right way of doing ethnographic research. Writing in the first person may be the only way to evoke raw emotions, impressions and sensibilities. At other moments a third-person narrative can best convey the flow of events. Sometimes the attention will be on the dialogue, and sometimes on silences.

All writing relies on conventions of rhetoric, voice and tense. The feminist scholars have long thought hard about the way researchers shape knowledge through their writing conventions. Committed to the principle of 'situated knowledges', Haraway cautions against what she calls the 'god trick' of appearing to take the detached third-person 'view from nowhere'. As she aptly notes 'The only way to find a larger vision is to be somewhere in particular' (1999, 130), and uses this to make a case for 'modest' witnessing and reliable testimony.

What counts as a 'good enough' grounding to knowledge claims? Ethnographic writing usually adopts a first person perspective, at least at certain moments, allowing the reader to see how the researcher is reacting and thinking. Whilst teaching at Makerere University in Uganda, David was upset and shocked by the misogynistic stance of many male students. In public debates, they would lambast feminist ideas and pour scorn on 'Western' ideas about gender equality. His fieldnotes recall his outrage and frustration, emotions that seemed to drown a scholarly empathy and methodological relativism. But rather than weigh into the debate, he stepped back, and began to think further about gender conflicts and the construction of masculinity. His analysis began to reveal the way in which local gender politics were defined through, and in opposition to, global development idioms (Mills and Ssewakiryanga 2002).

Writing in the first person has its own submerged dangers. One has to chart a course between narcissistic self-indulgence and the risky assumption that one's experience is self-evidently true. The rhetorical assurance that 'I was there and you can trust what I am telling you' is just a gambit, as a number of philosophical deconstructions of the 'authority of experience' have shown (e.g. Alcoff 1992). Developing a self-critical perspective on one's emotions is part of being a modest and accountable witness.

There is a growing interest in, and debate around, 'auto-ethnography' amongst educational ethnographers (Ellis et al. 2011). Ellis argues that it involves paying attention to physical feelings, thoughts and emotions through 'systematic sociological introspection and emotional recall to try to understand an experience' (1999, 671). Whilst it has its defenders, we question the need for another label, and share Delamont's critical perspective on this (Delamont 2007). We would argue that all ethnography involves this process of reflecting on bodily and emotional sensations, and finding a way to go between self and other.

It may be that one solution is to try writing notes in a range of different voices and genres. Emerson et al. (1995) highlight the importance of empathetic participation with a range of actors, and of shifting back and forth between one perspective and another in one's fieldnotes, suggesting that this is the best way to document the different voices in any setting.

If there are few answers, the advice is consistent. No matter what ethnographic tradition one finds oneself in, the recommendation is to write and write and write. Luker could not be more explicit: 'the one thing I insist on is that you absolutely, positively must write your notes before you talk to another human being about the work ... something magical happens when you write, and if you talk about it first, the magic can't happen' (Luker 2008, 165).

Putting fieldnotes to work

As well as being a chance to flex one's writing muscles, the process of writing and rewriting can also be a training in discipline and patience. The way one chooses to do this marks out one's methodological identity and epistemological purity. Those working within a sociological tradition of 'grounded theory' would argue that it is important to record one's memories and observations separately from the process of making creative and analytical sense of them. They suggest that the process of analysis needs to be made visible in order to be scientifically legitimate. This means documenting one's reactions and thoughts about what's going on, and reflections on people's motivations/values, as the start of the analytical process, and as separate from the 'data' itself.

The original proponents of 'grounded theory', Barney Glaser and Anselm Strauss, recommended the use of 'explicit coding' and the 'constant comparative method' as a way of making the generation of theory 'more systematic' (1967, 102). Their method has become highly codified, as we describe in Chapter 6. They recommend starting by 'noting categories on margins' of the fieldnotes, and then 'comparing the incidents applicable to each category', before going on to write short analytical memos to record one's observations and emerging thinking.

This iterative movement between fieldnotes and analytical writing does not require full and loyal adherence to the principles of coding, memoing and grounded theory that they advocate. Whilst we discuss the grounded theory movement in more detail in Chapter 6, every ethnographer moves backwards and forwards between thoughts, field-notes and writing. Repeated reflective fieldnotes and 'analytical memos' help to push one's thinking forward. You may find that writing a short memo summarising an encounter or an interview is a way to stand back and begin to organise the volume of material that ethno-graphic research generates.

Some – but not all – anthropologists make extensive use of cultural codes and categories in their work. This is particularly visible in work that draws on the Human Relations Area Files (HRAF) project. Founded in 1949 at Yale University by the cultural anthropologist Peter Murdock, this was a major collaborative initiative to code and classify ethnographic materials in order to facilitate synthesis and cross-cultural comparison. Involving a number of US universities, today more than 6000 ethno-graphic texts on 400 societies have been carefully coded using one of the 700 cultural codes (e.g. socialisation, breast-feeding, child-care, teaching) developed by Murdock in his grand scientific vision of a uni-versal cultural taxonomy. These ethnographic comparisons can be used to test hypotheses and used by some to document the range of cultural attributes for cross-cultural comparison. David Lancy uses the files in his work on the anthropology of childhood to show how contemporary Western childcare practices and benevolent attitudes to children tend to be exceptional (2008).

Many anthropologists are critical of HRAF, its scientific pretensions, its history of military funding patronage (Price 2008) and its treatment of cultures as autonomous entities. However, it does offer a huge, search-able ethnographic archive that one could use in a range of innovative ways (Tobin 1990). But it also illustrates the key weakness of any approach to coding: the extraction of information from one context and its insertion into a new context. This action presumes that the informa-tion is indeed isolable and comparable.

Are other approaches to making sense of one's materials possible? Some anthropologists shy away from formal coding. They recognise the difficulty of keeping data and analysis separate, seeing each are changed by the other. A statement on fieldnotes by the American Anthropological Association captures the essence of this position. Fieldnotes are to be seen as 'hybrid of research ideas, research observations, general thoughts', and as 'works in progress' that help 'clarify thought' and provide 'mental stimulation' (AAA 2003). Here, fieldnotes are less emergent findings than raw musings, food for analytical thought and work.

Anthropologists who subscribe to this position tend to treat the writing process holistically. Advocates of this approach are often less concerned to document every stage of the analytical process, or to record how they approached making sense of their materials. Whilst this leaves them open to accusations of obfuscation, they see ethnographic writing as an opportunity to creatively rework their materials and ideas, rather than to faithfully 'represent' empirical realities.

One example of this can be found in an innovative set of ethnographic portraits brought together by the cultural geographers Craig Jeffrey and Jane Dyson. Their *Telling Young Lives: Portraits in Global Youth* (2008) brings together ten accessible but theoretically sophisticated portraits of young people that show how social worlds shape individual lives, from gang-life in Brooklyn to war and displacement in Bosnia, from racism in Scotland to poverty in South Africa. The contributors were tasked with finding ways to portray the life of one young person whilst casting light on broader social forces, using the biographic form to document young people's lived experiences of political change and of war, poverty, crime, disability and racism. The initiative draws on David Arnold and Stuart Blackburn's 2004 project *Telling Lives* and their sense of the way in which single lives 'reveal insights not just into the experiences and attitudes of the individuals directly but also of the wider society or social segment of which they are a part' (2004, 43).

The strength of ethnographic portraits lies in the way they communicate the complexity of theoretical ideas through imaginative writing and individual stories. The very term 'portrait' is a helpful one, for it emphasises the deliberately crafted nature of the accounts. Portraits are not aspiring to be 'true' representations, holistic representations or complete 'life histories', but rather are deliberately partial accounts and encounters. Within the field of Education, Sara Lawrence-Lightfoot was an early proponent of the value of creative portraits (including poems, pictures and songs) for bringing the lived experiences of teachers and students in a school to life (Lawrence-Lightfoot 1983). A useful exercise for any aspiring ethnographer is to attempt an ethnographic portrait of one's own academic socialisation and training, using it as a chance to reflect on the relationship between biography, experience and knowledge. Do we need to give this genre of self-writing a new label, such as 'auto-ethnography'? Whilst the genre has been keenly promoted by some (Reed-Danahy 1996; Ellis et al. 2011), ethnography is a broad church, and the label is well able to cope with a range of approaches to writing about oneself in a way that also acknowledges others.

One can never fully 'choose' one's analytical strategies and writing techniques. One's peers, disciplinary training, career stage, intellectual interests and institutional surroundings all shape one's path. The doctoral thesis, for example, could not consist solely of ethnographic vignettes and portraits, no matter how beautifully crafted. Expectations about the explicitness of one's methodology will vary from one examiner and one disciplinary community to another. Is adding additional comments and queries to one's margins just another level of fieldnotes? Can one ever fully separate out 'data' from 'analysis'? Are personal asides about one's own mood and feelings best kept for one's diaries, or are they part of one's embodied experiences and 'data'?

Creating the ethnographic archive

For all their enthusiasm around method, ethnographers often come over as coy when discussing fieldnotes, seeing them as private affairs. The Association of Social Anthropology's code of ethics states that 'fieldnotes (and other forms of personal data) are predominantly private barring legal exceptions' (ASA 2009). The code goes on to suggest that anthropologists have a duty to 'protect all original records of their research from unauthorised access', as this is the most important way in which confidentiality and the anonymity of subjects is ensured. The American Anthropological Association similarly echoes their provisional and incomplete status, 'works in progress' for which ethnographers should ensure their security.

Living in close quarters with people, ethnographers take great care who sees their fieldnotes, especially if they contain information of a sensitive nature. Many go to great length to anonymise individuals' identities in their diaries, and ensure they are kept under lock or computer password key. But for how long should this last? At what point might they be valuable for a broader scientific public? If, one day, our own research notes may prove invaluable for other scholars, should we be thinking about how to keep and deposit these in future?

Against these ethical cautions, Marcus (1998) argues persuasively for the multiple potentials of the 'once and future ethnographic archive'. He suggests that in the 'realist' ethnographic archive of the present, ethnographic monographs act as the primary sources for the comparative work of others; whilst in the 'relativist' archive of the future the 'messy, constructed nature of ethnographic knowledge' becomes more obvious and open to critical reappraisal.

Marcus acknowledges that our diaries and fieldnotes are 'an extension of our anthropological selves, and rarely exposed to others'. But he also points out how, on formal deposition, such personal archives 'become potentially subversive sources in relation to the claim of prestige and authority for published ethnographic scholarship' (ibid., 53). Here he is thinking perhaps of Malinowski's diaries, or the dispute over Margaret Mead's work (Freeman 1983; di Leonardo, 1998). These unauthorised histories, uncovered through re-studies and the use of personal archives, Marcus suggests, demolishes the sole authority of published materials within the disciplinary archive.

For Marcus, this 'reconstituted, more complex and unwieldy' archive encourages new scholarly approaches and undermines older disciplinary certainties (see Tobin 1990). It is a vision that cultural historians are comfortable with, but ethnographers of a more 'presentist' bent have yet to fully grasp.

What does this mean for ethnographies of education? Pressing events in the present are always shaped by the past, and it highlights the value of returning to the fieldwork carried out by earlier scholars, especially where they have made their papers available for study. Anyone writing about education in rural Turkey today would benefit greatly from Stirling's detailed fieldnotes, reading them alongside his published work.

Recent work has affirmed the importance of what Marcus calls 'deep analytic work' within documents of all kinds. Increasingly, ethnographers are focusing less on single sites than on cultural assemblages – the interweaving of texts, policies, events and social networks. Stephen Ball's work on international advocacy networks promoting private education (Nambissan and Ball 2010) is informed by his ethnographic training, whilst Stambach (2010) explores the way that American evangelical values and approaches to education travel in East Africa. As ethnographers think about the power of documents in creative and new ways (Riles 2006), the existential immersion of fieldwork is no longer the only thing that matters.

Conclusion

For all the advice about the writing of fieldnotes, there is much one learns through fieldwork that is never captured in, or reducible to, writing. Hammersley and Atkinson caution that 'one should not become totally wedded to fieldnotes, as if they were the sum total of all available information' (2007, 147). Yet social and educational worlds are about so much more than mere information, and to think only in these terms is to limit one's imaginative possibilities. Emerson et al. capture this elegant dialectic between writing and being: 'a lived experience is not only preserved but also illuminated through writing about it' (1995, 63).

Given the twinned ambitions of evoking experience and creating analytical meaning, the relationship between ethnographic being and writing rewards consistent attention and reflection. Fieldnotes play an invaluable role in this process. For this reason they are worth keeping as fully, and as carefully, as possible.

Exercises

- Plan and carry out a twenty-minute observation in a public setting, keeping extensive notes. Write 'up' your notes more fully afterwards and then reflect on the following questions. If possible, compare them with those of a colleague who has done a similar observation.

    o How have you structured your observation note-taking? What voice and tense do you use? How much dialogue was there, and how much did you capture in writing?

    o How much were you able to write down, and how much more did you add/develop afterwards? How did you supplement your notes?

    o Do particular behaviours, conversations, actions or images recur? Did you focus on people, things, actions or settings?

    o To what extent did you record smells, sounds, and non-visual sensations?

    o To what extent do your notes dwell on your own reactions, emotions and thoughts?

    o Were you able to identify participants' feelings or emotions by their non-verbal communication and body language? What does this exercise reveal about the limits of non-participant observation?

    o Do your notes incrementally focus on key events or themes during the observation?

(Continued)

(Continued)

o Have you structured it as a coherent narrative or a series of discon-nected fragments? Would you now rewrite it differently?

o Can you see any emerging themes coming out of this material?

o Try writing a 100-word summary 'analytical memo' about the observation. Is this helpful in distilling your thoughts or taking your understanding further? Does it change the way you think about the observation?

o Develop some ideas for the next steps of your writing and thinking, or initial coding categories, with brief description and examples.

• Write an account of the situation or setting that you observed through the eyes of one of the participants.

o How does it feel to try and put oneself in this person's shoes?

o What insights does it offer into the possibilities (and risks) of interpretation?

• Review some of the ethnographic fieldnotes that are now available online, and reflect on how the genres of fieldnote taking has changed over time. How do they differ?

Further reading

The best ways to learn about fieldnotes is to start taking one's own. Keeping a regular journal or diary is the best way to develop one's skills and the habit of recording and writing. Reading the following guides (and in particular DeWalt and DeWalt 2011, or Emerson et al. (1995) to garner practical advice and field wisdom is highly recommended. Sanjek (1990) offers a fascinating set of anthropological reflections.

Hobbs, D. and Wright, R. (2006). *The Sage Handbook of Fieldwork*. London, Sage.

A sociological presentation of qualitative research in a range of field sites, with a focus on difficult places and sensitive topics (sexuality, science, sport, criminality). The book treats the notion of the field relatively literally, but the examples may be useful for thinking through access, participation and observation.

DeWalt, K. and DeWalt, B. (2011). *Participant Observation: A Guide for Fieldworkers*. Plymouth, AltaMira Press.

A compendious and detailed guide to the philosophy and practice of participant observation, written partly to champion the systematisation and objectivity of the method. The authors offer lots of advice on observation and interviewing, and are keen on grounded theory for 'reducing' and analysing 'data' and systematic approaches to coding. The book is helpfully leavened by excerpts from their own Latin American fieldnotes, tips on fieldwork with children and a useful discussion of anthropological ethics. This second updated edition also reflects on the potential for doing ethnographic research online.

Emerson, R. M., Fretz, R. I., and Shaw, L. (1995). *Writing Ethnographic Fieldnotes*. Chicago, University of Chicago Press.

A highly practical set of guidelines on writing and rewriting fieldnotes by three sociologists. Full of examples of unfinished 'working' notes, the authors show how they turn 'jottings' into full fieldnotes, and then how later they begin to code by writing first theoretical and then integrative memos to link together themes and categories. Fluently written and persuasive, this book remains an important and valuable resource for those new to ethnographic writing.

Agar, M. H. (1996). *The Professional Stranger*. San Diego, Academic Press.

A thoughtful and self-critical account of the nature of the ethnographic method – and why it is different from other social-science approaches. First published in 1980, the updated 1996 edition is slightly different in tone, defending its reliance on interviews and underscoring the importance of formalising approaches to methods and analysis. I preferred it the first time around.

Van Maanen, J. (1988). *Tales of the Field: On Writing Ethnography*. Chicago, University of Chicago Press.

Despite being a quarter-century old, John Van Maanen's pithy account of writing ethnography remains pacy and quick witted. He uses fieldnotes from research with the New York Police Department to illustrate different genres: realist, confessional and impressionist. Ahead of its time.

Sanjek, R. (ed.) (1990). *Fieldnotes: The Makings of Anthropology*. Ithaca, Cornell University Press.

Whilst now more than 20 years old, this remains an excellent and iconoclastic set of reflections on the art and science of taking fieldnotes, with reflective accounts by a range of influential anthropologists and some fascinating examples.

Additional online resources can be found at: www.sagepub.co.uk/beraseries.sp

CHAPTER 5

NEW TIMES, NEW ETHNOGRAPHIES?

What is in this chapter?

- A discussion of 'new' approaches to ethnography
- A focus on three recent trends: 'policy ethnography', 'sensory ethnography' and 'virtual ethnography'
- Reflections on the politics of methodological 'innovation' and its relationship to theoretical debates

Introduction

The world changes faster than academics can make sense of it. The growing complexity, self-reflexivity and communicative intensification of globalised societies have far-reaching implications for ethnographic practice. The explosion in the use of the internet, social media and mobile technologies offer new communicative worlds and relationships to explore. Previously distinct cultural forms and autonomous social worlds become interwoven through the migration of ideas, technologies and imageries. Ethnographers find themselves struggling to develop analytical concepts and tools adequate to the task. What chance is there for someone new to ethnographic research?

Scholarship rewards disciplined experimentation and targeted creativity, and ethnographers constantly tinker with tried and tested methods. Along the way, they have promoted a dizzying diversity of methodological specialisms and specialist subfields. The more unusual might include 'para-ethnography', 'performance ethnography', 'autoethnography' and 'ethno-drama', to name but a few. Some are associated with particular political or theoretical positions, and others with the politics of method. Some are driven by theoretical fashions, and others emerge in response to new dimensions and forms of sociality. This chapter reviews three emergent areas for ethnographic investigation, and discusses how in each case scholars develop new analytical framings and approaches to ethnographic research and writing.

Even where scholars aren't promoting new labels, the discourse of innovation is not far behind. A recent anthropological collection, enticingly entitled *Fieldwork is Not What it Used to Be* (Faubion and Marcus 2009), explores how new generations of anthropological fieldworkers are rethinking the ethnographic project. As one contributor, Kristin Peterson, puts it, space is no longer a 'limiting factor of research design'. This leads her to turn her attention to 'spheres of knowledge in which new analytical and epistemological domains have arisen as primary questions of the anthropological project' (2009, 43). This rethinking of fieldwork space has also shaped work on multi-sited ethnography discussed in Chapter 3.

The task that researchers face is not new. It is to find ways of understanding and depicting emergent developments and relationships without presuming that they represent a radical disjuncture with the past. Does the internet, for example, enable a fundamentally different method of sociality from face-to-face interactions? And is its use in classrooms and teaching really transformative? Or are the relationships it mediates assimilated into an established set of pedagogies? Earlier generations of researchers faced comparable epistemological dilemmas. To invoke the rhetoric of change, one has to assume that the alternative is continuity. Perhaps things are always changing.

How many of these new labels are really necessary? Despite the best efforts of their advocates, many of these innovative ethnographic 'flavours' will not stand the test of time. Other labels will disappear as the methods are gradually absorbed into the disciplinary mainstream. This leaves researchers facing difficult questions. If you are starting out on a project, how much should you 'invest' in a particular label or methodological school? Should your focus be on contributing to theoretical debates rather than to methodological dilemmas? Or are the two inter-linked? We explore the pressure on researchers and disciplines to innovate, cast a quizzical glance over the latest fashions, and ask how best to combine disciplinary stewardship with intellectual novelty.

How is this chapter structured?

In this chapter we choose three new fields of ethnographic endeavour for further investigation: 'Policy ethnography', 'Sensory ethnography' and 'Virtual ethnography'. Discussing recent examples of each, the chapter explores their relevance for ethnographic researchers in education. Our choice is illustrative rather than exhaustive. We ask why these new sub-fields have emerged, looking at a range of examples. The chapter explores how new methodological techniques and substantive fields revisit older theoretical conundrums, such as the relationship between the individual and the state, between structure and agency, or between the body and the mind.

Labelling is a risky affair. The chapter ends by suggesting that one can experiment whilst remaining wary of the fads and fashions of methodological debates. The core ethnographic gambit remains: to develop a theoretical and empathetic ethnographic sensibility, and to nurture research relationships that are responsible, reflexive and reciprocal.

Policy ethnography

Educational ethnographies can ill afford to ignore the state. In Europe and its colonies the early provision of universal formal education was a defining feature of responsible statehood. Over the last four decades, 'Education For All' has become a rallying cry for global humanitarian interventions and the development 'industry', and the provision of schooling has become one of the most basic expectations placed upon national governments. It should be no surprise that social theorists of all stripes have sought to theorise the relationship between the state, schooling and the individual.

Back at the start of the twentieth century, Durkheim argued that Education amounted to 'a continuous effort to impose on the child ways of seeing, feeling and acting at which he would not have arrived spontaneously' (quoted in Lukes 1973, 12). Understanding the effect of state and institutional educational 'structures' on the 'agency' of individual students and teachers has continued to motivate scholars ever since.

The intensity of what has been called the structure/agency debate tends to wax and wane. During the heyday of sociological interest in 'symbolic interactionism' during the 1970s, educational ethnographers focused on the 'micro' level of social life, and in particular on the roles, symbols and signs that shape social relations. The larger political economy was left somewhat implicit, and instead the focus was on the classroom dynamics being observed. The primacy accorded to recording fine empirical detail, especially of dialogue and social interaction, was seen as a key strength of this microethnographic tradition.

This theoretical tension over whether to emphasise the influence of institutional structures or the free will of individuals is prominent in the work of the influential educational scholars Basil Bernstein and Pierre Bourdieu. Both put Durkheim to work in their sociology of education, and both sought to address the problem in different ways. Bernstein, particularly influential in the UK, tried to explore the different ways in which educational institutions framed and classified pedagogic knowledge (e.g. Bernstein 1971, 1996). Bourdieu was more expansive, and sought to make sense not only of the role that culture and bodily practice played in reproducing inequalities (Bourdieu 1977, Bourdieu and Passeron 1977) but also of the hierarchical forms of knowledge production within the university itself (1984). Towards the end of his career he became more explicit about the role scholarship could play in questioning the inevitability of neoliberalism (Bourdieu and Ferguson 1999, Bourdieu 2003).

Does one have to follow the twists and turns of these theoretical debates in order to be a good educational ethnographer? No, but as they raise profound questions about the role of learning in society, they can be hard for educational ethnographers to ignore (Ashwin 2009). In what follows, we introduce the history of this debate, before explaining why 'policy ethnography' offers one way to study these changes.

Negotiating structure and agency?

Making sense of education policy discourses that surround education has kept several generations of scholars busy, generating a whole sub-field of educational policy. This attention reflects a growing recognition of the peculiar power of policy to shape subjectivities. In post-Second World War Britain, to take one example, governmental responsibility for the welfare state led to a constant policy anxiety over state education. The sweeping ambitions of the Education Act of 1949 gave way gradually to educational policy turmoil, growing debate about 'standards' and repeated U-turns. From Heath's famous 'Great Debate' of 1976 to Blair's

2007 election-call 'Education, Education, Education', the sector has rarely been out of the public eye. Education could both be blamed for society's ills and seen as an easy way to rectify these ills. Educational researchers have also come in for political criticism, most notably in the 1990s through a series of bad-tempered exchanges between the Chief Inspector of Schools in England, Chris Woodhead, and commentators of opposing political hues. This history matters, but does it need to be rehearsed and repeated in an ethnography of a classroom or a playground? The answer varies, depending on the ethnographer's interests in politics, in theoretical debates, and how they conceptualise the relationship between the state and the individual child.

Ethnographers have taken several different approaches (Walford 2003; Shore et al. 2011). One is to submit the seemingly abstract process of policy formation to ethnographic scrutiny. Anthropologists have long advocated 'studying up' (Nader 1974), taking policy seriously by doing ethnographic research on policy-making 'elites'. There are some precedents amongst ethnographers of education, such as Geoffrey Walford's studies of private schools (1991, 1993), or Tuchman's ethnography of university administrators (2009), or comparable studies of policy expertise in development institutions (e.g. Mosse 2005). However this path is fraught with stony dilemmas, especially around access and ethics (Walford 1994).

Another solution is to show how this larger policy context is not just a backdrop to an ethnography, but rather directly shapes consciousness and subjectivity. In the most determinist Marxist form of this position, the French theorist Louis Althusser famously argued that schools not only taught 'know how', but also taught 'know how' in 'forms which ensure subjection to the ruling ideology' (Althusser and Brewster 1971, 133). Drawing on Lacan, he argued that in capitalist societies the education system was a key ideological state apparatus (ISA) that 'hailed' or 'interpellated' individuals to act and think in particular ways. An ideology is somewhat akin to a policeman hailing you as you walk down the street. You assume it is you they are hailing, you turn, and so become subject to that ideology.

Viewing education simply as an ideology that reproduces an unequal society is overly simplistic, but Althusserian ideas inspired many other thinkers. The relationship between educational ideologies and individual subjectivities inspired much debate within Cultural Studies. Paul Willis (in Mills and Gibb 2000, 410) queried the 'trickle-down' logic that even weak deterministic arguments make. He also pointed out that merely analysing ideologies or policy discourses led to a 'very artificial and self justifying' rationalist understanding of subjectivity, and insulated one from 'the possibility of recording and understanding sensuous activities and processes as containing depth and dynamism'.

These problems with 'structuralist' ethnographies partly explain the huge appeal of Michel Foucault's theoretical work for many anthropological ethnographers and for social research more broadly. Foucault was a French philosopher and historian of science, but his brilliant ability to both theorise and carefully situate the complex histories of power–knowledge relationships has led to his work being taken up in many fields. He is perhaps best known for his insights into the nature of modern power (1980), for his concept of discourse (1972), and for his substantive histories of the changing nature of sexuality, mental illness and incarceration (Foucault 1967, 1977, 1978). Few are the social theorists and researchers who have felt able to ignore Foucaultian ideas and their relevance for the study of modern personhood, identity, education and governance. Insightful introductions to using Foucault can be found in the work of Rose (1999), Hunter (1994) or Donald (1992).

Amongst anthropologists of education, Cris Shore and Susan Wright have most consistently drawn on Foucault to explain the power of neoliberal policies as redefining both universities and academic senses of self. They have championed the ethnographic study of policy, arguing that policy is 'a fundamental organizing principle of society' (Shore, Wright and Pero 2011, 2). Writing about how discourses of audit and accountability reshape individual subjectivities, they have argued for the importance of ethnographically attending to how policy discourses work, the metaphors and language they use, and the way they seek to organise and make coherent the unpredictable complexity of political interventions. Their most recent collection, *Policy Worlds*, takes a less deterministic view, arguing that 'anthropology's more open and democratic approach emphasises not only the messiness of policy processes, but also the ambiguous and contested manner in which policies are simultaneously enacted by different people in diverse situations' (ibid., 2011, 8). But the puzzle facing ethnographers is knowing how best to write about the influence of international, national, regional and local education policy 'cultures' on everyday social worlds. How best does one trace ethnographic connections between the individual and larger practices of governance? Is the influence only one way? Is it possible to convey the influence of policy abstractions through ethnographic work that focuses on people's everyday lives?

One of the most influential social anthropologists of her generation, Marilyn Strathern has written extensively about the effect of what she calls a 'new cultural apparatus of expectations and technologies' on universities as sites of knowledge creation (1997, 305). Modest about her own ethnographic and theoretical achievements in feminist anthropology and Melanesian studies, she has also been writing about the changes affecting British universities since the 1980s. She draws on her own personal experience working as an academic, and fieldwork with close readings of an eclectic set of thinkers. She deploys her provocative and allusive writing style to make a powerful case about the ramifying effects of 'audit culture' (1997, 2000) and its virtues of 'transparency' and 'accountability'. Arguing that universities are 'increasingly subject to national scrutiny', her analysis goes one step further, and does not see this process as one simply imposed on universities, but rather acknowledges that the very origins of accounting lie in the written examination procedures first pioneered in eighteenth-century Oxbridge. As she cogently puts it, 'auditors are not aliens; they are a version of ourselves. The issues lie in commitment to the very values of academic excellence that educational auditors and practitioners share' (1997, 305). It is this twist that, she suggests, requires us to look again at ourselves: students and academics are not simply the victims of policy decisions decided far away. We are also part of this policy 'field' through our creative responses and interpretations.

What becomes clear from this range of recent ethnographies of policy is that ethnographers seek to find ways to make connections between abstract social forces and the intensity of lived experience. Not all assume that these discourses (be they of neoliberalism, racism or consumerism) overwhelmingly define our lives and identities. All face the same tasks: to rely on their own sensory abilities and emotional compass in order to conceptualise the sensations and feelings of others, and then to convey this through writing. Which brings us to the question of how best to do this.

Sensory ethnographies

Time for an experiment. Spend a moment thinking back about your first days at a new school. You would have been besieged by a range of sensations and experiences – sights, smells, sounds and tastes. Which sense memories are most vivid? The smell of the floor polish or the hydrochloric acid in the chemistry lab, the incessant ringing of bells, the taste of soya mince or warmed-over tinned tomatoes? If you are like us, your visual memories are likely to be less acute than the recollections of the whole gamut of bodily sensations that accosted you.

Some sensations and emotions are just impossible to put into writing. The anthropologist Renato Rosaldo was doing research on the Philippine island of Luzon with the Ilonggot, a people known for headhunting. He sought to articulate something of the 'rage of grief' that led him to murder a fellow man. This headhunter could only say that he needed somewhere to 'carry his rage'. At the time Rosaldo could make no analytical sense of this relationship between rage and grief. Fourteen years later the comment took on a whole new meaning. On a return visit with his wife, Michelle Rosaldo, she slipped off a path and fell to her death. Rosaldo describes how the intensity of his own grief, mixed in with feelings of acute anger, overwhelmed every aspect of his body. It was only when he finally began to recognise his own rage at being abandoned that he felt able to understand the Ilonggot passion that could drive a man to murder. His moving account of this gradual comprehension is at once 'an act of mourning, a personal report and a critical analysis of anthropological method' (1989, 168).

No one is suggesting that one has to go through such devastating events in order to convey the power of bodily experience. Yet his admonition remains. The art of writing fieldnotes is to capture something of participants' emotions and the way they are expressed, without over-interpreting what they might mean. From the outset, this means being attentive to the bodily comportment and language of others.

Again, ethnographic concern with bodily experiences, sensations and emotions is not new. More than a century ago, Durkheim's cousin Marcel Mauss wrote about 'habitus' and documented the different 'techniques of the body', noting differences between cultures in posture and even ways of walking (1934). Another early anthropologist, W. H. Rivers, carefully sought to experiment on his own body as part of an investigation into different cultural constructions of sensation. In his experimental Arcades project, the German-Jewish literary critic Walter Benjamin developed the notion of the 'sensorium' to capture the new forms of apperception that modern technologies had trained the senses to appreciate, creating new ways for humans to aesthetically appreciate and inhabit urban forms (such as the shopping mall). Within continental philosophy, the phenomenological tradition (and its exploration of the nature and meaning of experience and consciousness) shaped the work of many scholars. But in British and American academia, much of this experimentation was lost in the move to make social research more scientific, and the Cartesian dualism of mind over matter was reasserted.

Come the 1980s, with the growing influence of postmodernism and feminist critiques of disembodied rational scholarship, ethnographers once again turned their attention to reflexivity, emotions and bodies. Many began to revisit the phenomenological influence of mid-century scholars such as Levinas and Merleau-Ponty. An influential essay by the ethnographer Michael Jackson emphasised the 'inseparability of conceptual and bodily activity' (1983, 127). David Howes edited *The Varieties of Sensory Experience*, a collection that illustrated the range of 'sensory' ethnographies one could develop (Howes 1991), highlighting the potential rewards of attending to smell, feeling, taste and the pulse, amongst other sensations.

These initiatives opened up an awareness of the interconnected sensory genres researchers could draw upon, along with the importance of knowing in practice. It has also provoked discussion about how one might record and collect these sensations, and more recently has led to a growing interest in 'performance ethnography' (Fine 1997; Madison 2012) as a way of communicating ethnographic insight through drama and bodily practices. In her work Sarah Pink has argued that 'sensory ethnography' has rendered the 'conventional focus on observing, listening and writing as insufficient' (2010, 6), and necessitated a whole new set of ways of thinking about, collecting and understanding ethnographic work. For Pink, the interview becomes a 'multisensory event'. Debates about sensory approaches are increasingly influential: a telling sign of the times may be that even Harvard now has its own sensory ethnography lab.

Paul Stoller (1997) was one of the first to use the specific term 'sensuous ethnography' to describe his research with West African migrants peddling their wares on North American streets. He set out to think about how attending to 'experience-in-the-world' might 'awaken' the scholar's body. The first chapter finds him in a Manhattan coffee shop, retelling the stories of West African *griots* to a film-maker friend. Provoked into thinking about how best to capture the mutuality of the head and heart so visible in these tales, he decides to set out to rethink his own anthropology. His book begins by reflecting on how Songhay sorcerers in West Africa learn their craft not through the assimilation of texts but through mastery of the body and the tolerance of illness and pain. He goes on to show how, for these *griots*, history is not a subject to be learnt but a consuming bodily force, before taking a similar approach to understand the experiences of the Harlem street traders.

A more deliberately educational example of a sensory ethnography comes from Elizabeth Curtis, and her description of a primary school outing through the streets of Aberdeen (Curtis 2008). Part of a larger collection exploring an ethnography of walking (Ingold and Vergnunst 2008) Curtis describes how the children are expected to follow a heritage trail between sites of special historical interest, stopping to record their observations at set points along the way. But knowledge is not so neatly parcelled, nor is walking simply a means of getting from one place to the next. She watches the children wend their way in the regulation school 'crocodile' formation and realises that the children are absorbing sights, sounds, feels and smells of the streets as they go. Her argument is that every child is a 'miniature detective', that their eyes are always close to the ground, and that their knowledge is encountered precisely through moving. It is no wonder that taking a toddler for a walk can feel like a slow, distracted process. The intensity of sensation and experiences are powerfully embodied forms of learning about the world.

A very different example of embodied knowing comes from Natasha Myers' ethnography of the teaching that goes on within US molecular biology labs, and what she calls the 'body-work of modeling proteins' (2008, 163). Despite the rise of new imaging technologies for understanding protein structure and function, she describes the importance that senior research scientists still placed in 'cultivating a feeling for proteins' (ibid). She vividly captures the way these academics use their upper bodes, entwining arms and hands as they literally embody to their students and postdocs the complexity and viability of their protein models. This bodily pedagogy allows the teachers to point to the limitations of simply relying on computer-generated visual models.

One final ethnographic example comes from Veronique Benei's work on the sensory training received by primary school children in a school in Maharashtra in the west of India. She explores the role of the state in the production of a schooling 'sensorium', and the ways in which infants' and children's sensibilities are shaped by everyday songs and prayers at morning assemblies, daily yoga and physical education, and by the bodily deportment expected at school events and competitions (2008). Her aim is to go beyond seeing schools as agents of social reproduction, and rather to show how one might use them as sites to explore the links between 'banal nationalisms' (ibid, 18) and sensory socialisation.

Our focus so far here has been on sensory ethnography, but this is only part of a larger scholarly tradition of visual anthropology, anthropological film-making and visual ethnography. The earliest ethnographers took pictures to create a record of the research process, but today's educational ethnographers are far more attuned to the representational power of photography. Pictures can be used as research tools, as well as sources of evidence and a powerful means of representation. Ever since using photo-elicitation in her ethnography of Spanish female bull-fighters, Sarah Pink has been a methodological advocate for visual ethnography, and then for sensory ethnography more broadly (Pink 2007, 2009).

Louisa Allen found that encouraging students to take pictures and discuss them was a way of opening up sensitive discussions around sexual cultures in schools (2011a, 2011b), whilst ML White (2009) explored the potential of digital video journals as part of a collaborative approach to creating ethnographic representations with young people. However, just because visuality is integral to popular culture does not mean that visual methods are easy to pursue. Collecting and using visual data with young people presents particularly acute ethical dilemmas, especially in an age where one's visual traces are found in unexpected places.

YouTube and other social media have dramatically transformed the opportunities for young people to record and document their own visual representations, again challenging text-heavy ethnographic accounts. There is now a flourishing literature on the use and representation of visuality, and the readings at the end of this chapter point to useful further resources in this area. There are many opportunities to mix methods, and Thomson and Holland (2012) describe how they successfully encouraged young people to keep reflective 'memory-books', part written diary, part visual scrap-book, as a way of exploring their experiences of teenage transition.

Many academics are left scrambling to keep up. Most textbooks (this one included) fail to take up the opportunities to communicate visually. Galman's (2007) introduction to ethnography is a wonderful exception, as is Taussig's *I Swear I Saw This* (2011). There are many opportunities to not simply rely on observation but to put visuality at the centre of ethnographic research. We are limited only by our imagination.

Virtual ethnography

If there is an increasing expectation that ethnographies capture the full range of sensory and bodily experience, new communication technologies have also opened up a range of seemingly disembodied 'virtual' spaces, experiences and relationships. Some of the first researchers made utopian claims about the liberatory potentials of these new social worlds (e.g. Turkle 1984), and how they would free people from social conventions and bodily constraints.

As the internet opened up, the first ethnographies of online life began to emerge. Early ethnographies clung to place-based approaches, leading to ethnographies of online chat rooms or user groups. This approach still lingers. In his 2008 ethnography of 'Second Life', Boellstorff questions the assumption that also doing research on lives offline is even necessary. He argues that 'to demand that ethnographic research always incorporate meeting residents in the actual world for 'context' presumes that virtual worlds are not themselves contexts' (Boellstorff 2008: 61). However, the assumption that 'Second Life' or other online social environments could ever be totally isolated from 'offline' culture and society has also come in for criticism. Dana Boyd questions whether one could ignore 'First Life' but also notes that offline lives should not just be seen as the unmediated 'backstage', used to check the veracity of a more mediated 'front stage'. Instead the focus is now increasingly on exploring how these spaces interact. As Boyd puts it, we 'do ourselves a disservice if we bound our fieldwork by spatial structures—physical or digital—when people move seamlessly between these spaces' (2008, 53).

There are now a growing number of educational ethnographies of online environments. Some still take polemical positions. In his ethnography of university students' informal use of social media sites, Francis (2010) is very upbeat, arguing that they are transcending institutional boundaries by shaping their own virtually figured worlds and learning identities. In contrast to her earlier enthusiasm, the social psychologist Sherry Turkle is now far more cynical about young people's lives lived, as she puts it, *Alone Together* (2011).

Danah Boyd's doctoral ethnography of youth sociality (2008) seeks to find a middle way. She highlights the struggles of young people to create their own networked publics through social media. She also explores how the particular properties of mediated sociality – persistence, searchability, replicability and invisible audiences – have implications for understandings of public and private, as well as for young people's use of these media technologies.

Most ethnographers are wise enough to avoid deploying online/offline and real/virtual dichotomies. Instead they explore the rich and complex connections between cyberspace and face-to-face contexts and situations. They set out to understand the juxtaposition and simultaneity of different modes of sociality enabled by the internet, and to show how online interactions are reshaping educational practices or social lives more broadly.

Christine Hine was one of the first to write about the possibilities and methodological demands of online ethnography (2000), using social theory to downplay the rhetorical claims made about technologies' transformative possibilities. The contributors to her 2005 edited volume *Virtual Methods* highlight the importance of paying close ethnographic attention to the particular contexts of internet use, and how both informants and researchers interact across a range of online and offline spaces. As Hine puts it, 'appropriate sites for research are not obvious in advance, and technologies are not research sites in themselves' (Hine 2005, 111). Nor does all research exploring people's use of the internet need to start online.

The fluidity of movement and connections enabled by network technologies make marking out boundaries difficult. If culture isn't just (and never was) 'out there', the focus is increasingly on the networked community and relationships created by the researcher through her online interactions. The internet is now not just an analytical space but also a methodological tool. In the same way that most academics now have websites, one's online profile becomes an aspect of one's social identity, and may be key to establishing one's credentials and gaining access as a researcher.

A recent ethnographic dissertation (Kane 2012) explored the role of the internet and live video-streams for teaching Cornell medical students at a satellite campus in Doha, Qatar. Tanya Kane uses her analytical skills to go beyond neat oppositions of the virtual and the real, exploring how notions of absence and presence are reworked in the Doha teaching encounter, and in particular the role played by the technology support teams as 'boundary workers' facilitating this interplay. Rather than juxtapose the real and the virtual, she develops the notion of 'face-to-interface', and describes how the Doha students campaigned to be offered both live video-links with the Cornell campus in New York along with podcasts of the lectures. She explores the different forms of pedagogic inter-subjectivity possible through these different media.

Networked society undoubtedly opens up new forms of sociality and reshapes existing genres and relationships. Researching these social worlds makes new demands of the ethnographic method. We are in many ways more accountable and accessible. It forces us to reconsider the priority ethnographers may once have accorded 'unmediated' face-to-face interactions.

Just as the internet opens up new methodological possibilities, such as asynchronous interviews or collaborative approaches, it also comes with new ethical dilemmas for the researchers, particularly around what counts as 'public' knowledge. It might seem easy to gather ethnographic 'data' unobtrusively from social media sites, given the way online interactions leave indelible traces. But most researchers caution against taking unwarranted advantage of anonymity, and instead highlight the importance of developing relationships through online presence and engagement. The internet is also a set of texts as well as a set of interactions, and many of those who write blogs see themselves as engaging a range of networked publics and audiences. Each case and situation will be different.

Despite the best efforts of the Association of Internet Researchers (2002) to come up with a robust set of ethical guidelines, there is no one right way of legislating around issues of trust and privacy. For those unsure about what might be appropriate, there is a growing literature on online research ethics to draw upon (Busher and James 2012), along with sharp criticisms of over-zealous ethical 'policing' of qualitative online research (Orton-Johnson 2010).

The internet distils old methodological debates into new bottles. The potential it offers for thinking about ethnography differently, and for communicating and sharing ethnographic insights online, make the ethical dilemmas more palatable.

Conclusion: against labels?

In 1970 the anthropologist John Middleton edited a landmark volume entitled *From Child to Adult: Studies in the Anthropology of Education*. It offered a range of case studies of child-rearing in different parts of the world, from Ghana to New Guinea. Many emeritus professors and senior figures within British and US anthropology contributed a chapter, including Margaret Mead, Siegfried Nadel, Raymond Firth, Meyer Fortes and Melville Herskovits.

Few of the contributors would have defined themselves as anthropologists of education, or been described as such. Instead, their careers had flourished in parallel with the rise of the new fields of social and cultural anthropology. They had become standard-bearers for a discipline committed to theoretical holism (Thornton 1988; Mills 2008). With the publication of the first ethnographic monographs, they had left behind the Victorian theorists, and instead saw their role as convincing the world of the value of anthropological theorising and ethnographic writing: they had little need for what Andrew Abbott (2001) calls sub-disciplinary 'fractals' and divisions.

Fast-forward almost fifty years and the academic landscape looks rather different. Universities have expanded, as has funding for social research. Ethnographic methods are used across the social sciences, often in very different ways (Scott Jones and Watt 2010). A methodological 'label' is a way of bringing scholars together, of generating robust criteria for evaluating newer research, and for creating a sense of progress. But it is also a way to differentiate, divide and exclude. When schisms emerge, this can sometimes result in whole new fields of study emerging, leading to the reinvention of wheels and debates.

Why do some scholars champion methodological innovation, and do you need to do so? One reason is pragmatic: to promote one's career. The institutional growth of the social sciences has led to a booming literature on method, both to support new researchers and because publication is key to academic career progression. Given these institutional pressures, new hyphenated ethnographies will continue to emerge. There is thus much talk of 'innovative' ethnographic approaches in the literature, often aimed at recruiting followers amongst new educational researchers.

This process is aided (or abetted, depending on your point of view) by qualitative methods journals and publishing houses, each of which have their own agendas to consider. A label or title provides a theme around which scholars with a common interest can gather, share ideas, teach and debate, much as a conference brings together like-minded souls. New labels are also ways to launch journals and sell books. Looked at less positively, they fragment and polarise, with academic careers devoted to assembling and zealously defending a sub-field. Empathy needs to be leavened with judicious scepticism.

What does this mean for new researchers? It means realising that the methods social scientists use are never simply neutral and 'objective' scientific instruments. They come with their own histories of use and debate. They get entangled in politics, be it local, institutional or national. A method or approach seen as de rigueur in one university may be seen as inappropriate at another.

It is also worth remembering that methods are often developed and refined within one national context. Critics of 'methodological national-ism' (e.g. Beck 2005) have highlighted how the nation state has been taken as an implicit container of social and political processes. This has made it much harder to capture transnational dynamics. National bureau-cracies have also shaped the organisation of social scientific knowledge production in ways that limit their more general application. Savage (2008) goes further still, and suggests that the deployment of the survey method after the Second World War by a cadre of social researchers helped spread new social and class identities in Britain.

The internal logic of disciplinary knowledge formation deserves care-ful attention by new scholars. American sociologist Andrew Abbott has sought to make sense of what he calls this 'chaos of disciplines' (2001). Drawing on his own background in anthropology, he suggests that dis-ciplines are rather like kinship lineages: 'A lineage starts then splits, then starts again … people know only their near kin well' (ibid., 11). This might explain why academics often disagree most strongly with those who are intellectually closest to them, as it is only with one's immediate relatives that these differences are so marked.

He then combines this metaphor with imagery drawn from the scien-tific study of fractals, suggesting that each lineage dichotomy contains within it endless further ramifying distinctions. This allows him to offer an explanation of why graduate students are often encouraged to learn about their field of knowledge through a series of dichotomies. He also uses it to illustrate why seminars are so often full of 'endless misunder-standings' and unproductive discussions. On the other hand, his analogy also allows 'old ideas to return under new names' as the limits and omis-sions of each new framing become visible.

His cyclical model of knowledge divisions, conflict and renewal might feel a little cynical. It takes little notice of history, and does not help explain how ethnographic work has changed and developed over time. But it is a salutary introduction to academic life, and highlights why educational ethnographers need to think hard about the way they understand and conceptualise their knowledge.

We feel that it helps to understand why academics invest their energies both in generating new ideas, but also in donning methodological labels and erecting walls around sub-fields. It might help you decide whether to wear a label, and if so, when.

Exercises

- Take a page of a recent national government educational policy statement. Look closely at the key phrases and discourses adopted and refrained throughout. What metaphors and imageries do these seek to communicate? Think about how one might begin to explore the creation, circulation and reception of such policy documents ethnographically.

- Choose some family photographs to share with a colleague. Ask them to comment on the message or narrative that the photograph seeks to communicate, the emotions of the participants, and what they can read from clothes, facial expressions and background.

- Turn the sound off on a TV documentary or film. Try to reconstruct your own understanding of the events you see. The exercise highlights the importance of sound and other sensory experiences for contextualising and understanding experience. A similar ethnographic exercise is available online at www.elearning.lse.ac.uk/dart

- Take a walk. Think about how your experiences and sensations are changed through walking. How might one learn differently on a walk, as opposed to in a classroom?

Further reading

Given the new methodological departures and substantive destinations being travelled from and to by ethnographers, this list is a guide to just a few recent works. They are chosen for their attempt to experiment with new forms of representation and research.

Atkinson, P., Delamont, S. and Housley, W. (2008). *Contours of Culture: Complex Ethnography and the Ethnography of Complexity*. Walnut Creek, Calif., AltaMira Press.

This one-volume overview of sociological ethnographic practice addresses a range of new research sites and spaces, including the study of discourse, narratives, materials, places, and visual and sensory cultures. Whilst sensitive to these new sources of data, it still cleaves to the realist empiricism that characterises the 'Cardiff school' of ethnography.

Crang, M. and Cook, I. (2007). *Doing Ethnographies*. London, Sage.

This is a practical hands-on guide that began its life in 1993 as a photocopied booklet, written when the authors were both doctoral students in Geography. A no-holds-barred account of the complexity, frustration and rewards of doing ethnographic research, word soon spread amongst Geography postgraduates, and it became a *samizdat* classic. Now leading cultural geographers, the book maintains its freshness and its focus on their own doctoral dissertation writing. Cook's thesis started as a study of the cultural worlds surrounding the production and consumption of papayas, but ended up as an auto-ethnographic examination of his discipline's research practices and his own Englishness. Crang's thesis became a textual montage focusing on public understandings of heritage, and his contributions show how he dealt with a range of visual materials in his writing.

Delamont, S. (ed.) (2012). *Handbook of Qualitative Research in Education*. Cheltenham, Edward Elgar.

With forty-five contributions, dominated by current innovations in 'data collection' and 'analysis', this voluminous collection seeks to define the theoretical and empirical zeitgeist amongst qualitative educational researchers. The rich diversity of methods and approaches is fascinating but somewhat fragmented, partly because the contributions are relatively short. Best used as a place to find out about recent methodological experiments (from mobiles to digital video journals), and to get ideas for further reading.

Hine, C. (2000). *Virtual Ethnography*. London, Sage.
Hine, C. (ed.) (2005) *Virtual Methods: Issues in Social Research on the Internet*. Oxford: Berg.

Hine's *Virtual Ethnography* was an early attempt to reflect on the methodological implications of research online. *Virtual Methods* brings together the lessons learnt from a range of ethnographies of everyday internet use. The contributions point to the limitations of a strong online/offline distinction, and to the very different social situations in which online interactions are a part.

Ingold, T. and Vergunst, J. L. (2008). *Ways of Walking: Ethnography and Practice on Foot.* Farnham, Ashgate.

An intriguing set of contributions advocate an ethnography of walking, and demonstrate the insights that emerge from thinking about the embodied knowledge that comes from movement. The chapter on a school trip around Aberdeen is particularly provoking.

Kozinets, R. V. (2010). *Netnography: Doing Ethnographic Research Online.* London, Sage.

An upbeat but simplistic account of online ethnography by a professor of marketing. Kozinets makes the case that online social experiences are significantly different from face-to-face social interactions, and that there-fore ethnographic techniques (participation, fieldnotes, etc.) also need to change, hence his neologism 'Netnography'.

Law, J. (2004). *After Method: Mess in Social Science Research.* London, Routledge.

This is an iconoclastic text that highlights the way that research methods create the very reality that they seek to describe. Driven by the author's interests in actor network theory, it troubles conventional assumptions about social science, and argues for a pluralistic and creative approach to making sense of the complexity of social worlds.

Levinson, B. A., Foley, D. E. and Holland, D. C. (eds.) (1996). *The Cultural Production of the Educated Person: Critical Ethnographies of Schooling and Local Practice.* Albany, NY, State University of New York Press.

An important edited collection from the mid-1990s that seeks to recon-cile schools' 'structural' power to reproduce inequalities in society with a recognition of the 'agency' of individual teachers and students. In an extensive initial theoretical literature review, the editors propose seeing schools as sites of 'cultural production', linking local cultural practices to larger dynamics of the economy and the state. The case studies range from ethnographies of scientists to schools in the Amazon and the Nepalese mountains. Contributions to Levinson and Pollock (2011) similarly show how anthropologists approach policy agendas.

Madison, D. S. (2012). *Critical Ethnography: Method, Ethics, and Performance.* London, Sage.

D. Soyini Madison is a sociological ethnographer who also champions performance studies. This is a provocative coupling of sensible and practical advice on doing ethnographic research with a call for writing and analysis that adopts a performance paradigm. Her reflections on ethical ethnographic practice are refreshingly devoid of debates about codes and regulations.

Pink, S. (2007). *Doing Visual Ethnography: Images, Media and Representation in Research*. London, Sage.
Pink, S. (2009). *Doing Sensory Ethnography*. Los Angeles; London, Sage.

Sarah Pink's work has consistently sought to explore a range of innovative ethnographic approaches, finding ways of incorporating a range of visual and other sensory media into her writing. Her own doctoral research on female Spanish bullfighters deployed a range of recording technologies, and she has moved from an attention to visual ethnography to calling for a holistic sensory ethnography. Both books offer useful reviews of the literature and debates, but also focus closely on fieldwork practice and on techniques of representation and analysis. She raises the intriguing question of whether audiences need to be educated in new forms of multisensory knowing in order to engage with visual, acoustic and other media.

Shore, C., Wright, S. and Pero, D. (2011). *Policy Worlds: Anthropology and the Analysis of Contemporary Power*. Oxford, Berghahn.

This most recent collection by Cris Shore and Sue Wright brings together a range of creative ethnographic explorations of policy. More nuanced than their earlier work, it emphasises the contestations that surround policy, the spaces created by policy dicourses and the relationship of academic work to policy representations.

Spencer, D. and Davies, J. (eds). (2010). *Anthropological Fieldwork: A Relational Process*. Cambridge, Cambridge Scholars Press.

An innovative edited collection of pieces reflecting on the emotional entanglements and personal subjectivities of researchers themselves. The contributors discuss the emotional labour involved in fieldwork, together with the ways in which these emotions shape the relationships and ground the forms of knowing that ethnographers develop. Whilst some draw directly on psychoanalytical insights, others explore the knowledges that emerge from an attention to empathy and bodily experience.

Strathern, M. (ed.) (2000). *Audit Cultures: Anthropological Studies in Accountability, Ethics and the Academy.* London, Routledge.

An early collection of critical reflections on the changes facing universities with the rise of new forms of measuring and assessing scholarly practice, such as the Research Excellence Framework (and its predecessors) in the UK. The volume shows how anthropologists can turn their analytical lens on the policy discourses that shape their lives.

Web resources

There are a growing number of excerpts from ethnographic films and resources available online via YouTube and elsewhere on the web, as well as via the professional associations such as the Royal Anthropological Institute. Alexanderstreet.com hosts a wide range of accessible online textual and video resources and provides free trial access.

Additional online resources can be found at: www.sagepub.co.uk/beraseries.sp

CHAPTER 6

WHAT DO I DO NOW? MAKING ETHNOGRAPHIC MEANING

What is in this chapter?

- A comparison of different ways of approaching ethnographic analysis
- An introduction to 'grounded theory' and its critics
- A review of ethnographic portraits
- A new acronym (CAQDAS) and advice on using qualitative analysis software

Introduction

This chapter asks about what it takes to make one's ethnographic materials and experiences meaningful: the art and science of analysis. For the careful reader of this book, this may not be the challenge it once seemed. Throughout we have underscored the importance of conceptualising research design and analysis in a holistic way. Ethnographers, we suggest, should not be worried by the 'I've collected all my data, what do I do now?' question. If writing is always already a form of analysis, then it begins the first time you start to think about your work or prepare your research proposal, continues throughout your writing, and afterwards too. Malinowski's advice may be almost a century old, but remains prescient: 'Preconceived ideas are pernicious in any scientific work, but foreshadowed problems are the main endowment of a scientific thinker' (Malinowski 1922, 7). In this one sentence, he captures the delicate interplay of inductive and deductive reasoning that defines the ethnographic habit.

One can tell a great deal about the tradition in which an ethnographer has been trained by the way they discuss matters of analysis. You have probably already decided on your approach to analysis, possibly without realising it. If you are inclined, by supervisory expectation or disciplinary temperament, towards a more positivist analytical tradition, you may already have developed an extensive set of 'analytical memos' that bring your data together and that you are beginning to process and develop. The dominance of sociological ethnographers writing methods texts has ensured a wide audience for 'grounded theory', as we discuss below. Not all sociologists adopt this procedural approach to generating knowledge. In the US there is an influential school of postmodern sociological ethnographers that champions experimental and literary forms for representing fragmentary social knowledge. This work is best represented in the journal *Qualitative Inquiry* under the editorship of Norman Denzin and Yvonna Lincoln.

On the other hand, if you have been exposed to a more anthropological approach, you may not have been taught to think in terms of formally 'coding' one's fieldnotes. You may not even wish to use the term 'data' to describe that large and unwieldy folder of ethnographic notes, memories, experiences, documents and materials that you are in the midst of assembling. But there are no firm rules. Working in the tradition of Science and Technology Studies, Daniel Neyland's 2007 textbook *Organisational Ethnography* never mentions coding, whilst the cultural geographers Mike Crang and Ian Cook offer some wonderfully vivid pencil sketches of their own emerging code maps in *Doing Ethnographies* (2007), covered with scribbles and crossing-outs. Some ethnographers would insist that a formal approach to, and record of, coding is essential, whilst others remain very suspicious of its fetishisation as 'the right' approach to analysis. A healthy dose of ethnographic empathy to those who have a different view may be the answer.

How is this chapter structured?

In this chapter we explore a diversity of approaches to organising, thematising and thinking about one's ethnographic materials. We give a sense of the debates, as well as the possibilities for combining different approaches. In the first section, entitled 'Grounded theory 101', we begin by discussing the early work of American sociologists Barney Glaser and Anselm Strauss (1967), and their vision for generating theory that is grounded in, and 'emerges' from, the data. The approach has been hugely influential among educational researchers, but has also become increasingly controversial as successive generations of researchers have become aware of the contradictions it presents (see Thomas and James 2006). We describe the process of coding and categorising that is integral to this analytical process, as well as the criticisms and potential drawbacks of this method.

In 'Ethnographic Writing as Ethnographic Analysis' we describe a range of more intuitive and unstructured approaches to analysing materials and generating narrative. These approaches, often adopted by anthropological ethnographers, tack back and forth, sometimes in unpredictable and jarring ways, between theoretical concepts and empirical materials, experimenting with ideas and concepts. Scholars of a more postmodern persuasion go further still. Norman Denzin and Yvonna Lincoln have become influential sociological exponents of an approach to qualitative research that is 'endlessly creative and interpretive'. They envision the qualitative researcher as a 'bricoleur and quilt-maker' and advocate experimenting with a variety of writing genres and reflexive approaches in order to deal with 'the art and politics of interpretation and evaluation' (Denzin and Lincoln 2008, 34). For this school of US sociological ethnographers, if poetry, fiction or performance offer new ways of representing and communicating educational experiences, then so be it.

Grounded theory and ethnographic portraiture are but two contrasting positions one can occupy on the 'analytical spectrum'. There are many other possibilities. We offer illustrations of work that bridge these different approaches. Again, a degree of methodological empathy may be helpful in understanding why different ethnographic traditions take the approach they do.

No matter which analytical approach one adopts, the same initial principles apply. The first stage is always immersion: spending time with one's research materials through reading and re-reading transcripts, diaries, fieldnotes and artefacts. If these are extensive this can feel like a daunting task. This is one reason why some advocate using information technology to help. Another fault-line in the world of qualitative research is between those who are committed advocates of qualitative data analysis software and those who remain deeply sceptical. The debate remains a live one. In 'The CAQDAS movement' we discuss the range of software available, and the advantages and disadvantages of using particular products and computer-assisted software.

Finally, we turn to the most difficult questions that harry some ethnographers as they write: epistemological sniping over questions of representation, reliability and validity. In 'But is it true?' we discuss the linguistic battles that surround these words, and what can feel like a methodological 'war' over whether qualitative methods, and in particular ethnographic approaches, offer reliable and generalisable knowledge. Whatever one's view on objectivity and the status of ethnographic knowledge, one needs to be able to articulate a convincing case for one's analytical approach.

Grounded theory 101

Sooner or later, social research textbooks invoke the hoary division between inductive and deductive approaches to the generation of knowledge. Two pioneering American sociologists, W.I. Thomas and Florian Znaniecki, who co-wrote the monumental *The Polish Peasant in Europe and America* (Thomas and Znaniecki 1918), championed empirical induction. They insisted on the importance of approaching a problem with an open mind and as few preconceptions as possible, allowing the theory to 'emerge from' the data, a vision that inspired others in the Chicago School of Sociology.

With the rise of the behaviouralist sciences and quantitative paradigms after the Second World War, inductive thinking began to be neglected within Sociology, before being 'rediscovered' by Glaser and Strauss in the 1960s. Sociological ethnographers and qualitative researchers may well be familiar with the label Glaser and Strauss championed for their version of inductive reasoning: 'grounded theory'. Grounded theory is at once a principle and a set of procedures for generating theory that is closely 'grounded' in the data. In Chapter 4 we introduced 'analytical memos', a writing technique that they popularised. We highlighted their usefulness for developing one's thinking, whether or not one follows the methodological precepts that Glaser and Strauss advocate. In what follows we discuss the conceptual implications of their approach to analysis, as well as the problems with assuming any research can ever be purely inductive.

Within a grounded theory approach, empirical 'data' takes on a precious and primary status. Even if data collection and analysis go hand-in-hand, the concepts and 'codes' one uses to sort this data should 'emerge', and not be imposed by the analyst. Many working in this tradition talk of the importance of 'open coding'. The metaphor is telling. It encourages an 'openness' to one's 'data' and fieldnotes in order to see what ideas, thoughts and puzzles emerge. These codes and open memos should be little more than labels, scribbles or notes appended to the margins of fieldnotes. At this point they are best not to be separated from their initial context, and may resemble jottings about jottings.

How did Glaser and Strauss's vision become so influential within qualitative research? Their methodological paradigm has been reflected and promoted within textbooks. Most conform to established conventions now detailing the process of 'coding' data. This, combined with the subsequent process of comparing codes, developing new codes and writing analytical memos, has become methodological wisdom. Even Kirsten Luker's entertaining 2008 account of 'salsa dancing into the social sciences', for all its caricatures of 'canonical social science', sees coding as a key step.

The root of this coding–comparison–analysis sequence is in the influential methodological manifesto of Barney Glaser and Anelm Strauss. Glaser was a social psychologist with a background in quantitative methods trained at Columbia, whilst Strauss was a student in the Chicago School of interpretive Sociology. Frustrated by the limits of their respective traditions and the 'embarrassing' gap between them, and shaken by family tragedies, they began to work together in their 1965 study *Awareness of Dying:*

> ... what kinds of thing happen around patients as they lie dying in American hospitals? ... what are the recurrent kinds of interaction between dying patient and hospital personnel? What kinds of tactics are used by the personnel who deal with the patient? (ibid., 8)

Profound and difficult questions about modern Americans and their relationship with death were at the centre of their work. Both came at the 'problem' of death with raw emotions, the consequence of having recently lost parents. The book itself is less well-remembered than the methodology they developed as a result.

Their vision was that researchers 'study an area without any preconceived theory that dictates prior to the research, "relevancies" in concepts and hypotheses' (1967, 33). Rejecting hypothesis testing and *a priori* theorisation, they insisted on the importance of the 'discovery of theory from data systematically obtained from social research' (ibid., 2). This precept was hugely influential, and has been widely adopted and reinterpreted. Their vision was appealing. It adopted the language of science – 'systematic', 'data', 'theory' – and offered a set of rigorous and clear procedures to follow, such as the repeated comparison and contrasting of different aspects of these 'data'. At the same time, their insistence that theory could be 'discovered' necessitated staying close to one's materials and experiences.

In essence, there are three steps to their method: coding, comparison and the generation of theory. But despite their commitment to the simple, insistent question, 'what's going on here?' their book adopts an abstract and technicist language, leaving scope for different interpretations of notions of coding and comparison. Indeed, the two authors subsequently fell out over the very definition of 'data'. If they couldn't agree, it is no surprise that the method remains divisive. The book also never mentioned their own traumatic experiences, and how these affected the way they theorised different types of awareness of dying.

The first step, most researchers agree, is to read one's fieldnotes and materials again and again. This facilitates the process of what Anselm Strauss (1987) called 'open' coding. Coding in this sense is just a way to get to know one's 'data', to begin to make sense of its complexity, and decide what aspects of it are meaningful for your study. The notion of 'openness' is intended to convey the importance of not imposing one's own preconceptions on the material.

Amidst the many textbooks offering procedural accounts of grounded theory, O'Reilly (2009, 36) offers a gloss on the key terms. Pointing out that coding is just a 'euphemism for the sorting and labelling which is part of the process of analysis', she explains that 'labels are names or phrases that label phenomena'. She differentiates between open and focused coding, with focused coding allowing exploration of categories and insights in more depth.

Let us take an example. Imagine you are doing an ethnography of a community of doctoral students. After doing several interviews, you realise that the way the students conceptualise the relationship between their lives and doctoral study or work is something you'd like to explore further. One could then go through the interviews looking for certain moments at which they discuss this relationship, giving them labels (e.g. 'stress', 'pleasure', 'intensity'). The more detailed and nuanced the label, the richer their analytical potential. It might be that one simply indexes key words or phrases. Sticking closely to one interview transcript, Coffey and Atkinson (1996) provide graphic illustrations of all the labels they use to index an interview with an academic about the experience of doing anthropological fieldwork, and then demonstrate how they use this index to build up a picture of the way doctoral students are socialised within a disciplinary tradition (in this case anthropology).

All notes, labels, codes or themes (be it 'friendship' or 'teacher author-ity' or 'discipline') are abstractions and interpretations. Their purpose is to allow you to stand back and compare contexts and cases, to see whether the labels can be used in other situations. Glaser and Strauss called this the 'constant comparative method'. Knowingly or not, this process of moving between contexts and comparing knowledge is one that we all engage in.

Let us say that you've added the label 'co-operation' to a fieldnote about a primary school playground activity in which two girls from very different social backgrounds make a daisy chain together. One would then look to find other examples of 'co-operation' in other contexts in the school. Does it need to be refined (e.g. cross-gender co-operation, classroom co-operation) or renamed (e.g. friendship)? How do you clas-sify these examples? Perhaps you now need to change your labels or codes. This process of sifting will inevitably throw up places where the codes don't fit, or where there seems to be a case for making them more abstract, or even rethinking the question one is asking of the material. This is inevitably messy and repetitive: Agar (1986), calls it a 'madden-ingly recursive' process.

As one continues to compare and contrast, recurring themes and issues in the data become visible. These can be used to think about the different ways you might divide up one's material into 'piles' or 'chunks', each related to a different theme. You can use these categories to sort or 'code' your notes, whether manually or virtually, though researchers dif-fer on whether it is important to separate out these themes. The impor-tant aspect of analysis is figuring out what concepts make sense and then linking those concepts to each other, along with changing the concepts when the data do not support your original thinking.

Many researchers emphasise the iterative nature of this process: mov-ing from description to concept and back again. Perhaps you return to your fieldnotes and decide that co-operation is not the best way to begin to code the many different activities you have noticed in the playground. It may be that you decide to think about gender relationships more broadly. Thinking about the wider themes helps one to look for catego-ries of codes that are connected. It is important to keep asking: What's going on here? And why? O'Reilly (2009) goes on to explain that memos are just notes through which one can 'expand on these labels, where they come from, what they might mean, what the ethnographer was thinking when she decided to use a given code'. Loyal to the 'grounded' tradition, she insists that 'nothing should be chopped up and divorced from its context' (ibid, 36).

The method has been subjected to sustained critique and revisions, not least by Glaser and Strauss themselves, who fell out in a disagreement about definitions. Rejecting the reduction of 'grounded theory' to what he disparagingly called 'Qualitative Data Analysis', Glaser insists that 'all is data' and advocates a more creative approach to concepts that can be abstracted from space and time. Others have tried to simplify the process, or to emphasise the iterative link between inductive and deductive approaches. Srivastava and Hopwood (2009) insist that the researcher's role is to go between the two key questions 'What are the data telling me?' and 'What do I want to know?'

Some critics are dismissive of the whole assumption that one can ever be free of preconceptions, and argue that the grounded theory ideology constrains and distorts qualitative inquiry. Critical both of the notion that theory can ever be 'discovered' and of the 'folk model of scientific endeavour' that grounded theory adopts, Thomas and James point out that 'a preoccupation with method makes for mirages of some kind of reliable knowing' (2006, 791). They argue instead for a looser approach to analysis and for 'narrative told simply and clearly' with no pretence of 'methodological alchemy'.

One does not have to be either 'for' or against coding and grounded theory, though most anthropological ethnographers shy away from its formality. You may want to approach your material from a number of directions. Looking for themes and issues in an inductive way is one way to go, but you may also want to try a more systematic coding at a certain point. Codes can be a way to navigate or even talk about one's materials, rather than simply a means to reduce and summate 'data'. Any approach that facilitates active learning, that allows the unexpected to emerge, and that does not overdetermine the pace and direction of analysis, is to be welcomed. The only requirement is to keep reflecting on one's approach, to openly and honestly document it, and to see this account as integral to the scholarly process.

Using analytical memos

One does not have to sign up to every aspect of grounded theory to use elements of Glaser and Strauss's approach. A popular approach that they pioneered is the writing of analytical memos. As we explained in Chapter 4, an analytical memo is a short note or piece of writing that seeks to précis and distil one's emerging thinking and findings about a situation, event, person or concept. It could be a few words, a paragraph, or even a page or more, depending on the stage or amount of material.

One could write a single-paragraph memo about each interview or observation, recording in each case a few things that were particularly striking or noteworthy. As well as playing a mnemonic function, memos help you focus on where you have been, and where you are going with your thinking and research. As the analysis develops, these memos can serve as building blocks, and may even form key sections of your findings. Some would rather keep these reflections and developments integrated within one's fieldnotes, but others prefer to separate out 'memos' and label them accordingly.

Why would one write analytical memos? There are a number of reasons. A memo helps you make connections and links between your analysis and the literature, and back again. It can also summarise your thinking about the patterns you have seen, and explain which patterns and themes seem important. It may also be a place to reflect on the literature, and whether there is a concept that helps explain your findings.

What else can one do with an analytical memo? It can act as a record of your research, helping you document where are you are 'at' with your thinking at a certain point. In the same vein it can be a reminder to yourself of the next steps you should take, whether they be further sites for participant observations; potential interviewees, interview questions, documents to look for, etc. Some use lengthy memos to bring together one's thinking, and to document planned changes or refinements to a research question or design. It can help one remember how a decision to alter, or not to alter, a research question was grounded in the analysis carried out for a memo.

In 'Figuring out Fieldwork' (2009), Kim Fortun offers a creative reworking of the notion of *memoing*. She carried out her own research in the aftermath of the Bhopal disaster, and found herself trying to understand how the survivors began to group themselves together in order to pursue Union Carbide for compensation. In a highly complex transnational set of field sites, the first task was to work out who she would be researching. She has since developed a creative set of pedagogic techniques to help her students prepare for fieldwork. She encourages them to start writing memos *before* they even start 'formal' fieldwork, as a way of helping them imagine themselves into their projects. These include making lists of the different types of people in their research sites, and the ways they may be differentiated. She asks them to come up with a list of the 'force fields' they work within, the political, economic and social forces that enable or constrain what each group can say and do. She encourages her students to be as historically specific as possible, and not to take any 'group' for granted. She goes still further, and asks them to think about the different and contradictory cultural impulses and currents any one individual might have to negotiate. These 'laundry lists', as she calls them, are intended to give students 'a structured place to play with what can be overwhelming ideas' (2009, 170), and to encourage the openness to want they might encounter. This approach to memoing precisely reverses the approach adopted in grounded theory, where they are used to integrate and develop one's analysis. Fortun's work is a reminder that the techniques of coding, comparing and memoing can be reinterpreted and used in ways that work for individual researchers.

Ethnographic writing as ethnographic analysis

Words such as 'data', 'coding' and 'analysis' immediately define one's ethnographic identity and ethnographic fieldnotes in a particular way. 'Data' has a rigorous, technical feel; the term frames knowledge as something measurable, independent and detached from the observer. References to one's 'data' immediately create a different aura from mention of one's 'fieldnotes'. The procedural rules that surround data coding and analysis can be reassuring and provide a sense of rigour and objectivity. However, a thorough approach to coding does not guarantee insightful and profound analysis, and too much attention to getting one's coding tactics 'right' can also be a distraction.

Some anthropologists shy away from an explicit discussion of their approach to analysis. This may be a dislike of codification and procedures. More positively, this reluctance is a tacit admission that every stage of research involves thinking and therefore analysis, and that one is constantly learning and developing. For the researcher, all ethnographies are educational. Each interview, text and encounter take one's thinking forward. Each helps one reconsider and make sense of all one's materials in new and sometimes contradictory ways. Iteration and recursivity are not just ways of understanding the relationship between theory and 'data', but become embodied in the researcher. Your understanding of a research topic will have developed hugely between your first and last interview: are both to be treated equally as data to be analysed? What if one reads a piece of writing after having completed one's field research that transforms the whole way one understands one's materials? What happens to grounded theory at that point?

This understanding of the analytical process as emergent and ongoing is taken for granted by many anthropologists. As a result their deployment of theory can seem to be opaque and instrumental, leading to the accusation that they simply cite aspects of their field materials that back up their particular theoretical or political preconceptions.

Their analytical approach does not need to be mystified. Whilst not purely inductive, nor is it cheap opportunism. One way to understand this process is to start at the back and work forwards. By looking first at a bibliography or set of theoretical references drawn on in an article, report or book, one can see the ideas and concepts that the author is bringing to the research. It is likely that the author has read a range of theoretical literature, and has become interested in a particular set of debates that then inform the actual research being undertaken.

Take Andrew Kipnis's work on educational 'desire' in China. Having written about gift-exchange and selfhood in a northern Chinese village for his doctorate, he became increasingly interested in social change in China and the way, post-Mao and the Cultural Revolution, that people once again began to value formal education. This crystallised into a research focus on the cultural, political and economic origins of this desire for college education, along with the way that individual and community aspirations, and schooling practices, were shaped by provincial and national government policies. The result is an ambitious and wide-ranging ethnography, *Governing Educational Desire* (2011). His use of the word 'desire' is informed by his experience of the intensity of rural families' educational aspirations, and his evidence of the way that they were prepared to go into debt or make huge sacrifices for their children. Yet his use of the concept of desire did not emerge neatly from his fieldnotes. It was also inspired by his reading of the French philosophers Gilles Deleuze and Felix Guatarri, whose writing has sought to liberate desire from Freud's overtly sexual framing while retaining an attention to fantasy, the imagination and the unconscious. Kipnis found this new theoretical understanding captured the issues that emerged from his research with parents from a range of schools in one province (Zouping). He then juxtaposed these with interviews with head-teachers, policy makers and educationalists in regional government and with national policy agendas. The result is a set of case studies that stretch from insights into individual rural households to China as a whole.

Another example comes from our own work. David's reading on anthropological theories of globalisation and his interest in feminist theory influenced the way he carried out his research in Uganda. The juxtaposition of everyday institutional life in a rural secondary school with that at the elite Makerere University in the capital Kampala was stark. This led him to carry out participant observation in both institutions, teaching and doing research into student cultures and pedagogic environments. He ended up focusing particularly on how local under-standings of gender were shaped within these institutions. Overly theo-retically ambitious, the range of themes and issues made formal coding of all the research materials inappropriate, and instead led to a close analysis of several focus groups.

Not all anthropologists are sceptical of an overly rigid approach to coding and analysis. For Madden,

> an ethnography that is not informed by scientific principles (like systematic data collection, analysis and presentation) is not good ethnography, it's more like fiction; and an ethnography that is not informed by the art of prose-writing, argument, rhetoric, persuasion and narrative, is not ethnography, it's just data. (Madden 2010, 24)

But others dispute the deployment of 'science' in this context, and turn instead to feminist philosophical debate around the creation of located knowledge and 'partial' truths (Haraway 1988). Scholars working in the influential tradition of actor-network theory are similarly reluctant to fol-low agreed precepts and rules. As John Law notes, the 'world is not to be understood in general by adopting a methodological version of auditing' (2004, 6).

These contrasting approaches to analysis are best understood in rela-tion to the knowledge claims that different ethnographic schools seek to make. Are the theoretical ideas primarily defined by (or grounded in) the empirical material? Or is the ethnographer seeking to create an illuminating juxtaposition between 'what the data are saying' with 'what the theory is saying'. Both have their place, but the latter allows for creativity and experimentation, whilst the former privileges empirical accountability.

The CAQDAS movement

Ever since the development of qualitative analysis software in the early 1990s, its use has provoked strong feelings among qualitative research-ers. Did these new technologies mark a watershed in the manipulation of voluminous sets of fieldnotes and large amounts of data, or distance the researcher from their ethnographic materials? Many ethnographers were sceptical, seeing it as a threat to the ethnographic craft. In an early critique, Coffey and Atkinson (1996) pointed to the danger of viewing the process of coding data as an analytic strategy in its own right. Our trust in technology, they suggested, can lead one to think that the soft-ware can do the analysis.

Others – especially those trained in sociological traditions of grounded theory – were more positive, and argued that packages such as MAXQDA, NVivo and Atlas-ti provided invaluable help with the process of coding large volumes of data. The CAQDAS (Computer Assisted Qualitative Data Analysis Software) movement is now well established, and is robust in its insistence on the rigour and objectivity that this technical process provides.

The critiques and defences continue, even if they bypass many anthropological ethnographers. MacMillan (2005) points to the way in which her research team began to treat 'data' in a more objectified way when they used a software package, whilst Lewins and Silver (2005) defend their use. Ness (2008, 8) suggests that the software can act as a 'rhetorical device' to underscore the 'scientific, modern, and even objective nature' of the analysis.

Those who enter this debate become all too aware of the polemics and strong feelings it provokes. The skill is to not be put off by them. The next step is to find out more about the software itself. As Fielding (2001) points out, there are more than twenty such packages. Each has a slightly different history, purpose and function. If you are thinking of using them, it is worth putting some time into understanding how they work. NVivo was developed by two sociologists, and is more amenable to a more grounded theory approach. The database can be external or internal, and is modelled on Microsoft Outlook. ATLAS.ti was developed by a more quantitative German academic. Simpler in structure than NVivo, all the data are held in one external file. MAXQDA was designed for the analysis of political discourse, and uses a Microsoft Windows-style interface. TransAna is less well-known, but purports to be particularly useful for the analysis of ethnographic data, as well as visual data. Most were originally developed by individual enthusiasts rather than large corporations, and tend to retain the inevitable quirks and idiosyncrasies. Their enthusiasm usually sustains a committed and helpful community of users.

There is no one best package, and your decision on which software, if any, to use, partly depends on your materials and your approach to analysis. Each package will take a while to learn and much longer still to master, and it is only worth this investment if you are confident that it is the right package for you. If you do not plan to do more research in future, it may not be worth making this time commitment.

Some researchers use this software primarily for data-management purposes. Whilst there is no doubt that this in itself is a useful role, increasing computing power and functionality makes word-processing packages such as Microsoft Word more helpful.

If you do have a choice, you would be well advised to consult widely and to assess the different options. A good place to start in deciding which analytical software to use are the reviews produced by the CAQDAS networking project at the University of Surrey. They tend to take the value of these packages for granted, but they do offer a careful assessment of the strengths and weaknesses of each.

Team-based qualitative research is an area where computer assisted analysis comes into its own. The software can help with the complexities of team-working when several people are simultaneously engaged in coding and analysis, or collaborating across a range of settings. On the other hand, working as part of a larger team means there is less scope to change analytical focus or direction.

But is it true?

Sooner or later the ethnographer encounters difficult questions about the way they analyse and present their work. 'Are your findings representative of all the schools in this town/county/nation?' or 'Aren't these stories just anecdotes?' or 'What's the difference between this and journalism?' or 'How do we know you haven't just chosen examples to back up your hunches?' Being defensive does not help. Developing articulate and thoughtful responses is an important part of communicating a commitment to valid and accountable ethnographic knowledge.

There are several ways to respond. One is to seek to reinterpret words such as generalisability and validity, away from a narrowly scientific model that measures knowledge claims in statistical terms. There are many ways in which findings can represent broader truths without having to be 'representative'. O'Reilly (2009) suggests talking of 'modest generalisations', statements that can be expressed formally while remaining moderate in scope and open to modification. One could also talk of 'analytical generalisations', creating hypotheses that can be tested for their applicability to other settings.

Another response is to change scale and to defend the importance of case studies. This is to argue for the value of nuanced, detailed and fine-grained analyses that bring out the complexity and singularity of social worlds. This is the defence of the well-chosen case and the logical inferences one can draw from it. It is a defence based on bringing a range of background and contextual knowledge to bear on one's choice of an apposite case. The ethnographer is not a journalist, but rather is trained to apply their own substantive and theoretical knowledge of their discipline to an empirical site. A case is never either typical nor atypical. Instead it is chosen for the insights it offers into more general issues. The significance of the case is in the way it distils the accumulated experience and knowledge of the researcher. It is not the case in itself that is being generalised, but rather the whole corpus of knowledge that surrounds the case. The case is used to illustrate the range of possible dynamics or the complexity of the situation. In 1940 Max Gluckman famously published a vivid account of one such 'social situation' – a bridge-opening ceremony in South Africa (Gluckman 1940). He went on to use the case to explore and critique the racial complexities and inequalities of South African society more generally. This one article shaped a whole tradition of case-study research, and is still influential today (e.g. Burawoy 2009).

A final alternative is to create a new language for discussing the process of ethnographic knowledge production. Here feminist theorists of science have led the way in thinking about how to locate knowledge claims with concepts such as 'reflexivity', 'situated knowledges' and 'partial truths'. Writing about the possibilities for a more accountable science, Donna Haraway (1999, 130) argues that 'the only way to find a larger vision is to be somewhere in particular'. Rather than attempting to find objectivity through 'escape and transcendence', what she calls the 'God trick' or the 'view from above', she insists on 'positioned rationality'. This means being open about one's own preferences and predilections as a researcher, allowing the reader to assess the claims one makes.

It may seem a utopian vision of science, but increasingly scientists are being called to account by their many publics, and expected to publish all aspects of their data collection. For ethnographers, being open about the dilemmas of method, access, research and analysis is increasingly expected. Reflexivity about one's choices and strategies is no longer seen as self-indulgence, but rather the best way to convince the reader of the authority and authenticity of the ethnographic account.

Conclusion

Debates over analysis are at the heart of strongly held differences and disciplinary loyalties. We have tried to show that a range of analytical approaches is possible within ethnography, each with varying degrees of creativity and accountability. Yet the future for ethnographic methods is far from secure. Within educational research, the fashion is for randomised control trials, large-scale collaborations, 'evidence-based' policy and statistical reliability. There are strong funding and political constraints that mitigate against support for ethnographic scholarship. A modicum of methodological empathy and solidarity towards other ways of 'being ethnographic' remains vital.

Exercises

- Compare two different recent ethnographic monographs and discuss their approach to analysis. Which is most open about its methods? Which do you find most convincing and why?

- Choose a passage from an interview you have carried out. Explore the different possible codes, themes or approaches you could use to make analytical sense of this text. Compare how your ideas and approaches differ from those of a colleague.

Further reading

Many of the books already reviewed in earlier chapters tackle issues of ethnographic analysis. This list offers a few further suggestions, both to help with your thinking and the practicalities of analysing ethnographic materials.

Becker, H. (1998). *Tricks of the Trade: How to Think About your Research While you're Doing it*. Chicago, Chicago University Press.

This book shows how we can at once think about our conceptualisation and our writing. Full of helpful imageries and examples of theoretical generalisations, it should be required reading for all social scientists.

Boeije, H. (2010). *Analysis in Qualitative Research*. London, Sage.

A very hands-on contribution to the literature on analysing qualitative research, Hennie Boeije has written a textbook that provides a structure to the analytical process that she calls the 'spiral of analysis'. A little directive in places.

Murchison, J. M. (2010). *Ethnography Essentials: Designing, Conducting, and Presenting your Research*. San Francisco, Jossey-Bass.

A down-to-earth introductory guide to ethnographic research by an anthropologist who has worked in Africa with his students, this book combines examples and advice through a clear set of 'how-to' instructions. Several aspects of the book stand out: advice on capturing spatial dimensions of culture through ethnographic mapping, and a discussion on documenting relationships through kinship charts. One of the few textbooks that bridges methodological cultures, even if coding gets taken somewhat for granted.

Additional online resources can be found at: www.sagepub.co.uk/beraseries.sp

CHAPTER 7

ETHNOGRAPHY THAT MAKES A DIFFERENCE

What is in this chapter?

- Advice on ethnographic exits and departures
- How does one know when has one has done 'enough' fieldwork?
- Suggestions on giving something back: communicating insights and sustaining relationships
- Introductions to 'action research', 'participatory research' and 'paraethnography'
- Reflections on the relationship between scholarship and politics: can one be an activist educational ethnographer?

Introduction

It is hard to make a research methods textbook look messy. The clean headings and careful typesetting present social research as an organised and tidy affair. One writes a research proposal and design, gets a grant, carries out fieldwork, conducts the analysis, and then 'writes up' the findings for publication.

This book has sought to show that ethnographic work is rarely so straightforward. Often we decide to do research on a topic precisely because we are already emotionally or politically involved in a situation, whether through work, travel or personal experience. We may have been frustrated by our own experiences at school, angry about glaring educational inequalities, or intrigued by the belief and commitment of the world's poorest to education. These prior attachments and entanglements become 'the grit in the oyster', and provide the energy and determination to tackle a topic. Carrying out and writing up ethnographic research spur new questions, new demands and new forms of engagement. None of this makes it easy to end a period of fieldwork or to detach oneself from a research situation. But then nor is education a straightforward process. In Bruner's unforgettable words, 'Education is risky because it fuels the sense of possibility' (1997, 42). Ethnography ensures that this sense of possibility and risk is sustained.

In this chapter we explore these personal and political 'entanglements', seeing them as ethnographic strengths rather than flaws in the methodology. They make it harder to draw boundaries around a scholarly 'project'. A particularly thorny problem is knowing when one has done 'enough' fieldwork. This is never straightforward. If ethnographic research is an iterative combination of disciplined curiosity and unexpected insight, any end-point is arbitrary. There may not be a 'last goodbye'. You may be forced by disciplinary expectations or bureaucratic timetables to formally 'finish' fieldwork. But insight does not sit neatly in institutionally approved packages. This time pressure to submit a dissertation or final report can be productive, but your own thinking about a topic is likely to continue to develop long after submission.

If it is hard to know *when* to finish, it is also hard to know *how* to finish fieldwork. Ethnographic research thrives on the quality of insight developed during fieldwork. These insights come from and through relationships. But what happens to these relationships after one has left? How does one handle the social and intellectual obligations that have accumulated through fieldwork? And what if your field is less a place than a dense network of relationships and collaboration? What ethical dilemmas does this create? What obligations remain?

The world is changing. Social research is no longer a mysterious concept. Educational ethnographers are more likely to encounter resistance or rejection than an innocent welcome. Amidst the welter of demands placed on them, schools and teachers may be resistant to the logistical demands created by what they see as irrelevant research. Few methods textbooks reflect on the implications of these changing power relations for ethnographic research, or on the relationship between scholarship and politics.

For this reason, this chapter offers ways of doing ethnographies of education differently. In one sense all ethnographic research is collaborative, but these contributions are often not acknowledged by the authors. The protagonists of participatory ethnography redefine ethnography as a shared and collectively owned approach to research. 'Collaboration', 'participation', 'engagement' and 'impact' are the current buzzwords. Their implications for research strategies are still being worked through. It is much easier to talk about participatory research than to put it into practice; much easier to take a strong political stand than to stay attuned to the complexities of power. We go on to ask whether these techniques of action research or participatory research are appropriate for those new to research.

We also explore the practicalities of working alongside people like oneself. Educators and students have their own explanations, analyses and interpretations. Does it matter if their interpretations and theorisations are different from yours? And how might one incorporate their 'para-ethnographic' insights into your work?

There is no way to avoid the power relations that are part of all social research. Once this is acknowledged, one can open up broader debates about the relationship between scholarship and politics. Many ethnographers of education have been influenced by the strong position taken by the eminent Martyn Hammersley, who seeks to protect the division between the two domains. He feels that 'we live in dangerous times for research', with funders seeking to define the goal of research 'in terms that subordinate the pursuit of knowledge to other goals'. He insists that researchers 'should be committed primarily to the pursuit of knowledge, and should be as neutral as they can towards other values' (2000, 12). In this book we have gently questioned the possibility of neutrality. But does that mean one can and should combine research with activism? Is it possible to sustain the integrity of both scholarship and one's political commitments? Opinions remain polarised.

How is this chapter structured?

This chapter starts with the simple question, 'When does fieldwork end?' Anthropological ethnographers have long celebrated the value of extended long-term fieldwork, arguing for the importance of spending at least a year or so, though many go on to whole careers working in, or returning to, one place. Others argue that the quality of the research and analysis matters more than the time one spends in a place.

We go on to look at the responsibility of researchers to those one has worked and researched with. In the section 'Giving something back' we look at different ways of doing this, from presenting findings to discussing the issues that arise. We also make practical suggestions for finding ways of contributing to policy debates.

One way of avoiding the 'cutting' of social relations is to simply keep going back. We explore the opportunities for sustaining relationships in one's 'field site'. There is no doubt that scholarship is greatly enhanced by the depth of analysis that comes from repeated and long-term engagement. But what if this research site is one in which you will continue to work as a practitioner? We offer examples from ethnographic accounts and also reflect on the dilemmas that may arise.

In 'These natives can speak for themselves' we explore the possibilities for making ethnographic research more participatory and collaborative. We draw on a range of examples, highlighting the risks that surround working with professional communities who may like the principle of ethnographic attention more than the consequences. The final section is entitled 'From scholarship to politics, and back again', in which we reflect on the history of ethnographic attempts to reconcile scholarship and political influence.

When does fieldwork end?

Reflecting on the influence of his work on other educational ethnographers, Paul Willis admitted that his use, in the late 1960s, of reel-to-reel tape recorders was somewhat unorthodox:

> I saw it at the time as 'For god's sake get something, get some data!' I wanted to have a form of working where I could get data and use it, do it quickly ... you could imagine it as the beginning of the corrosion of serious fieldwork. (Quoted in Mills and Gibb 2000, 407)

This has led anthropologists to accuse Willis of taking short-cuts and misappropriating 'their method' by promoting what some see as high-speed 'drive-by' ethnography. Educational ethnographers have also criticised this strategic use of ethnography to illuminate prior theoretical and political agendas, suggesting that it foregrounds Willis's own concerns rather than those emanating from the field. For both sets of critics, the theoretical flair of this work may have come at the expense of a commitment to empirical depth and grounded analysis.

Even within anthropology, a debate has emerged about just how long fieldwork needs to be. Classically, anthropology students spent at least a year in their field site, justified by the need to live through a full seasonal cycle. Ethnography has moved on, but the re-imagination of the field less as a period of dwelling than as a set of empirical and conceptual spaces is controversial. In his provocative *How Short Can Fieldwork Be?* George Marcus (2007) questions the value of an extended period of fieldwork as a disciplinary rite of passage, a shibboleth of scholarly rigour and a source of academic capital (see also Delamont et al. 2000).

Is the length of one's fieldwork a fair measure of the quality of one's ethnographic insights? In theory, one could spend a year in a field site without learning the local language or developing deep insight. Perhaps ethnographies should be judged on their quality, not on the length of fieldwork. Indeed, Geertz (1989) calculates that Evans-Pritchard spent only four months doing the fieldwork that led to his classic 1940 monograph *The Nuer*.

If your research is defined by a critical event, such as the events around the launch of a new educational charity (Mills 1999b) or the trial of a nanny accused of murdering a child in her charge (Hine 2000), then the timetable may be defined by the scope of the research.

For most researchers, the length of fieldwork is defined primarily by pragmatic concerns – running out of money, the pressure to write the dissertation or book, the need to look after family or friends. But whenever the time is right to 'exit' the field, the departure needs careful preparation. You may well have developed a number of close relationships and friendships. Will you try and sustain these after 'leaving'? Do you stay in touch by email or phone? Will the people you have worked with expect you to reciprocate in some way? It is worth remembering that whilst 'fieldwork' may have formally finished, you may well still have unanswered questions or things to check up, and you wish to explore. Your connections and emotional attachments are not going to suddenly come to an end. You may also want to ensure that you can return at some future point.

After leaving Uganda, David continued to stay in touch with many of the teachers he had got to know, helping a close friend to first study for an MSc and then pay for medical treatment for a sick relative. As well as sponsoring one student through school, he later helped set up a small educational charity to provide secondary school scholarships. As well as being a modest attempt at reciprocity, these links also provided insight into the changing financing of Ugandan schools and the pressures facing parents. In his discussion of 'exits' Neyland highlights how the end of his formal period of research on a university allowed him to then negotiate a new role working more closely with key practitioners and professionals. He characterises this shift from ethnography 'of' an organisation to ethnography 'for' and 'with' an organisation (2007, 170).

Many ethnographers return again and again over their careers to the same research site, and are able to offer valuable understandings of change. In a recent collection entitled 'Returns to the Field', Howell and Talle (2012) describe this as 'multitemporal fieldwork', and suggest that it gives rise to a 'multitude of ethnographic presences' and several different 'ethnographic presences'. Going back over time is both a way to develop the longitudinal research perspective that is often lacking and to develop a better understanding of change.

The question of 'leaving' is rather different for teacher researchers who continue to work in their research sites. They are not leaving at all, but instead seeking to sustain two different identities. Little discussed within the methods literature, seeing oneself as simultaneously research 'outsider' and practitioner 'insider' can be disorienting. But the shift between the two can serve to 'keep the familiar strange', and would seem to be a prerequisite for scholarly detachment, and the ability to stand back from everyday assumptions and taken-for-granted practices.

Giving something back

There are many ways in which one can reciprocate, both during and after fieldwork. Reciprocity during fieldwork was addressed in Chapter 3, but here we discuss possible ways to 'give something back' when fieldwork comes to an end. Endings are also beginnings, and offer new ways of relating and working with people.

One form of reciprocity is material, as discussed above. Another form of reciprocity is more integral to the research: bringing one's research back to the community, sharing insights and findings. Whilst this is an important ethical principle, this is easier said than done. At one level it can be a chance to check one's interpretations and insights, and to take one's thinking forward. But it is vital to think about one's audience. Academic genres of presentation are unlikely to be appropriate for communicating with school teachers, a parent–teacher association or a group of students. Better to do a two-page policy briefing for teachers, a talk at assembly or an article in the school magazine.

Beyond the research, most ethnographers have forms of expertise and professional knowledge that will be invaluable to those with whom we work. Whether it is your knowledge of national educational policy processes, or just having the confidence and cultural capital to stand up in front of school governors, these are the contributions that make a difference. These interventions might also lead to new possibilities for fieldwork, or spark new projects.

It may not be what you do, but how you do it that counts. In her *Critical Ethnography* (2012) Soyini Madison draws on performance and social theory to come up with creative ideas for physically staging and performing one's findings, and encourages ethnographers to think about writing as a performance too.

These natives can speak for themselves

The stakes surrounding engaged ethnographic research are increasingly high. At one San Francisco anthropological conference in the early 1990s, a group of AIDS activists decided to blockade a session at which prominent anthropologist theorists were giving papers on the social power of discourses around AIDS. Incensed at the session title 'Aids and the social imaginary' at a time when so many people were dying, they arrived wearing T-shirts that read 'These natives can speak for themselves'.

Their action pointed to a central dilemma for all ethnographers: the relationship between power and knowledge. A scholarly text may aspire to be a neutral or objective rendition of a social world, but the complex power relationship that is contained within any scholarly representation has led some ethnographers to adopt more participatory and collaborative approaches to research.

Within anthropology, there is a long tradition of action research, first pioneered by Sol Tax in his work on the Fox project in the late 1940s. He set this up to provide University of Chicago anthropology students with field experience. As they worked with the Fox tribe of American Indians they became aware of the pressures facing that community because of white encroachment on Fox lands. Their discussions about whether and how to intervene led them to pioneer a theoretical framework for action that became known as action anthropology, and led to a number of educational programmes. Whilst the organisational psychologist Kurt Lewin is usually credited with developing the concept of 'action research' (Gaventa et al. 2001), there is evidence that he was influenced by the reformist efforts of an Indian Bureau Commissioner called John Collier (Cooke 2006). Collier had long worked with anthropologists, saw research as a tool of action, championed the 'Indian New Deal' and championed Native American rights.

A number of anthropologists of education have fruitfully drawn upon these traditions of participatory research. The first protagonists saw themselves working in the radical educational tradition of the Brazilian activist and writer Paulo Freire and his 1972 *Pedagogy of the Oppressed*. Freire put his philosophical training to work pioneering an approach to literacy instruction that emphasised conscientisation and politicisation. Inspired partly by Frantz Fanon, it was a heady combination of anti-colonial Marxism, and a vision for the way knowledge could in itself be emancipatory. As he put it, 'the oppressed must be an instrument in their own redemption' (Freire 1972, 54). Insisting that education was always political, he is best known for challenging what he called the banking model of education, in which the student is seen as an empty vessel and 'receiving object' (ibid., 70). A period of exile as an academic in the US and Europe ensured that his vision of 'critical pedagogy' remains very influential, especially amongst researchers.

There are many strands to his influence, but his vision has been taken up by educators and reformers committed to democratising research, many of whom have sought to involve children and young people in the research process. Best known today by the acronyms PRA (Participatory Rural Appraisal) or PAR (Participatory Action Research), these traditions embrace a range of collaborative approaches to research, usually foregrounding the active participation of groups or collectives in representing their shared knowledge, often with an explicit aim of empowering marginalised groups or challenging external representations and agendas (Cornwall and Jewkes 1995).

Among educational ethnographers, participatory methods have been particularly championed by those committed to critical pedagogy. Julie Cammarota (2008) describes how she uses it as the basis of a youth empowerment programme with Latino students in Tucson, Arizona, where they conduct research together and then present the results in creative ways – through drama, observations, poetry. One student she worked with went around taking pictures of his school to illustrate the language discrimination and informal exclusion experienced by Mexican immigrant students. This documentation was used to mount a legal challenge to state law forbidding bilingual education.

One of the risks of this sort of politicised research is that, even in careful hands, it can oversimplify questions of power and voice. As Ellsworth notes in her influential 1989 piece *Why Doesn't This Feel Empowering?*, work in this tradition tends towards highly abstract notions of 'domination' and 'emancipation' and to assume that 'rationalistic dialogue' will in itself be enough to address these inequalities. She describes running a course at the University of Madison-Wisconsin that set out to address campus racism, after a fraternity was suspended for racial slurs. She decided to do so in a way that was explicit about her own politics, did not hide behind the code words 'critical pedagogy', and did not presume to understand the very specific racial positionings and experiences that faced students in her class. The article describes the complexities of running a course in a way that helped students develop a more nuanced understanding of difference and their own affiliations.

She goes on to suggest that, at worst, the 'critical pedagogy' movement becomes another 'repressive myth' perpetuating relations of domination (1989, 298). She also questions the seductive assumption that research can simply access the authentic voices and representations of the most marginalised. If research was simply a question of giving voice to the voiceless, social inequalities would have long disappeared. Other feminist writers have made similar interventions. Questioning the promises made by the influential 'student voice' research movement, Bragg and Manchester argue that 'voice should be understood as enacted within and through specific sites and practices, and in terms of the subjectivities and narratives it offers to teachers, students, artists and others involved' (2011, ix). They acknowledge that the very process of articulating such voices can have unpredictable political effects.

Working together over the twenty years, Lois Weis and Michelle Fine have done most to respond to these critiques, and to develop the theoretical rationale and methodological tactics for the use of participatory methods that can 'situate analyses of inequity, power, privilege and deprivation' (2004, ix). They describe their accounts as 'compositional studies', research that demonstrates how larger structural formations 'seep through the lives, identities, relations and communities of youth and adults' (2004, xx). Aware of the risks of characterising 'a' single community perspective, their methodological approach is to first map the whole community, and then 'fracture' these to show the many competing stories that can be told within one institution. Their work in schools, prisons and grass-roots organisations has sought to investigate the experiences of 'communities under siege', and to open up what they call 'spaces of possibility'.

One project, entitled 'From within and beyond prison bars', involved women prisoners researching their experience of studying for a degree whilst incarcerated. The team developed a research methods course to be delivered within the prison, and ensured the inmate researchers became integral to the project, writing up their findings in one voice. Their reflections highlight how 'insiders know more, know better, and know in more complicated detail', whilst outsiders have the relative freedom to speak a kind of truth to power' (2004, 118). Attentive to the limitations of their own politics, Weis and Fine collaborate closely with their participants, be they parents, students or immigrant children. In another project, they describe how students from schools at either end of the social spectrum visit each other's schools in order to reflect on the huge gap in privilege between the two.

The techniques of participatory research have proved popular beyond academia, and practitioners within environmental and development charities were the first to turn the principles into a set of practical tools (Chambers 1983). Whether drawing maps in the sand, using piles of beans to rank concerns, sorting cards or guided walks to promote discussion, these methods have been adopted by an ever-growing range of non-academic organisations and practitioners. Mosse (2005) hints at one reason why: participation is the word that can travel easily and translate well. Superficially apolitical, it seems to allow compromise, multiple definitions of success, and allows ideological differences to be set aside.

Used uncritically, 'participation' simply becomes another buzzword, a methodological orthodoxy, and as Cooke and Kothari (2001) suggest, 'a new tyranny'. Where once the social representations generated through participatory research were seen in themselves to be emancipatory knowledges that could speak 'truth to power', scholars are now rather more critical about the assumption that participation in and of itself untangles the tight weft between knowledge and power. Increasingly, ethnographers need to study the process and products of knowledge production as much as the people involved.

What of teacher inquiry more broadly? One can trace the principle of teacher inquiry back to John Dewey, and his insistence that experience, action and reflection are linked. The key pioneer of research by and for teachers was Lawrence Stenhouse. As well as writing about curriculum reform (1967), he pioneered the Humanities Curriculum Project, an innovative approach to classroom power relations. Through curriculum materials and guidance notes, the project sought to equip the teacher with the ability to bring controversial issues into the classroom and to lead discussions without imposing their own agendas or opinions, and led to a wider set of debates about the role of the teacher. He argued that teachers should study their own work, and that 'curriculum research and development ought to belong to the teacher' (Stenhouse 1975, 142).

Today, the principles of action research still inform some professional teacher education programmes. For others, 'action research' has become synonymous with practitioner research and is consequently disparaged. This is not just because of the problematic assumptions made by some of its protagonists about 'empowerment'. There is also the realpolitik of institutional life to consider. If there is no tradition of critical ethnographic practice in your department or school, this may be because historically Education departments have prioritised more immediately palatable, policy-relevant research.

Working in teams and across disciplines

Another aspect of the politics of participation emerges when working in a multi-disciplinary research team. *Shane, The Lone Ethnographer* is the catchy title for a pioneering comic-book introduction to ethnographic research in education by an award-winning cartoonist (Galman 2007). It plays upon the iconic American trope of the plucky lone-ranger astride her saddle, whilst revealing something of how anthropologists tend to imagine themselves: alone with their vocation.

Like most caricatures, the joke hides a partial truth. Ethnographers have long relied on the advice and guidance of collaborators, and worked with others in creating their accounts, even if they have not always been frank about the contributions their colleagues have made.

Whilst this may not be possible for doctoral researchers, increasingly ethnographers are communicating across disciplinary divides. There are many different ways to collaborate. In a three-year ethnographic research project looking at university IT cultures, Daniel Neyland began to appreciate the complexity and messiness of organisational change. He decided to start writing an ethnographic article with one of the participants in the research, an IT manager with many years of professional experience. He even involved the research funders as co-authors. His rationale was that the impact of the final report would be enhanced through working closely with those who would go on to assess the report. He realised that the best measure of his contribution would be a collaboratively written report and its 'impact' within higher-education policy circles rather than a single-authored academic journal article (2007).

Whilst Neyland proved highly adept at redefining the expectations of his collaborators and funders, other educational ethnographers have found it rather harder to work in multidisciplinary teams. Increasingly collaboration has become an end in itself, with research teams cobbled together in order to meet funder expectations or policy targets. Collaboration is never straightforward, especially when seeking to work across different analytical and disciplinary frameworks (e.g. Strathern 2004); Barry, Born and Weszkalnys 2008). If ethnographers are not to simply provide the 'cultural icing' on a pre-defined research cake they have to find ways to represent their disciplinary perspectives and insights to those unfamiliar with the field. They also have to be wary of their disciplinary expertise being appropriated or disputed in unexpected ways.

The experience of the anthropologist David Mosse is salutary. His ethnography of the deployment of development 'expertise' within an international organisation (2005) benefitted from the close collaboration with the organisation's employees and 'knowledge workers'. But when presented with the findings, they denigrated his account, seeing it as inaccurate, disrespectful and defamatory of their professional reputation. The dispute focused on the very notion of professionalism that he, and they, deployed. For them, professionalism meant a detached, rational expertise, whereas his research showed that in practice their skills included the difficult emotional labour of negotiating expectations, facilitating bureaucratic processes and the off-script. They accused him of using his personal relationships with them for his own ethnographic purposes. As a result his former colleagues sought to prevent the publication of findings, and accused him of unethical behaviour. Whilst he was defended by his professional association, the case demonstrated the complexity of carrying out collaborative work (Mosse 2011).

So is para-ethnography the answer?

In their study of Wall Street's investment bankers, Holmes and Marcus become intrigued by the way that ethnographic approaches to symbolic analysis are not dissimilar to the abstractions and cultural practices of our 'expert subjects' (2006, 41) They go on to suggest that this 'convergence' marks the gradual end of a more positivist research paradigm, blurs the 'us'/'them' distinction, and forces us all to adopt a more collaborative and participatory approach to knowledge creation. They advocate treating experts as counterparts, and finding ways of accessing the 'illicit, marginal social thought' (ibid., 248) that circulates amongst professionals whose lives are dominated by official and technical discourse. Used critically, these thoughts could then 'provide' a bridge to more fundamentally anthropological knowledge.

Whilst the attempt by Holmes and Marcus to call an epistemological tipping point is somewhat overdone, their work reminds us that those we work with are also engaged in theory, analysis and reflection. Their answer is to advocate 'substantively collaborative projects', and they are optimistic about the possibilities of what they call 'para-ethnography'. The term was first used in 1988 by James Clifford to describe early para-ethnographic genres of writing, such as missionary accounts and travel reports, from which academic ethnographers sought to distance themselves. A century and a half later, academic researchers are now blurring these distinctions once again in the name of citizen science, knowledge exchange and research impact.

This does not mean that *the* solution to the ethical and epistemological dilemmas at the heart of ethnography is para-ethnography, any more than it is participatory research. Each approach offers new possibilities and creates new threats. Para-ethnography is perhaps less of a methodological vision than an acknowledgement that in a global, media-saturated knowledge culture ethnographers are not the only analysts and theorists. The likelihood is, as Mosse discovered when he sought to publish a piece of collaborative research, that the politics of ethnographic knowledge production and reception become ever more complex and fraught.

From scholarship to politics, and back again

Ethnographers have long had worldly ambitions. As well as proselytising about social anthropology, Bronislaw Malinowski took every opportunity to influence policy debates about education. Seeking church mission funding and colonial office patronage for his research in Africa, he wrote influentially about education 'being bigger than schools' (Malinowski 1936, 1943), pronounced on the risks of 'transculturation', and lobbied Western educators to take into consideration 'native' systems of informal education. Earlier interventions around colonial policy had led to several large research grants. But at one 'New Education Fellowship' conference in Cape Town in 1934 (Johnson 1943), he even advocated 'the possibility of developing an equitable system of segregation' (Malinowski 1936). His post at the London School of Economics, an institution established with a commitment to social reform, made these connections into the world of colonial policy easy to sustain.

Many of his students also sought to deploy anthropology to shape educational policy. Amongst them was Audrey Richards, who became one of the key architects of colonial university policy in the years after the war. Not all academics approved of the close links between LSE and the Colonial Office, and even those who did become involved in educational policy were frank about their frustrations. Writing in the 1950s, Margaret Read roundly criticised both anthropologists and educationalists for not working together, bemoaning that anthropologists felt they had 'more interesting and more urgent problems in cultural change to investigate', whilst educationists were 'impatient with their [anthropologists'] outspoken criticisms and unwilling to revise their aims and methods in the light of these criticisms' (1955, 74). Such caricatures may no longer hold true, but the relationship between academic knowledge and governmental knowledge remains fraught.

If combining scholarship and politics is not new, there is now a growing community of ethnographers who write specifically about understanding and shaping fast-moving policy processes. The contributors to *Adventures in Aidland* (Mosse 2011) reflect on the contested spaces that academic knowledge (and in particular ethnographic expertise) occupy within the World Bank, the World Health Organization and the UK Department for International Development. Stephen Ball's work has sought to critically map the new transnational policy networks and their connections (Ball 2008; Nambissan and Ball 2010). Drawing together his twin expertise as a public health doctor and anthropologist, Paul Farmer is one of the most prominent of those ethnographers who has managed to combine a critical analysis with professional engagement in a field of public policy (Farmer 1999).

Whilst the new global philanthropies (such as the Gates Foundation) champion transparency and the role of expert research and scientific evidence to inform policy, the frank insights that ethnography might offer into their organisations do not sit easily with their carefully crafted self-images. If ethnographers were once courted, this is no longer the case. The Foucaultian ambition to speak 'truth to power' remains a necessary and difficult undertaking.

Conclusion

It is increasingly difficult to separate out sites of knowledge collection, production and consumption. The university is no longer the sole arbiter of academic knowledge, and ethnographers can find themselves working in organisations that are equally dedicated to producing 'para-ethnographic' knowledge. We have highlighted a range of methodological shifts that have accompanied this recognition. One's fieldwork is no longer spatially detached or bounded in time, but may always be ongoing, defined by an institutional workplace or set of friendships. Collaboration is an integral part of any ethnography, or a way of sustaining relationships and access.

Scholars have long sought to sustain their political principles and their scientific vocation. This was never an easy task, especially in Education departments that bring together scholars of a range of epistemological and political persuasions. A commitment to social justice makes one more aware of power and social inequality, but politics alone is no guarantee of ethnographic attentiveness.

Exercises

- Prepare a policy briefing about your research or an ethnographic monograph that you have read. How would you seek to represent its findings in a one-page executive summary? What are the consequences of trying to do so?

- Try out some of the techniques used in participatory research, e.g. drawing up a set of cards to rank food likes and dislikes. What might be the advantages and disadvantages of these methods?

Further reading

Armbruster, H. and Lærke, A. (eds.) (2008). *Taking Sides: Ethics, Politics, and Fieldwork in Anthropology*. Oxford, Berghahn.

Raw accounts from anthropologists committed to social advocacy and activism, the contributors seek to balance political commitments with ethical responsibilities.

Conteh, J., Gregory, E., Kearney, C. and Mor-Sommerfeld, A. (2005). *On Writing Educational Ethnographies: The Art of Collusion*. London, Trentham.

A powerfully honest set of reflections on planning, researching, writing and publishing educational ethnographies of education by four UK academics committed to progressive political change. They use collusion in a positive sense – to invoke their determination to work together against 'those promoting simplistic answers to collecting, analysing, or interpreting data involving real people' (xxiii).

Gaventa J., Cornwall, A., Reason, P. and Bradbury, H. (eds.) (2001). *Handbook of Action Research: Participative Inquiry and Practice*. London, Sage.

Participatory research techniques have been explored in a range of scholarly traditions: this book offers a critically thoughtful guide to putting these techniques to work.

Sanford, V. and Angel-Ajani, A. (2006). *Engaged Observer: Anthropology, Advocacy and Activism*. London, Rutgers University Press.

A hard-hitting set of pieces by ethnographers reflecting on research in zones of conflict. The contributors put a political commitment to challenging social injustice and oppression at the heart of their research practice.

Weis, L. and Fine, M. (2000). *Speed Bumps: A Student-friendly Guide to Qualitative Research*. New York, Teachers College Press.
Weis, L. and Fine, M. (2004). *Working Method: Research and Social Justice*. New York, Routledge.

Lois Weis and Michelle Fine are part of a US community of 'critical educators' who see research as a key route to social justice. Both books offer very clear approaches to research design, and in particular see participatory methods as a key tool for emancipatory research.

Additional online resources can be found at: www.sagepub.co.uk/beraseries.sp

CHAPTER 8

WRITING AGAIN: COMMUNICATING ETHNOGRAPHIC INSIGHTS

What is in this chapter?

- A manifesto for ethnographic writing
- A discussion of ethnographic narrative styles
- Blogging: communication or participation?
- Reflections on public ethnography

Introduction

There are many ways to write an educational ethnography. There are also many other writing genres that ethnographers can use to good effect: fieldwork blogs, review essays, journal articles. Each genre has its role, each its expectations. Scholarly publishing conventions are also changing, under pressure from publishers struggling with the demands of open access and the costs of print runs. Academic monographs are under threat from the rise of bibliometrics. Individual scholarship is measured by the number of articles published in peer-reviewed journals, each with their own ranking and 'impact factor'. On the other hand, there are many new online journals, and the internet offers dramatically new ways to communicate. The landscape for academic writing is rapidly shifting, and doctoral pedagogies are often slow to keep up.

Nurturing an academic career was never easy. Max Weber famously commented that he 'knew of no other career in which chance played such a role' (1948 [1918]). Surviving in today's universities means thinking early and hard about the potential 'impact' of your work, and writing in ways that engage policy makers and other potential 'users' of research. This means learning the dark arts of writing funding proposals, punchy consultancy reports and measured policy briefings.

In this chapter we return to the discussion of ethnographic writing with which we began this book. We highlight different approaches to structuring an ethnographic narrative, and make the case for also learning to write for audiences beyond the academy. We also reflect on what distinguishes ethnographic writing from the best journalism or travel writing. We end by asking whether ethnographers of education should prioritise their scholarly audiences, a policy community or the broader reading public. And is it possible to write for several audiences simultaneously?

How is this chapter structured?

Ethnographic writing, suggest Gay y Blasco and Wardle (2007, 20), is 'akin to a conversation with many participants, rather than merely a dialogue between ethnographer and subjects'. This is an appealing vision, acknowledging that ethnographies are always in dialogue with other ethnographies, and with scholarship more generally, as well as those with whom we have lived and worked. Yet what if the conversations adopt different registers and use different languages? Can theoretical ideas and engaging description really be combined?

In 'A manifesto for ethnographic writing' we explore different genres of writing about educational experiences and institutions. Is it possible to distinguish ethnographic writing from comparable narrative genres, such as investigative journalism? We identify three writing virtues that ethnographers aspire to – modesty, honesty and analytical insight.

In 'Narrating ethnography' we discuss different genres of ethnographic writing, and encourage you to think about your own ethnographic voice. Developing a range of narrative skills is a great way to improve one's ethnographic writing, and helps make one's reading more critical and thoughtful. We explore the ethnographic conventions that shape writing practices, and the different ways educational ethnographers present their work. We reiterate a point made at the start of this book, that it is never too early to start writing and experimenting with one's own ethnographic voice. Rather than turn to the growing number of self-help guides to learn how to write 'properly', see writing as both a form of thinking but also a way to develop a scholarly identity. A research career may depend on honing the skills of writing punchy abstracts and research proposals, but the ability to articulate one's voice requires finding an ethnographic genre to match.

Finally, we turn to the question of audience, and how best to communicate. In 'Public ethnography' we highlight ethnographers and other educational scholars who have sought to write for a range of broader publics, and explore why this may be increasingly difficult for researchers in education.

A manifesto for ethnographic writing

Katharine Boo is an investigative journalist and the author of *Behind the Beautiful Forevers* (2012), an acutely observed narrative of the 'life, death and hope' faced by children in a makeshift Mumbai slum. Overlooked by glitzy new hotels and a new international airport, her searing account of life in Annawadi offers poignant insight into the way India's new wealth affects the poorest living in its shadows.

Contributing to a fine US tradition of documentary reportage, what makes this book special? It is her empathy and ability to sensitively convey the violence and trauma that surrounded the Muslim and Hindu families at the heart of her narrative. Her commitment and dedication to understanding the worlds of children fractured by poverty, caste and religion is evident. She spent three years in Annawadi researching the book, working with local co-researchers to do an enormous number of interviews, constantly fact-checking and verifying, trying to get to the bottom of complex social relationships and enmities. This level of dedication and patience marks her out from most non-anthropologists. Her prose is gripping, and her interpretations of the inner emotional lives of the children and young people she spends time with are both audacious and convincing. She also writes in a way that most ethnographers could only dream of doing. Where does this work leave ethnography? Do we welcome her as an ethnographer manquée despite her lack of paperwork, or do we dismiss this as highbrow journalism?

A moment of reflection reveals that this is not a new dilemma. A century ago the Victorian Britons who collected some of the first anthropological materials had day jobs as missionaries, administrators or explorers (Stocking 1987). With little or no academic patronage or support, their main role was to proselytise or organise, but both were done best by asking questions. Many were committed amateur scholars, and regularly sent letters and drawings to London for publication in the journals of the Royal Anthropological Institute. Their handbook was the 1874 *Notes and Queries on Anthropology*, which sought to 'promote accurate anthropological observation on the part of travellers' (Garson and Read 1874, v). Their amateur scholarship was synthesised by armchair theorists such as James Frazer. Even Emile Durkheim, sociological theorist, rarely left France. He based his hugely influential *Elementary Forms of the Religious Life* (1915) on missionary and traveller reports of Aboriginal religious practice, along with first-hand accounts by other anthropologists.

It was only with the rise of the academic disciplines of Sociology and Anthropology that ethnographic description began to be codified through an emergent set of scientific principles and scholarly conventions. Core to these was the importance of extended periods of fieldwork and a commitment to a holistic account of societies and cultures. The first academic anthropologists were also quick to reject the evolutionist and racial hierarchies of Victorian science, and instead began to write in the present tense, focusing on societies as 'going concerns'. James Clifford's work (1997) has explored the tropes and conventions that ethnographers have used to mark out this divide between 'proper' scholarship and travelling, and how these have changed over time.

Rather than try to erect boundaries around 'proper' ethnographic writing, our manifesto proposes three textual aspirations that are integral to an empathetic ethnographic research practice: modesty, honesty and analytical insight.

Why a manifesto of writing virtues rather than political principles? When new researchers are introduced to the professional ethical codes governing social research, the focus is on following the rules: informed consent, confidentiality, anonymity. Whilst these ethical principles have been honed through long and sometimes bitter experience, they oversimplify the dilemmas of ethics in practice. Many researchers feel that these principles, largely transplanted from medical research, tend to presume a relatively contractual and time-limited research engagement. They are rather less useful when negotiating the complex moralities and responsibilities of ethnographic research. They also neglect to consider the ethical virtues that researchers could aspire to. Without downplaying the political aspects of ethnographic writing and representation, we explore these virtues further.

Our first virtue is modesty. This is an easy virtue to espouse, and rather more difficult to explain and put into practice. Our understanding of this virtue comes from the figure of the 'modest witness' that historian of science Donna Haraway (1999) sees as central to early Enlightenment science. Experimenters such as Robert Boyle had to find ways of reporting their work in ways that were convincing. Boyle's answer, she suggests, was to adopt a voice that was neutral, detached and invisible – a subjectivity that evokes objectivity. They 'lose all trace of their history as stories' and the narratives 'have a magical power' (1999, 24). Haraway appropriates this history to insist that today's modest witness has to be embodied, located and accountable: 'the only way to a larger vision is to be somewhere in particular'. The fashionable if overused buzz-word is reflexivity – acknowledging enough of oneself to allow the reader to judge the veracity of one's account.

Another aspect of this modesty is to appreciate other scholars and writers, showing how one's own work builds on their contributions. Critique does not have to be negative, but rather is a way of acknowledging the strengths and limitations of existing work, in order to identify how it might be developed and taken forward. This is also a way of living up to what Haraway calls the 'joining of partial views and halting voices' (1999, 199).

The second writerly virtue, honesty, leads on from the first. The ethnographer retells their world through writing but is also accountable for the 'honesty' of this representation. Honesty means being frank about one's own scholarly ambitions and motivations, about the limits of the research, about the things that could have been done better. It also means nurturing a quiet scepticism about analyses that confirm pre-existing hunches or conventional wisdoms. Sometimes the answer was not expected.

The third virtue is analytical insight. What distinguishes academic writing from other genres is the way the narrative and analysis is framed within larger scholarly debates. This is not always easy, and may involve changing key and frame as one shifts from example to abstraction, from vivid case to theoretical explanation. Each has to be accountable to the other.

Can one be ethnographic without engaging theory? In her history of the Rhodes Livingstone Institute in Zambia (2001), a key training ground for many Manchester School anthropologists, Lyn Schumaker recounts that the worst insult one could be accused of was being a 'mere ethnographer'. The idea that one could 'merely' collect and represent data without a guiding theoretical question was anathema to Max Gluckman.

Working closely with extended research teams, the Institute conducted pioneering social surveys and ethnographic studies of urban identity politics in the new Copperbelt mining towns.

Ethnographic work is still disparaged. Ethnographers face accusations of being anecdotal and therefore partial. This is partly because ethnographic writing is often lively and 'easy' to read. Good ethnography tries not to hide behind technical language (though some may be inevitable), and instead offers telling cases and individual situations or events that illustrate more general themes and issues. The aim is to combine theoretical exploration with engaging description, respecting the integrity of both.

Narrating ethnography

There are many ways to weave ethnographic narratives. In Chapter 1 we offered some particularly vivid examples of educational ethnographic writing and analysis (e.g. Willis 1977) that combined description with theoretical contributions. Some develop extended descriptive case studies; others juxtapose analysis with telling vignettes or individual portraits. Sociological ethnographers and linguistic anthropologists have tended to work in the micro-ethnographic tradition, providing transcripts of conversations or discussions in order to provide a sense of dialogue. Ethnographers in the social anthropological tradition are more likely to adopt more holistic or encompassing narratives, focusing less on particular speech events than on social forms. They too have developed a number of literary conventions and tropes, such as 'arrival scenes' (like the first day at school described in Chapter 1), illustrative 'vignettes' or portraits.

Writing immediately raises questions of voice and tense. A common approach among many ethnographers has been to use the present tense to communicate a sense of immediacy and 'presence'. This convention was pioneered by Malinowski. Whilst 'presentism' has its appeal, it can also downplay history and change. A commitment to 'realistic' portrayals also raises questions of voice and person. Do you use the active or passive tense? Should the narrator be in the third person, or is there a role for a more confessional approach, through the use of the first person? Staying alert to these choices, and finding ways to deploy them effectively, ensures a convincing narrative style.

Whatever one's narrative choice, all ethnographic writing is made much easier by having a rich set of materials, insights and findings from which to work. As Madden notes, 'doing the practical stuff properly makes finding your ethnographic muse a whole lot easier' (2010, 153). He emphasises the importance of having one's 'data organised and marshalled behind you' (ibid.).

Murchison develops the useful distinction between writing 'from' and writing 'with' one's ethnographic materials. As he notes, 'ethnographers can run into trouble when they choose to write *with* the data instead of writing *from* the data' (2010, 175). The challenge is not simply to turn to one's fieldnotes when you want to find a supporting quote or example, but rather to treat your field materials as a whole.

The genre you adopt may well reflect the extent to which you tend towards explanation as opposed to interpretation. A desire to explain might require you to provide a more formal account of your approach to analysis, whereas a more humanistic emphasis on interpretation might be more informal. But even here, interpretations need to be justified and warranted. One of the risks that Boo (2012) takes in her book is to evoke, in novelistic depth, the inner emotional worlds of her protagonists. This leaves her open to charges of over-interpretation, but she responds by insisting that these feelings were described to her in conversation.

If interpretation is risky, might autoethnography be one possible answer? There is a growing interest in this approach among educational researchers, who see it as a mode of writing that allows one to draw critically on personal experience. Ellis is clear about what autoethnography offers: 'When researchers do autoethnography, they retrospectively and selectively write about epiphanies that stem from, or are made possible by, being part of a culture and/or by possessing a particular cultural identity' (Ellis et al. 2011, 3).

Why has the autoethnography label become popular? At one level it opens up fieldwork practices, allowing the practitioner to draw on and analyse everyday professional worlds beyond the confines of a formally defined piece of research. Its strength is in its recognition that the researcher's own embodied experience matters. Its weakness is that it is yet another label. All ethnography should be focused on both the self and the other, reflective and outward-looking, and use the ethnographic self to offer insight into the practices of others. Ethnographic empathy needs more than an unhealthy dose of self-regard.

When should I start writing?

It is never too early to put fingers to keyboard. Even a first research proposal or a course application are opportunities to flex the writing muscle. One's first fieldnotes are not just neutral records of observations, but also an ethnographic genre in themselves, representing events in certain ways. By recording one's own reactions and feelings into field-notes, one can sustain the sense of bewilderment that also allows the emergence of new understanding. The following excerpt from Valerie Hey's ethnography of schoolgirl friendship captures this perfectly, leading her to recognise the sense of loss and confusion that lasted throughout fieldwork:

> Felt foolish 'cos I couldn't recollect the names of all the staff with whom I'd just been liaising. I kept calling Mrs Harris Mrs Taylor, felt like a new girl, overwhelmed by the bureaucratic nightmares that schools are (to newcomers). Not only do you have to remember the [layout of] buildings but also staff names; statuses; subjects; time-tables; timings; routines; protocols and facilities. (Hey 1997, 14)

One's first fieldwork and thesis is a key moment of genre negotiation. Each education department or supervisory relationship will have its own expectations around the presentation of ethnographic material, expectations that can be gently subverted or provoked. Supervisors and dissertation committees will have their own opinions, but should nonetheless also listen to a convincing critique of their own scholarly predilections.

This is a good time to read what ethnographers have to say about writing. From his earliest ethnographic research describing student cultures at Kansas University in the 1950s, Howard Becker has had an illustrious writing career, and his advice on writing rewards reading. In his quirkily excellent *Writing for Social Scientists* (1986, xii) he points out that graduate students 'seldom see anyone writing, seldom see working drafts and writing that isn't ready for publication'. As a result, writing becomes invisible, a mystery, as does the emotional labour, sweat and tears that lie behind any book. Becker sets out to remove the mystique and to help students see that 'the work they read is made by people who have the same difficulties that they do' (1986, viii). Full of autobiographical asides, the book is refreshingly frank, offering advice on developing one's confidence about writing, on how to 'let go' of a text and on not being 'terrorised' by the literature. If writing is a way of thinking, it is also a way of developing a scholarly identity and persona.

There are now many 'self-help' guides to dissertation writing on the market. Unlike Becker's tolerance, they may reinforce the assumption that there is one 'right way' to put a dissertation together. Often full of breezy confidence, they can have the opposite effect to that intended, reinforcing feelings of insecurity and uncertainty. Barbara Kamler and Pat Thompson, like Becker twenty years earlier, are not convinced that how-to guides are the answer. They argue for writing together with a supervisor, for sharing one's work, and for nurturing the connection between text work and identity work (Kamler and Thomson 2006).

What ever your topic, opening up a conversation with the scholarly literature can feel intimidating: what right have you to question the views of experts? Here the reflective account of analytical moves by Graff and Birkenstein (2006) is a helpful guide to position taking. In *They say/I say* they show how many academic texts sketch a set of opposing positions in order to open up a space for a new contribution. These analytical and argumentative moves can feel somewhat exaggerated or strong readings of particular positions, but they are also key to making a contribution that builds on the work of others.

A final thought? Ultimately the best way to write convincingly is to write and write. Voracious and critical reading across a range of scholarly and popular genres can only help.

Ethnographic blogs: communication or participation

The democratisation of ethnographic writing has many positive consequences. Journals such as *Cultural Anthropology* are able to supplement their print editions with a range of extra online material (cultanth.org), promoting interaction and debate. Open-access online journals offer alternatives to the commercial publishing monopolies, and are able to combine the scholarly values of peer review with the dynamism of new approaches.

But the internet also allows individual academics the chance to promote their own work and make it more accessible to broader publics. Online CVs, downloadable writings, Wikipedia entries and personal websites abound, allowing interested readers to understand an individual piece of work within a larger intellectual trajectory. Whilst self-publishing risks a cacophony of eccentricity, it also shakes up scholarly practice and draws attention to the less palatable aspects of the publishing industry.

In the fickle world of 2.0 communication, blogging has endured as a way to explore possibilities and to create dialogues. There are a whole range of possibilities, from the raw polemics of individual activists to the slightly worthy blogs set up by scholarly associations like the American Anthropological Association. Blogs can be tentative and unpolished, allowing experimentation away from scholarly gatekeepers and disciplinary conventions. They allow one to rethink the relationship between the public and the private, to connect with like minds and to get feedback on one's ideas.

As Price points out (2010), the best blogs are multi-voiced, allowing for a diversity of opinions and voices. One of the first anthropological blogs – Savage Minds – started in 2005 and continues to foster cutting-edge debates. Others of note include Open Anthropology Cooperative, Zero Anthropology and Ethnography Matters, but new blogs are constantly appearing and developing.

A blog is much more than a way of communicating one's findings. In an increasingly wired world, it is also a way of developing one's research personae. It can be a way for potential research participants to find out about you and your work, facilitating access and discussion about his project. A blog can also be a way of being accountable to the community where one is researching, allowing a responsiveness and dialogue to develop. Blogs can also be highly political. *Zero Anthropology* brings together a series of unflinching contributions drawing attention to the growing military patronage of anthropology.

Much as with writing more broadly, there is no one right way to blog. Their importance will depend on the area in which you work and your own willingness to invest time and energy in developing new genres of writing. Their potential remains to be explored.

Public ethnography

Can one go from being an academic ethnographer to being a 'public' ethnographer? The towers within universities are often erected by academics. Under pressure from funders and the public alike, these barriers are beginning to come down. Academics are no longer just researchers, but are also consultants, teachers, op-ed writers, policy entrepreneurs, bloggers and activists. Public ethnography becomes about much more than writing.

Where does one look for inspiration? Gillian Tett, Managing Editor of the *Financial Times* at time of publication, is perhaps one of the best known of today's public anthropologists. On the back of her research for her best-selling book *Fools's Gold* (2009) on the roots of the 2008 banking crisis, she has her own *FT* column entitled 'An anthropologist in America'. Despite being fascinated with otherness of other cultures and doing research on Tajikistan marriage practices for her DPhil, she left academic anthropology because she felt she was committing 'intellectual suicide' (McKenna 2011). Only when she developed her career as an investigative financial journalist did she realise that anthropological perspectives on 'tribal' loyalty helped explain a dysfunctional banking culture. Whilst depicting bankers as an exotic tribe risks a rather old-fashioned mystification of contemporary financial elites, she admits in her defence that she is now only an amateur anthropologist. However, she has harsh words for academic ethnographers, insisting that they are trained to absorb information, rather than project it. She calls for her university colleagues to 'come out from their bushes' and to 'emit' knowledge, to project and to perform.

Who are the public intellectuals within Education? Historically, John Dewey is perhaps the best known of the early-twentieth-century philosophers of education, and his theoretical writings remain hugely influential. He was also an active educational reformer, setting up a number of influential educational institutions and rights-based organisations. One can think of similar big-name thinkers – such as Jerome Bruner, Jerome Piaget, Jane Addams or Paulo Freire.

It is not easy to define public ethnography. The 'big names' in academic circles may have little cachet amongst broader reading publics. For a while in the 1950s and 1960s, British anthropologists such as Mary Douglas (famous for her 1970 book *Purity and Danger*) were household names, but today the late Clifford Geertz is the only anthropologist to make it into the top 100 in a recent list of public intellectuals in *Prospect* magazine. On the other hand, Kate Fox's populist ethnography of everyday English manners, conversation and ritual *Watching the English* (2005) has sold more than 50,000 copies. Well written (if repetitive), her insights into pub rituals and conversational gambits are amusing, if anodyne. Yet most academic ethnographers have little time for her work, partly because it is only loosely grounded in academic debates. It primarily draws on rather determinist socio-biological explanations of culture for which her father – Robin Fox – built his academic reputation (Tiger and Fox 1972).

Influential ethnographers of education have often been great communicators. This is not without risks. Certainly, Margaret Mead's comparisons of adolescent sexuality in the US and in Samoa may have been hugely popular, but to what extent did it perpetuate a set of problematic popular stereotypes about 'otherness', as well as reinforce American notions of superiority (di Leonardo 1998)? Whilst less well-known outside the community of educational ethnographers, Harry Wolcott's engaging writing and wise advice remains influential. In *Anthropology Off the Shelf* (Waterston and Vesperi 2009), leading anthropologists reflect on their passion for the craft of writing but also on the dangers that can accompany 'populist' ethnographic genres.

Pierre Bourdieu is perhaps the best example of an engaged intellectual, and his work on forms of cultural domination, embodied practices and symbolic violence has been highly influential. Always a provocative intellectual presence, his early work on education sought to explore how schools and universities reproduced inequalities. His account of French academic life *Homo Academicus* (1984) skewers the status hierarchies and epistemological snobberies that pervade universities.

Towards the end of his life he became increasingly involved in writing for broader publics, and became a prominent critic of neoliberal economic policies. Arguing that scholars should bring their knowledge to bear on social and political issues, he famously commented that sociological knowledge was akin to a combat sport or 'martial art', a means of self-defence. One of his last projects was *The Weight of the World* (Bourdieu and Ferguson 1999), a collaborative project that seeks to represent the social suffering faced by those left behind in an unequal society. The book consists of a series of short vignettes – the life of a steel worker sacked after twenty years in the same factory; the story of an Algerian family coping with the racism of the Parisian *banlieues* (suburbs); the experience of a school teacher confronted with urban violence; and many others as well. The book is a political statement as much as a piece of social analysis.

For our purposes, public ethnography is perhaps best defined by Tedlock as 'research and writing that directly engages with the critical social issues of our time' (Tedlock 2005, 473). Few of us will ever be best-selling authors, but we can take up the gauntlet by communicating scholarly ideas and debates in a range of ways. By thinking through our responsibilities to both the republic of letters and a reading public, ethnographers can be engaged intellectuals. This can take many forms beyond writing sparkling prose or a glitzy media profile. Everyday engagement might mean quietly defending someone's right to voice unconventional or unpopular opinions, or questioning the latest educational fashion.

Joining policy debates

As we demonstrated at the end of Chapter 7, the first ethnographic studies of education came out of a tradition of engaged and applied anthropology. As the field developed within universities, this history has largely been left behind. But a few educational ethnographers have consistently sought to shape policy. David Hargreaves, author of *Social Relations in a Secondary School* (1967), arguably the first UK school ethnography, written while he was a student in Manchester, went on to an influential career in educational policy and administration, and was often outspoken in his criticisms. An iconoclastic and original thinker (Wilby 2009), his determination to help schools transform their learning cultures led him to promote the new specialist schools and academies that now increasingly dominate secondary educational provision in England. Paul Willis took his own political vision to raise the cultural aspirations of young people into the community, working as a youth-policy advisor, and authoring the *Youth Review* (Willis et al. 1988) that shaped UK youth policy nationally.

Education policy in many countries is increasingly politicised, and this makes public interventions complex and fraught. Within Britain and the US, public debates on education tend to be overshadowed and overwhelmed by the political divide between right and left on the appropriate role of the state. Jeffrey Henig's 2008 account of how educational researchers became entangled in conflicts over charter schooling is a salutary reminder of the funding strings and expectations (Henig 2008). The vivid descriptions of the conflicts over state schooling by Melissa Benn (2011) stand in stark contrast to the libertarian rhetoric of James Tooley and his case for low-cost private schooling in poor communities (2012). There is little middle ground, and the politicisation of debate makes for unproductive dichotomies and a search for one-size-fits-all solutions. Nor are educational researchers immune, and the 1990s were marked by repeated attacks on the quality of educational research by public figures. It is perhaps no surprise that some educational ethnographers have tended to steer clear of such debates. But there is a growing expectation on academics to show how their writing and research has a broader social impact: it is incumbent on us to find scholarly genres of writing that can do exactly that.

Conclusion

Take a look at a range of recent educational ethnographies published by major American university presses: work that is accessible, readable and engaged (Lukose 2009; Stambach 2010; Fong 2011). Scholarly books that are also a pleasure to read would seem to be the future for ethnographic writing. If online writing, blogs, position pieces, journalism and other forms of experimental writing all help to develop scholarly insight, then these different genres are complementary, and the ethnographic genre looks secure. Good writing is unlikely to go out of fashion any time soon.

Exercises

- Review a recent educational ethnography published by a major US academic press and compare it with a monograph of, say, two decades ago. How do they differ? What conventions have changed? Which do you feel is more scholarly and why?

- Compare two or three different ethnographic blogs. Which ones sustain a sense of intellectual engagement and why? Can you find examples of the ways in which these blogs inform the author's scholarship more broadly?

Further reading

This chapter has highlighted the range of different writing styles and audiences that ethnographers may need to cultivate. As academia changes, it is more important than ever to communicate clearly and effectively beyond one's own disciplinary community, and to think of oneself as a writer as much as a researcher. To help you develop your skills, Becker's (1986) advice remains as pithy and prescient as ever, whilst Waterston and Vesperi (2009) bring together a sparkling collection of essays on how anthropologists handle the demands of writing for a broader set of publics.

Becker, H. (1986). *Writing for Social Scientists*. Chicago, Chicago University Press.

Sage and often humorous advice on the habits that lead to good social research and accessible writing, and how to deal with the task of getting it all down on paper.

Clifford, J. and Marcus, G. (eds.) (1986). *Writing Culture: The Poetics and Politics of Ethnography*. Berkeley, Calif, University of California Press.

The 'classic' postmodern challenge to the anthropological canon, Clifford and Marcus point to the role of writing in creating and shaping ethnographic 'realities'. Still provocative and rewarding reading, even if many of the debates and insights have now been taken up across the disciplines.

Rabinow, P., Marcus, G. E., Faubion, J. and Rees, T., (2008). *Designs for an Anthropology of the Contemporary*. Durham, NC; London, Duke University Press.

Extended theoretical conversation between Paul Rabinow, George Marcus and two younger scholars, pointing to some of the possibilities that lie ahead for ethnography.

Waterston, A. and Vesperi, M. D. (2009). *Anthropology Off the Shelf: Anthropologists on Writing*. Chichester, Wiley-Blackwell.

A passionate defence of accessible writing by eighteen leading North American anthropologists. Contributors describe the navigation between the formal constraints of disciplinary canons and academic careers and their desire to tell a good story. Strongly recommended.

Willis, P. (2000). *The Ethnographic Imagination*. Oxford, Polity Press.

Willis likes to think of himself as an 'academic vandal', and this unusual book mixes up social theory, methodological musings and empirical substance. Playing off C. Wright Mills's *The Sociological Imagination*, Willis champions the importance of 'sensuous ethnography': aesthetic and creative sensibility when making sense of ethnographic data. He returns to the 'lads' of *Learning to Labour* to inform his musings. Eclectic, abstract and often profound, but not to everyone's taste.

Wolcott, H. F. (2008). *Ethnography: A Way of Seeing*. Lanham, Md., AltaMira Press.

Whimsical, stylish and perceptive set of anecdotal reflections on the ethnographic method and Wolcott's own anthropological career. Particularly valuable for those familiar with methodological debates, Wolcott combines advice on key research dilemmas with thoughts on other scholars' approaches to dealing with these dilemmas.

Web resources

There are a range of well-established blogs dedicated to writing and commenting on ethnographic research for new audiences. Some of the best include Zero Anthropology, Savage Minds and the Open Anthropology Cooperative, though they vary greatly in style, authorship and politics. The professional associations also have their own blogs, though these tend to be rather less engaging.

Additional online resources can be found at: www.sagepub.co.uk/beraseries.sp

CONCLUSION:

BEING AN EVERYDAY ETHNOGRAPHER

What is in this chapter?

- Advice on 'acting like an ethnographer'
- Ethnographic perspectives on teaching and on reciprocity in the classroom
- Suggestions on narrative and ethnographic-like approaches to assessment
- Thoughts on cultivating an 'everyday' ethnographic sensibility

---

Introduction

Are you still an ethnographer once you have finished your thesis and your course? Can you use your ethnographic skills in other aspects of your professional and personal life? Is it possible to sustain one's ethnographic sensibility and empathy as a teacher, administrator or policy professional? Yes, yes and emphatically yes. Whilst some scholars disparage the rise of corporate ethnography, or declaim that if you have left the university you are 'no longer one of us', many more are committed to putting skills learnt in the academy to work in the world. This may not involve high-visibility 'public ethnography', but rather a quiet everyday commitment to modest pedagogy and located practice.

What does an 'everyday' ethnographic sensibility look like? We suggest it involves reflecting openly, engagingly and critically on the mundane and everyday. This final chapter offers thoughts on packing one's ethnographic habit on every journey. We explore how to put hardearned ethnographic skills to work in professional settings, particularly in Education. We highlight educational ethnographies that offer insights into learning and classroom cultures, and provide practical examples of 'ethnographically informed' curriculum interventions, drawing on a set of New Zealand curriculum initiatives in which Missy has been involved.

How is this chapter structured?

In 'Acting like an ethnographer' we restate our book's moral vision, and argue for sustaining ethnographic sensibilities in a range of professional settings. We go on to explore what that might mean in methodological and moral terms.

In 'Taking ethnography back to school' we highlight the different ways that an ethnographic sensibility can be put to use in educational settings. In particular we focus on teaching and assessment. We introduce the way that ethnographic insights around gift-giving can be used to highlight the dialogical and relational aspects of teaching and learning. We go on to suggest ways that an ethnographic sensibility can inform approaches to assessment. In both cases we draw on examples from policy innovations in New Zealand, but similar principles could be applied to schools and colleges in other educational settings.

Acting like an ethnographer

This book began with arguing for the importance of developing an ethnographic sensibility in one's being, seeing and writing. To start with, we left the ethnography 'label' open, diffuse and encompassing. Nine chapters later, we are willing to defend our own understanding of the term. Our definition of ethnography has become sharper and more focused.

We see ethnography as both a scholarly habit and a moral disposition: quietly attentive, modest, critical and above all empathetic. Throughout we have argued for the importance of analytical and methodological empathy. Empathy is not the easy assumption of shared feelings and experiences, but the rather more difficult task of trying to understand other people's experiences on their own terms.

This moral disposition makes its own demands on time. Ethnographic insights demand, and reward, patience. Yet institutional and bureaucratic demands for accountability make time a precious commodity. They privilege particular forms of research and ways of judging the quality of educational research. The new educational environment is one that is ruled by numerical measures of effectiveness and statistical definitions of evidence. Universities are not immune. Pressures for productivity measures have led to a push for rapid doctoral and master's thesis completion that potentially squeezes the time needed for the ethnographic craft.

It also comes with the need to remain constantly open to new possible scales, connections and linkages. Each of the 'landmark' educational ethnographies discussed in this book remind us of the importance of looking beyond the classroom in order to understand what is going on within them. *Learning to Labour* (Willis 1978) draws our attention to the gendered bodies, history and power, to tacit knowledges and the hidden curriculum of the school. *Making the Grade* (Becker et al. 1968) asks us to think about how other factors influence what is learnt. *Wannabe U* (Tuchman 2009) makes us think about how universities are changing under commercial pressure and corporate expectations. An ethnographic sensitivity to connections reminds us of the diversity of lives and experiences brought together in the classroom.

Taking ethnography back to school

Here is a thought experiment. Imagine being asked to teach a lesson ethnographically. How would it be structured and delivered? What forms of pedagogy and learning would an ethnographic sensibility seek to nurture? What would your lesson plan look like?

One way to answer this question is to think about the attributes that teaching and ethnographic research share in common. Teaching, like fieldwork, is a form of engagement with difference, a means of learning and sharing through experience. Both professions cultivate the skills of observation and reflection. Both understand that knowledge is co-constructed, partial and created within relationships. And both demand sensitivity to relationships, meanings and emotions. At their best, teaching and research inculcate a critical awareness of the subtle complexities of power, whether in classrooms or other social worlds. In what follows we think through the implications of this for our own approaches to teaching and to assessment, and to the values of bringing research and pedagogy more closely together.

What can we learn from ethnographic practice for our own teaching? One lesson is methodological: to see teaching as a form of participant observation. All teachers learn to 'read' the mood of their class, and classroom observations and structured reflections are an important part of teacher training. This observation has parallels to ethnographic observation, even if this book has argued for making participatory techniques and approaches integral to education. It reminds us that knowing is a process, that we are constantly learning anew, and that we need to understand the meanings and understandings that our students are crafting. The ethnographic practice of 'participant-observation' is an apt one to describe the lived engagement between students and teachers, reminding us how teaching is also a process of learning. Even in the middle of a lesson or a lecture, the good teacher seeks to step back and reflect on the dynamics unfolding around them. How better can one understand the meanings that our students are crafting about knowledge, about themselves and about us?

The second lesson for our classrooms is the importance of cultivating a sense of potential connections. The best ethnographies of education highlight the range of forces and networks that shape classroom interactions. They remind us of the importance of looking beyond the classroom in order to understand what is going on inside. An ethnographic sensibility reminds us of the diversity of lives, experiences and identities shaped and refashioned within the classroom, a fractal of the wider world.

Teaching as gift-giving

The apple on the teacher's desk is the quintessential expression of appreciation. Beyond the imagery, it helps us think a bit further about the exchanges that go on in the classroom. Anthropological ethnographers have long been fascinated by the interweaving of the social and material aspects of relationships. Emile Durkheim's cousin Marcel Mauss was the first to make this point in his famous essay *The Gift* (1990 [1926]). In it he explores the 'spirit of the gift', drawing on a range of examples from the ethnographic literature, to demonstrate the social relationship it opens up between the giver and the receiver. The best-known example is the one he takes from an explanation by a Maori lawyer called Tamati Ranaipiri. Ranaipiri describes how all personal possessions are animated by a *hau* (spirit). If one is given a gift (*taonga*) one is obligated to make a return because the gift is still part of the giver, and has some power over the receiver. Even if the gift is then passed on to a third person the obligation is to return the *hau* of the *taonga* to the original giver. All things, especially things of the forest, are seen to possess this spirit, and this *hau* wants to return to its origin. Mauss uses this example to explain the phenomenon of the circulation of wealth visible in many Polynesian societies, but also to underscore the social relationships embedded in objects and in the obligation to give and to receive.

Whilst Karl Marx wrote about how human labour was hidden in objects and commodities, Mauss captured the moral obligations and dependencies inherent in exchange relationships, the way that the gift contained within it the obligation to return. Much more than his uncle Emile Durkheim, he was an engaged public intellectual, writing critically about capitalism. Mauss demonstrated that rather than see gifts as selfless and altruistic gestures, they create ongoing relationships of reciprocity and indebtedness. Since his time, philosophers and theorists have repeatedly returned to the questions he raised about reciprocity, dependency and social obligation.

What does gift-giving have to do with teaching? Whilst one does not need to be a talented ethnographer to teach well, an ethnographic sensibility reminds us that teaching is a practice of reciprocity and indebtedness. Thinking of it as a gift relationship draws attention to classroom hierarchies, and the possibility that they might be overcome. Gift-giving, like learning and teaching, involves an inevitable asymmetry of experience and knowledge between the giver and the receiver (Galea 2006, 128). But it also sets up a relationship that does not expect an immediate or direct return. The last thing one wants is a gift (or one's teaching) returned, unwrapped, unexamined or unwanted.

This perspective helps us dispute any overly reductive interpretations of education to a process of cultural transmission and social reproduction, despite the somewhat bleak picture painted by critical sociologists such as Bourdieu and Willis. Even if, from one perspective, education remakes society, individual teachers hope to be given something different back.

A commitment to thinking of teaching as a gift-giving relationship allows us to do two things. It directly contests the banking metaphor to knowledge so criticised by Paulo Freire, and undercuts a stark commodity logic that seems increasingly to be redefining the attitudes of students and policy makers. As teachers, we give part of ourselves in the classrooms. This is not a relationship that ends when the bell goes. The memories and experiences our students take from us may last years, and one of our rewards is the sense of having shaped the personhood of others. Giving isn't easy: it is an art, as Neitzsche pointed out, and needs great skill in order to avoid feelings of indebtedness. Reciprocity too is unpredictable and difficult to manage. But both are hugely rewarding. A bit like teaching.

What does this mean in practical terms for teachers? It does not need qualitative research to affirm the importance of the teacher–student relationship for learning. However, New Zealand teacher education has put this insight to work, directly drawing on Maori understandings of reciprocity and ways of knowing to inform teacher education. The notion of *Te Kotahitanga* (Unity) is a 'culturally responsive pedagogy of relations', a professional learning process that encourages teachers to examine how they develop relationships with their Maori students and the role of reciprocity in these relationships. As Berryman and Woller point out, teachers' failure 'to recognise the importance of their students' own prior experiences can severely restrict the student's ability to engage actively in their own learning through meaningful relationships and interactions with others' (Berryman and Woller, 2011, 12). The New Zealand evidence is indisputable.

The lesson for teachers is clear: by acknowledging and making an effort to understand students' social backgrounds and prior experiences, teachers can strengthen these relationships and help students actively engage in their own learning. Missy put this principle to work in her qualitative research class 'How do postgraduate students in Education make sense of/negotiate/interpret their experiences?' The course involves carrying out observations and writing analytical memos. At the end of one course, feedback from the students underscored the value of involving them in designing and carrying out a project to investigate their experiences. As one commented, 'What a shame the course is ending now, we are only just getting to know each other.' Missy used this feedback to re-think the ways she ran the class and online activities so that she can explicitly support students 'getting to know each other' from earlier on in the course.

This example shows how the findings of ethnographic research can inform the teaching of qualitative research. It also highlights how ethnographic attentiveness can shape pedagogy more broadly. A chance comment by a student enabled her to rethink how she used feedback to inform her planning and curriculum design. This incident has led Missy to reaffirm the importance of meaning-making at the centre of ethnographic research methodology as well as teaching and learning.

An ethnographic approach to assessment

There is growing interest in finding ways of assessing students that adequately capture the complexity of teaching and learning activities.

In New Zealand, as we have shown, sociological and anthropological understandings have been used to inform curriculum, pedagogy and assessment for more than a decade. They have been a feature of *Te Whāriki*, the national early childhood education curriculum, since 1996. Like Tamati Ranaipiri's explanation of the gift that inspired Mauss almost a century earlier, the curriculum affirms that 'children learn through responsive and reciprocal relationships with people, places, and things'.

Neither Ranaipiri nor anthropologists can claim all the credit here. The New Zealand vision also draws on the 'pedagogy of listening' developed in schools in the Reggio Emilio area of Italy (Berger, 2008). Developed originally by a primary school teacher called Loris Malaguzzi, the Reggio Emilia philosophy contests the idea of learning as something that only happens inside the learner, and the notion of teaching as transmission of knowledge, between expert teacher and novice student. Instead the emphasis is on placing the child at the centre of their learning, with an emphasis both on sensory learning, on the importance of relationships between children, and on seeing the teacher as a co-learner.

Ever since the early work of Vygotsky, Dewey and Bruner, scholars have questioned overly individualistic models of learning. James (2006, 46) insists that 'interactions between people, and mediating tools such as language, are now seen to have a crucial role in learning'. This has implications for thinking about assessment, given the integral relationship between styles of assessment and approaches to learning. She goes on to suggest that assessment of learning outcomes should 'take more account of the social as well as individual processes through which learning occurs', and draw on the disciplines of social-psychology, sociology and anthropology (2006, 48).

Yet the seemingly impossible task facing traditional forms of assessment is to figure how exactly to 'take account' of these social contexts. Typically our focus is on individual students' performance in assessment, ideally achieved without any external influence or help. In New Zealand one solution has been to use what has been called 'narrative assessment', to notice, recognise and respond to children's learning. Drawing on this focus on noticing, recognising and responding, researchers have supported teachers, students and their families to write stories about learning, both in and beyond the classroom. These stories become ways of assessing the child.

In New Zealand there are now sets of resources, called curriculum exemplars that support teachers as they learn to use narrative assessment. Curriculum exemplars take examples of student learning, and show how these examples link to the curriculum. The exemplars offer illustrations of teachers' thinking about the aspects of the curriculum that are evident in a given example of a student's learning.

Examples of these narratives are included in *Curriculum Exemplars for Students with Special Educational Needs* and *Narrative Assessment: A Guide for Teachers* (Ministry of Education, 2009). The development of these exemplars was informed in part by key tenets of Disability Studies in Education, in particular a rejection of the medical discourse of disability in favour of presumptions of competence, privileging the interests, agendas and voices of people labelled with disability/disabled people.

Through this approach, teachers are invited to look at their students' learning through a largely ethnographic lens. The approach to assessment is based on an understanding of curriculum and meanings as co-constructed, contextual and interactional, and goes beyond more traditional understandings of learning as demonstrating progression. It gently questions the assumption that teachers should already know what learning will look like for every student, and that assessment is simply about looking for evidence of that learning.

In narrative assessment, a different kind of attention is called for. This is the ability to attentively listen to a student or group of students. In a collaborative research project that Missy was involved in, teachers were encouraged first to write little jottings or take photos of what they considered to be 'wow' moments in the life of their special needs classroom. Along the way teachers were supported to notice things the students had done. Teachers and researchers then met as a group, to share and talk about these 'wow' moments in their classrooms or on the playgrounds. In describing why the moment was 'wow' for them, the teachers described what they thought they knew about the students in the stories, how they had previously documented students' learning (or lack of learning) and how this had led to a lowering of expectations.

The next step was to encourage teachers to elaborate their jottings and stories: what else was going on? What were they, the teachers and storywriters, doing at the time? They were gently encouraged to put themselves, their ideas and feelings, into the stories. They then met with other teachers involved in curriculum planning and so familiar with all aspects of the New Zealand curriculum. Together the planners and the teacher storywriters began to identify how these stories linked to the various learning areas of the curriculum. The teacher storywriters began to see that these 'wow' moments demonstrated moments of student learning that the teachers were only able to recognise in retrospect. The teachers working together on this project were co-constructing new understandings of learning and learners, re-interpreting students' behaviours. Where once these behaviours were seen as, at best, irrelevant, their newly shared frameworks for interpretation allowed them to see the ways their students actively made sense of their worlds and lives.

For those involved in the development of these exemplars, the experiences of fully noticing and recognising students' learning were electrifying. Teachers repeatedly expressed the opinion that they saw their students 'through different eyes', ascribing them identities as learners. The teacher storywriters also saw themselves differently; as both learners and advocates for their students.

The development of these curriculum resources offers a chance to embed ethnographic ways of thinking and strategies in teachers' practices. Ideally teachers would gain an insight into qualitative research practices in their own training, in order to help them appreciate its value. It also highlights the importance of weaving together theory and practice, both as a researcher and a teacher.

Conclusion

The ethnographic endeavour doesn't suddenly end with a publication of one's results. One can constantly return to one's materials and experiences in the light of new insights and debates, often unlearning in order to relearn. Throughout this book we have argued that the ethnographic habit equips one with the empathy and versatility to keep learning in new professional contexts.

We have argued in this final chapter that ethnographic insights into gift-giving and relationships can be particularly useful for teachers and others involved in education. The teaching vocation is increasingly cast adrift in a sea of numbers, accountability and 'evidence-based' practice. To have moral value as a vocation, pedagogy has to be more than a one-sided or one-off exchange, more than a purchased service or commodity relationship. Teachers hope to be given something different back: new horizons and inspiration, personal as well as professional growth. The ethnographer's attention is to relationships rather than numbers, quality rather than quantity, empathy rather than rights. The practical New Zealand examples we have discussed, with their emphasis on reciprocity and sensitivity in teaching and assessment, puts this vision into practice.

Our closing message? We would encourage you to think beyond the current dissertation or research project. Think about the responsibilities it places upon you, but also the limits to all academic forms of knowing. Think instead about your ethnographic sensibility as a transferable skill, useful in new contexts and for taking up new roles. And finally, think about the everyday ways that ethnographic empathy can make a difference.

Further reading

Fetterman, D. M. (2010). *Ethnography: Step-By-Step*. Thousand Oaks, Calif.; London, Sage.

Third edition of a clear (if programmatic) account of applied ethnographic research by an educationalist with a career in evaluation, assessment and contract research. Its strengths are in its lists of web resources and evaluation tools, many of which can be found on www.davidfetterman.com.

Lee, W. and Carr, M. (2012). *Learning Stories: Constructing Learner Identities in Early Education*. London, Sage.

Margaret Carr is not an ethnographer, but her influential promotion of learning stories parallels the ethnographic commitment to narrative. This updated text highlights the latest findings from research with teachers on learning dispositions and learning power, showing how learning stories can construct learner identities in early childhood settings and schools.

Nolan, R. (2003). *Anthropology in Practice*. Boulder, Col., Lynne Riener publishers Inc.

A useful guide to the possibilities of using ethnographic research and writing skills in careers and professions outside the academy. Whilst a decade old, this book is full of practical advice and guidance on applying for jobs and working within organisations.

Pink, S. (ed.) (2006). *Applications of Anthropology: Professional Anthropology in the Twenty-first Century*. Oxford, Berghahn.

A diverse set of contributions by applied anthropologists on how they put their academic training and skills to work.

Schensul, J. J. and LeCompte, M. D. (1999). *The Ethnographer's Toolkit*. Walnut Creek, Calif., AltaMira Press.

This nine-volume 'toolkit' seeks to cover the whole range of techniques and skills employed in applied anthropology and ethnographic evaluations. Upbeat in its tone, it doesn't dwell on the conundrums that accompany 'compressed' designs or participatory research as much as it might.

Schensul also contributes an up-to-date overview of Applied Educational Anthropology in Levinson and Pollock 2011.

Smith, D. E. (2005). *Institutional Ethnography: A Sociology for People*. Walnut Creek, Calif., AltaMira Press.

An unusual and powerful argument for an 'alternative sociology' of the institutions we live within, attending to the gendered nature of everyday experiences and knowledge and the possibility of using ethnography. The focus is particularly on language, and on research for social change.

Web resources

Professional associations for practising ethnographers include practicinganthropology.org, the website of the US-based NAPA (National Association for the Practice of Anthropology), www.sfaa.net (Society for Applied Anthropology) and www.theasa.org.uk/apply (Association of Social Anthropologists of the UK and Commonwealth Network of Applied Anthropologists).

Other web resources include www.throughdifferenteyes.org.nz, the learning stories resource at www.inclusive.org.nz

Additional online resources can be found at: www.sagepub.co.uk/beraseries.sp

BIBLIOGRAPHY

AAA (American Anthropological Association). (2003). 'Statement on the confidentiality of fieldnotes.' Retrieved 1 August 2012, from http://www.aaanet.org/stmts/fieldnotes.htm.

ASA (Association of Social Anthropologists) (2009). *Association of Social Anthropologists of the UK and Commonwealth Ethical Guidelines for Good Research Practice*. London, ASAUK.

Abbott, A. D. (2001). *Chaos of Disciplines*. Chicago, University of Chicago Press.

Abu El-Haj, T. R. (2006). *Elusive Justice: Wrestling with Difference and Educational Equity in Everyday Practice*. New York, Routledge.

Agar, M. (1986). *Speaking of Ethnography*. London, Sage.

Agar, M. H. (1996). *The Professional Stranger*. San Diego, Academic Press.

Alcoff, L. (1992). 'The Problem of Speaking for Others.' *Cultural Critique* 20: 5–32.

Alexander, C. (1996). *The Art of Being Black*. Oxford, Clarendon Press.

Allen, L. (2011a). '"Picture This": Using Photo-methods in Research on Sexualities and Schooling.' *Qualitative Research* 11(5): 487–504.

Allen, L. (2011b). 'The Camera Never Lies?: Analysing Photographs in Research on Sexualities and Schooling.' *Discourse: Studies in the Cultural Politics of Education* 32(5): 761–777.

Althusser, L. and B. Brewster (1971). Ideology and Ideological State Apparatuses. *Lenin and Philosophy, and Other Essays*. London, New Left Books: 127–188.

Anderson-Levitt, K. M. (ed.) (2003). *Local Meanings, Global Schooling: Anthropology and World Culture Theory*. New York; Basingstoke, Palgrave Macmillan.

Anderson-Levitt, K. M. (ed.) (2011). *Anthropologies of Education: A Global Guide to Ethnographic Studies of Learning and Schooling*. Oxford, Berghahn.

Armbruster, H. and Lærke, A. (eds.) (2008). *Taking Sides: Ethics, Politics, and Fieldwork in Anthropology*. Oxford, Berghahn.

Arnold, D. and Blackburn, S. H. (2004). *Telling Lives in India: Biography, Autobiography, and Life History*. Delhi, Permanent Black.

Asad, T. (ed.) (1973). *Anthropology and the Colonial Encounter*. London, Ithaca Press.

Ashwin, P. (2009). *Analysing Teaching-Learning Interactions in Higher Education: Accounting for Structure and Agency*. London, Continuum.

Association of Internet Researchers (2002). 'Ethical Decision-Making and Internet Research: Recommendations from the AoIR Working Committee.' Retrieved from *aoir. org* 03.11.12.

Atkinson, P., Coffey, A. and Delamont, S. (2003). *Key Themes in Qualitative Research: Continuities and Changes*. Walnut Creek, Calif., AltaMira Press.

Atkinson, P. and Delamont, S. (eds.) (2009). *Representing Ethnography: Reading, Writing and Rhetoric in Qualitative Research*. Sage Benchmarks in Social Research Methods series. London, Sage.

Atkinson, P., Delamont, S., Coffey, A., Lofland, L. and Lofland, J. (eds.) (2007). *Handbook of Ethnography*. London, Sage.

Atkinson, P., Delamont, S. and Hammersley, M. (1988). 'Qualitative Research Traditions: A British Response to Jacob.' *Review of Educational Research* 58(2): 231–250.

Atkinson, P., Delamont, S. Housley, W. (2008). *Contours of Culture: Complex Ethnography and the Ethnography of Complexity*. Walnut Creek, [CA], AltaMira Press.

Ball, S. (1990). *Politics and Policy-making in Education: Explorations in Policy Sociology*. London, Routledge.

Ball, S. (2007). *Education plc: Understanding Private Sector Participation in Public Sector Education*. London, Routledge.

Ball, S. (1981). *Beachside Comprehensive: A Case Study of Secondary Schooling*. Cambridge, Cambridge University Press.

Ball, S. J. (2008). *The Education Debate: Policy and Politics in the 21st Century*. Bristol, Policy Press.

Barry, A., Born, G. and Weszkalnys, G. (2008). Logics of Interdisciplinarity. *Economy and Society* 37(1): 20–49.

Bartlett, L. and Garcia, O. (2011). *Additive Schooling in Subtractive Times: Bilingual Education and Dominican Immigrant Youth in the Heights*. Nashville, Tenn., Vanderbilt University Press.

Beck, U. (2005). *Power in the Global Age: A New Global Political Economy*. Cambridge, Polity.

Becker, H. (1986). *Writing for Social Scientists*. Chicago, Chicago University Press.

Becker, H. (1998). *Tricks of the Trade: How to Think About Your Research While You're Doing It*. Chicago, Chicago University Press.

Becker, H., Geer, B. Hughes, E. and Strauss, A. (1961). *Boys in White: Student Culture in Medical School*. Chicago, Chicago University Press.

Becker, H., Geer, B. and Strauss, A. (1968). *Making the Grade: The Academic Side of College Life*. New York, Wiley.

Becker, H. S. (1971). 'Great Tradition, Little Tradition and Formal Education.' *Anthropological Perspectives on Education*. S. D. M. Wax and F. Gearing (eds). New York, Basic Books.

Benei, V. (2008). *Schooling Passions: Nation, History and Language in Contemporary Western India*. Stanford, Stanford University Press.

Benn, M. (2011). *School Wars: The Battle for Britain's Education*. London, Verso.

Berger, J. (1972). *Ways of Seeing: Based on the BBC Television Series with John Berger*. London, British Broadcasting Corporation and Penguin.

Berger, J. (2008). *Ways of Seeing*. London, Penguin.

Bernstein, B. (1971). *Class, Codes and Control: Theoretical Studies Towards a Sociology of Language*. London, Routledge and Kegan Paul.

Bernstein, B. (1996). *Pedagogy, Symbolic Control and Identity: Theory, Research, Critique*. London, Taylor and Francis.

Berryman, M. and Woller, P. (2011). 'Learning about Inclusion by Listening to Māori.' *International Journal of Inclusive Education*. 1–12 (iFirst Online journal).

Blommaert, J. and Jie, D. (2010). *Ethnographic Fieldwork: A Beginner's Guide*. Bristol, Multilingual Matters.

Blumer, H. (1969). *Symbolic Interactionism*. Los Angeles, UCLA Press.

Boeije, H. (2010). *Analysis in Qualitative Research*. London, Sage.

Boellstorff, T. (2008). *Coming of Age in Second Life: An Anthropologist Explores the Virtually Human*. Princeton, Princeton University Press.

Bogdan, R. and Biklen, S. K. (1992). *Qualitative Research for Education: An Introduction to Theory and Methods*. Boston, Allyn and Bacon.

Bogdan, R. and Biklen, S. K. (2007). *Qualitative Research for Education: An Introduction to Theory and Methods*. Boston, Mass. London, Pearson A & B.

Boo, K. (2012). *Beyond the Beautiful Forevers*. New York, Harper Collins.

Bourdieu, P. (1977). *Outline of a Theory of Practice*. Cambridge, Cambridge University Press.

Bourdieu, P. (1984). *Homo Academicus*. Stanford, Stanford University Press.

Bourdieu, P. (2003). *Firing Back: Against the Tyranny of the Market 2*. London, Verso.

Bourdieu, P. and Ferguson, P. P. (1999). *The Weight of the World: Social Suffering in Contemporary Society*. Cambridge, Polity.

Bourdieu, P. and Passeron, J.-C. (1977). *Reproduction in Education, Society and Culture*. London, Sage.

Boyd, D. (2008). *Taken Out of Context: American Teen Sociality in Networked Publics*. Berkeley, University of California Berkeley PhD Dissertation.

Bragg, S. (2007). '"But I listen to Children Anyway!"—Teacher Perspectives on Pupil Voice' *Educational Action Research,* 15(4): 505–518.

Bragg, S. and Manchester, H. (2011). 'Doing it Differently: Youth Leadership and the Arts in a Creative Learning Programme.' *UNESCO Observatory Multi-Disciplinary Research in the Arts* 2(2): 1–11.

Brewer, J. (2000). *Ethnography*. Buckingham, Open University Press.

Bruner, J. (1997). *The Culture of Education*. Cambridge MA, Harvard University Press.

Bulmer, M. (1984). *The Chicago School of Sociology: Institutionalisation, Diversity and Professionalism*. Chicago, University of Chicago Press.

Burawoy, M. (2009). *The Extended Case Method: Four Countries, Four Decades, Four Great Transformations, and One Theoretical Tradition*. London, University of California Press.

Burgess, R. G. (1983). *Experiencing Comprehensive Education: A Study of Bishop McGregor School*. London, Methuen.

Burgess, T. (1977). *Education After School*. London, V. Gollancz.

Busher, H. and James, N. (2012). 'In Cyberspace: Qualitative Methods for Educational Research.' *Handbook of Qualitative Research in Education*. S. Delamont. Cheltenham, Edward Elgar.

Cammarota, J. (2008). "The Cultural Organising of Youth Ethnographers; Formalising a Praxis-based Pedagogy." *Anthropology & Education Quarterly* 39(1): 45–58.

Campbell, A. (1995). *Getting to Know Waiwai: An Amazonian Ethnography*. London, Routledge.

Cerwonka, A. and Malkki, L. H. (2007). *Improvising Theory: Process and Temporality in Ethnographic Fieldwork*. London, University of Chicago Press.

Chambers, E. (2000). 'Applied Ethnography.' *Handbook of Qualitative Research*. N. K. Denzin and Y. S. Lincoln. Thousand Oaks, Sage.

Chambers, R. (1983). *Rural Development: Putting the Last First*. Harlow, Longman Scientific.

Cheney, K. (2009). *Children, Youth and National Development in Uganda*. Chicago, University of Chicago Press.

Classen, C. (1997). 'Foundations for an Anthropology of the Senses.' *International Social Science Journal* 49: 401–412.

Clifford, J. (1988). *The Predicament of Culture: Twentieth-century Ethnography, Literature and Art*. Cambridge, Harvard University Press.

Clifford, J. (1990). 'Notes on (Field)notes'. *Fieldnotes: The Makings of Anthropology*. R. Sanjek. London, Cornell.

Clifford, J. (1997). *Routes*. Berkeley, University of California Press.

Clifford, J. (2003). *On the Edges (of Anthropology)*. Chicago, Prickley Pear Paradigm.

Clifford, J. and Marcus, G. (eds.) (1986). *Writing Culture: The Poetics and Politics of Ethnography*. Berkeley, CA, University of California Press.

Coe, C. (2005). *Dilemmas of Culture in African Schools: Youth, Nationalism and the Transformation of Knowledge*. Chicago, CUP.

Coffey, A. and Atkinson, P. (1996). *Making Sense of Qualitative Data: Complementary Research Strategies*. London, Sage.

Conteh, J., Gregory, E., Kearney, C. and Mor-Sommerfeld, A. (2005). *On Writing Educational Ethnographies: The Art of Collusion* London, Trentham.

Cook, J., Laidlaw, J. and Mair, J. (2009). 'What if there is No Elephant? Towards a Conception of an Un-sited Field. *Multi-sited Ethnography: Theory, Praxis and Locality in Contemporary Research* M.-A. Falzon. Burlington, Ashgate.

Cooke, B. (2006). 'A Foundation Correspondence on Action Research: Ronald Lippitt and John Collier.' *IDPM Working Papers*. Manchester, IDPM: 1–12.

Cooke, B. and U. Kothari (2001). *Participation: The New Tyranny?* London, Zed Press.

Cornwall, A. and Jewkes, R. (1995). 'What is Participatory Research?' *Social Science and Medicine* 41(12): 1667–1676.

Crang, M. and Cook, I. (2007). *Doing Ethnographies*. London, Sage.

Curtis, E. (2008). Walking Out of the Classroom: Learning on the Streets of Aberdeen. *Ways of Walking: Ethnography and Practice on Foot*. T. Ingold and J. L. Vergunst. Farnham, Ashgate.

Delamont, S. (2007). Arguments Against Auto-ethnography. *Qualitative Researcher*. Issue 4, 2–3.

Delamont, S. (2008). 'For Lust of Knowing: Observation in Educational Ethnography.' *Ethnography and Education*. G. Walford. London, Tufnell Press.

Delamont, S. (2009). 'The Only Honest Thing: Autoethnography, Reflexivity and Small Crises in Fieldwork.' *Ethnography and Education* 4(1): 51063.

Delamont, S. (ed.) (2012). *Handbook of Qualitative Research in Education*. Cheltenham, Edward Elgar.

Delamont, S. and Atkinson, P. (1980). 'The Two Traditions in Educational Ethnography: Sociology and Anthropology Compared.' *British Journal of Sociology of Education* 1(2): 139–152.

Delamont, S. and Atkinson, P. (1995). *Fighting Familiarity*. Creskill, NJ, Hampton.

Delamont, S., Atkinson, P. and Parry, O. (2000). *The Doctoral Experience: Success and Failure in Graduate School*. London, Falmer.

Denzin, N. and Lincoln, Y. S. (2008). The Discipline and Practice of Qualitative Research. *Strategies of Qualitative Enquiry*. N. Denzin and Y. Lincoln. Thousand Oaks, Sage.

Denzin, N. K. (2003). *Performance Ethnography: Critical Pedagogy and the Politics of Culture*. Thousand Oaks, CA, Sage.

Denzin, N. K. and Lincoln, Y. S. (2005). *The SAGE Handbook of Qualitative Research*. Thousand Oaks, Calif. London, Sage.

DeWalt, K. M. and DeWalt B. R. (2002). *Participant Observation: A Guide for Fieldworkers.* Plymouth, AltaMira Press.

DeWalt, K. M. and DeWalt, B. R. (2011). *Participant Observation: A Guide for Fieldworkers.* Plymouth, AltaMira Press.

di, Leonardo, M. (1998). *Exotics at Home: Anthropologies, Others, American Modernity.* Chicago, Chicago University Press.

Dicks, B. (2005). *Qualitative Research and Hypermedia: Ethnography for the Digital Age.* London, Sage.

Dingwall, R. (2006). 'Confronting the Anti-Democrats: The Unethical Nature of Ethical Regulation in Social Science.' *Medical Sociology Online* 1: 51–58.

Donald, J. (1992). *Sentimental Education: Schooling, Popular Culture and the Regulation of Liberty.* London, Verso.

Douglas, M. (1970). *Purity and Danger.* London, Routledge.

Durkheim, E. (1915). *Elementary Forms of Religious Life.* London, George Allen and Unwin.

Ministry of Education, New Zealand (2009). *Narrative Assessment: A Guide for Teachers.* Wellington NZ.

Ellis, C. (1999). 'Heartfelt Autoethnography.' *Qualitative Health Research* 9(5): 669–683.

Ellis, C., Adams, T. and Bochner, A. (2011). 'Autoethnography: An Overview.' *Forum Qualitative Sozialforschung / Forum: Qualitative Social Research* 12(1): 1–12.

Ellsworth, E. (1989). 'Why Doesn't this Feel Empowering? Working Through the Myths of Critical Pedagogy.' *Harvard Educational Review* 3(59): 297–324.

Emerson, R., Fretz, R. and Shaw, L. (1995). *Writing Ethnographic Fieldnotes.* Chicago, University of Chicago Press.

Evans, G. (2007). *Educational Failure and Working Class White Children in Britain.* London, Palgrave Macmillan.

Evans-Pritchard, E. E. (1940). *The Nuer.* Oxford, Oxford University Press.

Falzon, M.-A. (ed.) (2009). *Multi-sited Ethnography: Theory, Praxis and Locality in Contemporary Research.* Farnham, Ashgate.

Fardon, R. (ed.) (1990). *Localising Strategies: Regional Traditions of Ethnographic Writing.* Edinburgh, Scottish Academic Press.

Farmer, P. (1999). *Infections and Epistemologies: The Modern Plagues.* Berkeley, University of California Press.

Faubion, J. D. and Marcus, G. E. (2009). *Fieldwork is Not What It Used to Be: Learning Anthropology's Method in a Time of Transition.* London, Cornell University Press.

Ferguson, J. (2011). 'Novelty and Method: Reflections on Global Fieldwork.' *Multi-sited Ethnography: Problems and Possibilities in the Translocation of Research Methods.* S. Coleman and P. Von Hellermann. New York; London, Routledge: vi, 219 p.

Fetterman, D. M. (2010). *Ethnography: Step-By-Step.* London, Sage.

Feyerabend, P. (1975). *Against Method: Outline of an Anarchistic Theory of Knowledge.* London, New Left Books.

Fielding, N. (2001). 'Computers in Qualitative Research.' *Handbook of Ethnography.* P. Atkinson, S. Delamont, A. Coffey, J. Lofland and L. Lofland. London, Sage.

Fine, M. (1997). *Off White: Readings on Race, Power, and Society.* New York; London, Routledge.

Firth, R. (1951). 'Contemporary British Social Anthropology.' *American Anthropologist* 53: 474–489.

Foley, D. (2002). 'Fifty Years of Anthropology and Education 1950–2000: A Spindler anthology.' *American Anthropologist* 104(1): 381–382.

Fong, V. (2011). *Paradise Redefined: Transnational Chinese Students and the Quest for Flexible Citizenship in the Developed World.* Palo Alto, Stanford UP.

Fortun, K. (2009). 'Figuring out Ethnography.' *Fieldwork is Not What It Used to Be: Learning Anthropology's Method in a Time of Transition.* J. D. Faubion and G. E. Marcus. Ithaca; London, Cornell University Press: xiv, 231.

Foucault, M. (1967). *Madness and Civilization: A History of Insanity in the Age of Reason.* London, Tavistock.

Foucault, M. (1972). *The Archaeology of Knowledge.* London, Tavistock.

Foucault, M. (1977). *Discipline and Punish: The Birth of the Prison.* Harmondsworth, Penguin.

Foucault, M. (1978). *The History of Sexuality.* New York, Pantheon.

Foucault, M. and Gordon, C. (1980). *Power/Knowledge: Selected Interviews and Other Writings, 1972–1977.* New York, Vintage.

Foucault, M. and Howard, R. (2001). *Madness and Civilization: A History of Insanity in the Age of Reason.* London, Routledge.

Foucault, M. and Hurley, R. (1978). *The History of Sexuality. Vol.1, The Will to Knowledge.* London, Penguin.

Fournier, A. (2012). *Forging Rights in a New Democracy: Ukrainian Students Between Freedom and Justice.* Philadelphia, U Penn Press.

Fox, K. (2005). *Watching the English.* London, Penguin.

Francis, R. J. (2010). *The Decentring of the Traditional University: The Future of (self) Education in Virtually Figured Worlds.* London, Routledge.

Freeman, D. (1983). *Margaret Mead and Samoa: The Unmaking of an Anthropologist.* Cambridge, MA, Harvard Univ Press.

Freire, P. (1972). *Pedagogy of the Oppressed.* London, Penguin.

Galea, S. (2006). 'Iris Marion Young's Imaginations of Gift-giving: Some Implications for the Teacher and the Student.' *Educational Philosophy and Theory* 38(1): 83–91.

Galman, S. C. (2007). *Shane, The Lone Ethnographer.* Lanham, MD, AltaMira Press.

Garcia, M. (2005). *Making Indigenous Citizens: Identities, Education, and Multicultural Development in Peru.* Stanford, Calif., Stanford University Press.

Gardner, A. and Hoffman, D. M. (2006). *Dispatches from the Field: Neophyte Ethnographers in a Changing World.* Long Grove, Ill., Waveland Press.

Garson, J. and Read, C. (1874). *Notes and Queries on Anthropology.* London, Royal Anthropological Institute.

Gaventa, J., Cornwall, A. Reason, P. and Bradbury, H. (eds.) (2001). *Handbook of Action Research: Participative Inquiry and Practice.* London, Sage.

Gay y Blasco, P. and H. Wardle (2007). *How to Read Ethnography.* London, Routledge.

Geertz, C. (1973). *The Interpretation of Cultures: Selected Essays.* New York, Basic Books.

Geertz, C. (1974). '"From the Native's Point of View": On the Nature of Anthropological Understanding.' *Bulletin of the American Academy of Arts and Sciences* 28(1): 26–45.

Geertz, C. (1983). *Local Knowledges: Further Essays in Interpretive Thought.* New York, Basic Books.

Geertz, C. (1989). *Works and Lives: The Anthropologist as Author.* Palo Alto, Stanford University Press.

Geertz, C. (1991). 'Clifford Geertz on Ethnography and Social Construction (Olson, Gary A., interviewer).' *Journal of Advanced Composition* 11(2): 245–268.

Geertz, C. (1998). 'Deep Hanging Out.' *New York Review of Books* 45(16): 69–72.

Geertz, C. (2000). *Available Light: Anthropological Reflections on Philosophical Topics.* Princeton, Princeton University Press.

Glaser, B. G. and Strauss, A. L. (1965). *Awareness of Dying.* Transaction, New Brunswick.

Glaser, B. G. and Strauss, A. L. (1967). *The Discovery of Grounded Theory: Strategies for Qualitative Research.* Chicago, Aldine Publishing.

Gluckman, M. (1940). 'Analysis of a Social Situation in Modern Zululand.' *Bantu Studies* 14(1): 147–174.

Goffman, E. (1961). *Asylums: Essays on the Social Situation of Mental Patients and Other Inmates*. Garden City, N.Y, Anchor Books.

Goody, J. (1977). *The Domestication of the Savage Mind*. Cambridge, Cambridge University Press.

Gore, J. (2003). 'What We Can Do for You! What Can "We" Do for "You"?: Struggling over Empowerment in Critical and Feminist Pedagogy.' *The Critical Pedagogy Reader*. A. Darder, M. Baltodano and R. D. Torres. New York, Routledge.

Graff, G. and Birkenstein, C. (2006). *'They Say/I Say': The Moves that Matter in Academic Writing*. New York, W. W. Norton.

Gupta, A. and Ferguson, J. (1997). *Culture, Power, Place: Explorations in Critical Anthropology*. Durham, Duke University Press.

Hammersley, M. (1992). *What's Wrong with Ethnography? Methodological Explorations*. London, Routledge.

Hammersley, M. (1995). *The Politics of Social Research*. London, Sage.

Hammersley, M. and Atkinson, P. (1983). *Ethnography: Principles in Practice*. London, Tavistock.

Hammersley, M. and Atkinson, P. (1989). *Ethnography: Principles in Practice*. London, Routledge.

Hammersley, M. and Atkinson, P. (1995). *Ethnography: Principles in Practice*. London, Routledge.

Hammersley, M. and Atkinson, P. (2007). *Ethnography: Principles in Practice*. London, Routledge.

Hammersley, M. (2000). *Taking Sides in Social Research: Essays on Partisanship and Bias*. London, Routledge.

Haraway, D. (1988). 'Situated Knowledges: The Science Question in Feminism and the Privilege of Partial Perspectives' *Feminist Studies* 14(3): 575–599.

Haraway, D. (1999). *Modest Witness@Second Millenium: FemaleMan Meets Oncomouse*. London, Routledge.

Hargreaves, D. (1967). *Social Relations in a Secondary School*. London, Routledge.

Harris, M. (ed.) (2007). *Ways of Knowing: Anthropological Approaches to Crafting Experience and Knowledge*. Oxford, Berghahn Books.

Hatch, J. A. (2007). *Early Childhood Qualitative Research*. New York, Routledge.

Hedgecoe, A. (2008). 'Research Ethics Review and the Sociological Research Relationship." *Sociology* 42: 873–886.

Henig, J. (2008). *Spin Cycle: How Research is Used in Policy Debates: The Case of Charter Schools*. New York, Russell Sage Foundation.

Hey, V. (1997). *The Company She Keeps: An Ethnography of Girls' Friendship*. Buckingham, Open University Press.

Hine, C. (2000). *Virtual Ethnography*. London, Sage.

Hine, C. (eds.) (2005). *Virtual Methods: Issues in Social Research on the Internet*. Oxford, Berg.

Hobbs, D. and Wright, R. (2006). *The Sage Handbook of Fieldwork*. London, Sage.

Holmes, D. R. and Marcus, G. E. (2006). 'Fast Capitalism: Para-ethnography and the Rise of the Symbolic Analyst.' *Frontiers of Capital: Ethnographic Reflections on the New Economy*. M. Fisher and G. Downey. Durham, Duke University Press.

Hostetler, J. A. and Huntington, G. E. (1971). *Children in Amish Society: Socialization and Community Education*. New York, Holt, Rinehart and Winston.

Howell, S. and Talle, A. (2012). *Returns to the Field: Multitemporal Research and Contemporary Anthropology*. Bloomington, Ind., Indiana University Press.

Howes, D. (1991). *The Varieties of Sensory Experience: A Sourcebook in the Anthropology of the Senses*. Toronto; London, University of Toronto Press.

Humphreys, L. (1970). *Tearoom Trade: A Study of Homosexual Encounters in Public Places*. London, Duckworth.

Hunter, I. (1994). *Rethinking the School: Subjectivity, Bureaucracy, Criticism*. New York, St Martins Press.

Inda, J. (2006). *Anthropologies of Modernity: Foucault, Governmentality, and Life Politics*. Oxford, Blackwell.

Ingold, T. and Vergunst, J. L. (2008). *Ways of Walking: Ethnography and Practice on Foot*. Farnham, Ashgate.

Israel, M. and Hay, I. (2006). *Research Ethics for Social Scientists: Between Ethical Conduct and Regulatory Compliance*. London, Sage.

Jackson, J. (1990). 'I Am a Fieldnote.' *Fieldnotes: The Makings of Anthropology*. R. Sanjek. Ithaca, Cornell University Press.

Jackson, M. (1983). 'Thinking Through the Body: An Essay on Understanding Metaphor.' *Social Analysis* 14: 127–148.

James, M. (2006). Assessment, Teaching and Theories of Learning. *Assessment and Learning*. J. M. Gardner. London, Sage.

Jeffrey, C. (2010). *Timepass: Youth, Class, and the Politics of Waiting in India*. Stanford, Calif., Stanford University Press.

Jeffrey, C. and Dyson, J. (2008). *Telling Young Lives: Portraits in Global Youth*. Philadelphia, PA, Temple University Press.

Jeffrey, C., Jeffery, P. and Jeffrey, C. (2008). *Degrees Without Freedom? Education, Masculinities and Unemployment in North India*. Stanford, Calif., Stanford University Press.

Johnson, C. (1943). 'Education and the Cultural Process: Introduction to Symposium.' *American Journal of Sociology* 48(6): 629–632.

Kamler, B. and Thomson, P. (2006). *Helping Doctoral Students Write: Pedagogies for Supervision*. London, Routledge.

Kamler, B. and Thomson, P. (2008). 'The Failure of Dissertation Advice Books: Toward Alternative Pedagogies for Doctoral Writing.' *Educational Researcher* 37(8): 507–514.

Kane, T. (2012). 'Transplanting Education: A Case Study of the Production of "American-style" Doctors in a Non-American Setting.' Edinburgh: University of Edinburgh. PhD.

Kaplan, S. (2006). *The Pedagogical State: Education and the Politics of National Culture in Post-1980 Turkey*. Palo Alto, Stanford University Press.

Kendall, L. (2002). *Hanging Out in the Virtual Pub: Masculinities and Relationships Online*. Berkeley, UCP.

Kenway, J. and Fahey, J. (2008). 'Imagining Research Otherwise.' *Globalising the Research Imagination*. J. Kenway and J. Fahey. London, Routledge.

Kenway, J. and Fahey, J. (2009). *Globalizing the Research Imagination*. Milton Park, Abingdon, Oxon; New York, NY, Routledge.

Kipnis, A. B. (2011). *Governing Educational Desire: Culture, Politics, and Schooling in China*. Chicago, Ill. London, University of Chicago Press.

Knorr-Cetina, K. (1999). *Epistemic Cultures: How the Sciences Make Knowledge*. Cambridge, MA, Harvard University Press.

Kozinets, R. V. (2010). *Netnography: Doing Ethnographic Research Online*. London, Sage.

Kvale, S. (2009). *InterView: Learning the Craft of Qualitative Research Interviewing*. Los Angeles, Sage.

Lacey, C. (1970). *Hightown Grammar*. Manchester, MUP.

Lambart, A. (1976). 'The Sisterhood.' *The Process of Schooling*. M. Hammersley and P. Woods. London, Routledge.

Lancy, D. (2008). *The Anthropology of Childhood: Cherubs Chattel and Changelings* Cambridge, Cambridge University Press.

Latour, B. and Woolgar, S. (1979). *Laboratory Life: The Social Construction of Scientific Facts*. Beverly Hills, Sage.

Law, J. (2004). *After Method: Mess in Social Science Research*. London, Routledge.

Lawrence-Lightfoot, S. (1983). *The Good High School: Portraits of Character and Culture*. New York, Basic Books.

LeCompte, M. D. and Schensul, J. J. (2010). *Designing & Conducting Ethnographic Research: An Introduction*. Lanham, Md., AltaMira Press.

Lee, W. and Carr, M. (2012). *Learning Stories: Constructing Learner Identities in Early Education*. London, Sage.

Levinson, B. A., Foley, D. E. and Holland, D. C. (eds.) (1996). *The Cultural Production of the Educated Person: Critical Ethnographies of Schooling and Local Practice*. Albany, SUNY Press.

Levinson, B. A., Borman, M., Eisenhart and Foster, M. (eds.) (2000). *Schooling the Symbolic Animal: Social and Cultural Dimensions of Education*. Oxford, Rowman and Littlefield.

Levinson, B. A. and Pollock, M. (eds.) (2011). *A Companion to the Anthropology of Education*. Oxford, Wiley-Blackwell.

Lewins, A. and Silver, C. (2005). *Choosing a CAQDAS Package*. Unpublished working paper (3rd edition) Guilford, University of Surrey.

Luker, K. (2008). *Salsa Dancing into the Social Sciences: Research in an Age of Info-glut*. Cambridge, Mass. London, Harvard University Press.

Lukes, S. (1973). *Emile Durkheim, his Life and Work: A Historical and Critical Study*. London, Allen Lane.

Lukose, R. A. (2009). *Liberalization's Children: Gender, Youth, and Consumer Citizenship in Globalizing India*. Durham, Duke University Press.

Lutkehaus, W. (1990). 'Refractions of Reality: On the Use of Other Ethnographers' Fieldnotes.' *Fieldnotes: The Makings of Anthropology*. R. Sanjek. Ithaca, Cornell University Press.

Luttrell, W. (2010). *Qualitative Educational Research: Readings in Reflexive Methodology and Transformative Practice*. New York, Routledge.

MacMillan, K. (2005). 'More Than Just Coding? Evaluating CAQDAS in a Discourse Analysis of News Texts. Forum Qualitative Sozialforschung / Forum: Qualitative Social Research Volume 6, No. 3, Art. 25.' *Forum Qualitative Sozialforschung / Forum: Qualitative Social Research* 6(3): 25.

Madden, R. (2010). *Being Ethnographic: A Guide to the Theory and Practice of Ethnography*. London, Sage.

Madison, D. S. (2012). *Critical Ethnography: Method, Ethics, and Performance*. London, Sage.

Malinowski, B. (1922). *Argonauts of the Western Pacific: An Account of Native Enterprise and Adventure in the Archipelagoes of Melanesian New Guinea*. London, George Routledge and Sons.

Malinowski, B. (1936). 'Native Education and Culture Contact.' *International Review of Missions* 25: 480–515.

Malinowski, B. (1943). 'The Pan-African Problem of Culture Contact.' *The American Journal of Sociology* 48(6): 649–665.

Malinowski, B. (1967). *A diary in the Strict Sense of the Term*. New York, Harcourt, Brace and World.

Malkki, L. H. (1989). *Purity and Exile: Transformations in Historical-national Consciousness Among Hutu Refugees in Tanzania*. Harvard University, PhD.

Marcus, G. (1995). 'Ethnography in/of the World System: The Emergence of Multi-Sited Ethnography.' *Annual Review of Anthropology* 24: 95–117.

Marcus, G. (1998). 'The Once and Future Ethnographic Archive.' *History of the Human Sciences* 11(4): 49–63.

Marcus, G. (2006). 'Where Have All the Tales of Fieldwork Gone?' *Ethnos* 71(1): 113–122.

Marcus, G. (2007). 'How Short Can Fieldwork Be?' *Social Anthropology* 15(3): 353–357.

Marcus, G. (2009). 'Notes Towards an Ethnographic Memoir of Supervising Graduate Research Through Anthropology's Decades of Transformation.' *Fieldwork is Not What It Used to Be: Learning Anthropology's Method in a Time of Transition*. J. Faubion. Cornell, Cornell University Press: 1–32.

Mason, J. (2002). *Qualitative Researching*. London, Sage.

Mauss, M. (1934). 'Les Techniques du Corps.' *Journal de Psychologie* 32: 3–4.

Mauss, M. (1990 [1926]). *The Gift: The Form and Reason for Exchange in Archaic Societies*. London, Routledge.

McIntyre, A. (2008). *Participatory Action Research*. London, Sage.

McKenna, B. (2011). 'How Will Gillian Tett Connect With the Natives of the US Left?' *Counterpunch*. 4 March 2011. Downloaded from www.counterpunch.org 04.11.12.

Mead, M. (1928). *Coming of Age in Samoa*. New York, W Morrow and Company.

Mead, M. (1951). *The School in American Culture*. Cambridge: Harvard University Press.

Mertens, D. M. and Ginsberg, P. E. (2009). *The Handbook of Social Research Ethics*. London, Sage.

Middleton, J. (1970). *From Child to Adult: Studies in the Anthropology of Education*. Garden City, N.Y. Published for the American Museum of Natural History [by] the Natural History Press.

Mills, D. (1999a). '"The Nation's Valiant Fighters Against Illiteracy": Locations of Learning and Progress.' *Social Analysis* 43(1): 3–17.

Mills, D. (1999b). 'Progress as Discursive Spectacle: But What Comes After Development?' *Modernity on a Shoestring: Dimensions of Globalisation, Consumption and Development in Africa and Beyond*. R. Fardon, W. V. Bimsbergen and R. V. Dijk. London and Leiden, EIDOS (European Inter-University Development Opportunities Study Group): 91–116.

Mills, D. (2003). '"Like a Horse in Blinkers?" A Political History of Anthropology's Research Ethics.' *The Ethics of Anthropology: Debates and Dilemmas*. P. Caplan. London, Routledge.

Mills, D. (2003). 'Relativism and Cultural Studies.' *Think: The Journal of the Royal Institute of Philosophy* 1(3): 29–32.

Mills, D. (2005). 'Made in Manchester? Methods and Myths in Disciplinary History.' *Social Analysis* 49(3): 129–143.

Mills, D. (2008). *Difficult Folk: A Political History of Social Anthropology*. Oxford, Berghahn.

Mills, D. and Gibb, R. (2000). 'Centre and Periphery: An Interview with Paul Willis.' *Cultural Anthropology* 16(3): 388–414.

Mills, D. and Ratcliffe, R. (2012). 'After Method: Anthropology, Education and the Knowledge Economy.' *Qualitative Research* 12(2): 147–164.

Mills, D. and Ssewakiryanga, R. (2002). '"That Beijing Thing": Challenging Transnational Feminisms in Kampala.' *Gender, Place and Culture: A Journal of Feminist Geography* 9(4): 385–398.

Mills, D. and Ssewakiryanga, R. (2004). 'No Romance Without Finance: Masculinities, Commodities and HIV in Uganda.' *Readings in Gender in Africa*. A. Cornwall. Oxford, James Currey Ltd.

Miner, H. (1953). 'Body ritual amongst the Nacirema.' *American Anthropologist* 58(3): 503–505.

Ministry of Education (2009). *Narrative Assessment: A Guide for Teachers*. Wellington, New Zealand.

Mitchell, T. (2002). *Rule of Experts: Egypt, Techno-politics, Modernity*. Berkeley, University of California Press.

ML White (2009) 'Ethnography 2.0: Writing with Digital Video,' *Ethnography and Education* 4(3): 389–414.

Moffatt, M. (1989). *Coming of Age in New Jersey: College and American Culture*. New Brunswick, NJ, Rutgers University Press.

Mosse, D. (2005). *Cultivating Development: An Ethnography of Aid Policy and Practice*. London, Pluto Press.

Mosse, D. (2011). *Adventures in Aidland*. London, Pluto Press.

Murchison, J. M. (2010). *Ethnography Essentials: Designing, Conducting, and Presenting Your Research*. San Francisco, Jossey-Bass.

Myers, N. (2008). 'Molecular Embodiments and the Body-work of Modelling in Protein Crystallography.' *Social Studies of Science* 38(2): 163–199.

Nader, L. (1974). 'Up the Anthropologist — Perspectives Gained From Studying Up.' *Reinventing Anthropology*. D. Hymes. New York, Vintage Books.

Nambissan, G. and Ball, S. J. (2010). 'Advocacy Networks, Choice and Schooling of the Poor in India.' *Global Networks: A Journal of Transnational Affairs* 10(3): 324–343.

Narayan, K. (1993). 'How Native is this Native Anthropologist?' *American Anthropologist* 95(3): 671–686.

Nathan, R. (2005). *My Freshman Year: What a Professor Learnt by Becoming a Student*. Ithaca, Cornell University Press.

Ness, K. (2008). 'Computer Assisted Qualitative Data Analysis Software (CAQDAS): A Personal View' Unpublished paper.

Neve, G. and Unnithan-Kumar, M. (2006). *Critical Journeys: The Making of Anthropologists*. Maidenhead, Ashgate.

Neyland, D. (2007). *Organisational Ethnography*. London, Sage.

Nolan, R. (2003). *Anthropology in Practice*. Boulder, Col. Lynne Riener Publishers Inc.

O'Reilly, K. (2009). *Key Concepts in Ethnography*. London, Sage.

O'Reilly, K. (2011). *Ethnographic Methods*. London, Routledge.

Okely, J. (2007). 'Response to George Marcus "How short can fieldwork be?".' *Social Anthropology* 15(3): 357–361.

Orton-Johnson, K. (2010) 'Ethics in Online Research; Evaluating the ESRC Framework for Research Ethics Categorisation of Risk.' *Sociological Research Online* 15(4): 13.

Pelto, G. and Pelto, H. (1978). *Anthropological Research: The Structure of Inquiry*. Cambridge, Cambridge University Press.

Perec, G. (2010 [1974]). *An Attempt at Exhausting a Place in Paris (Translated by Marc Lowenthal)*. Cambridge, MA, Wakefield Press.

Peshkin, A. (1972). *Kanuri Schoolchildren; Education and Social Mobilization in Nigeria*. New York; London, Holt, Rinehart and Winston.

Peshkin, A. (1986). *God's Choice: The Total World of a Fundamentalist Christian School*. Chicago, University of Chicago Press.

Peshkin, A. (2001). *Permissible Advantage? The Moral Consequences of Elite Schooling*. Mahwah, New Jersey, Lawrence Erlbaum.

Peterson, K. (2009). 'Phantom Epistemologies.' *Fieldwork is Not What It Used to Be: Learning Anthropology's Method in a Time of Transition*. J. D. Faubion and G. E. Marcus. Ithaca; London, Cornell University Press: xiv, 231 p.

Pink, S. (eds.) (2006). *Applications of Anthropology: Professional Anthropology in the Twenty-first Century*. Oxford, Berghahn.

Pink, S. (2007). *Doing Visual Ethnography: Images, Media and Representation in Research*. London, Sage.

Pink, S. (2009). *Doing Sensory Ethnography*. Los Angeles; London, Sage.

Pink, S. (2010). *What is Sensory Ethnography? An NCRM Working Paper*. Southampton, NCRM.

Pole, C. and Morrison, M. (2003). *Ethnography for Education*. Buckingham, Open University Press.

Powdermaker, H. (1966). *Stranger and Friend*. London, Secker and Warburg.

Price, D. (2008). *Anthropological Intelligence: The Deployment and Neglect of American Anthropology in the Second World War*. Durham, Duke University Press.

Price, D. (2010). 'Blogging Anthropology: Savage Minds, Zero Anthropology, and AAA Blogs.' *American Anthropologist* 112(1): 140–148.

Rabinow, P., Marcus, G. E., Faubion, J. and Rees, T. (2008). *Designs for an Anthropology of the Contemporary*. Durham, Duke University Press.

Radcliffe-Brown, A. R. (1938). 'Applied Anthropology.' *Oxford University Summer School in Colonial Administration*. Oxford, Oxford University Press.

Read, M. (1955). *Education and Social Change in Tropical Areas*. London; New York, Thomas Nelson.

Read, M. (1959). *Children of their Fathers: Growing Up Among the Ngoni of Nyasaland*. London, Methuen.

Reed-Danahay, D. (1996). *Education and Identity in Rural France: The Politics of Schooling*. Cambridge, Cambridge University Press.

Riles, A. (eds.) (2006). *Documents: Artifacts of Modern Knowledge*. Ann Arbor, University of Michigan Press.

Rizvi, F. (2009). 'Mobile Minds.' *Globalizing the Research Imagination*. J. Kenway and J. Fahey. Milton Park, Abingdon, Oxon; New York, NY, Routledge: viii, 144 p.

Robben, A. C. G. M. and Sluka, J. A. (2007). *Ethnographic Fieldwork: An Anthropological Reader*. Malden, MA; Oxford, Blackwell.

Rosaldo, R. (1989). *Culture and Truth: Remaking Social Analysis*. Stanford, Stanford University Press.

Rose, N. S. (1999). *Powers of Freedom: Reframing Political Thought*. Cambridge, Cambridge University Press.

Rose, N. S. (1999). *Governing the Soul: The Shaping of the Private Self*. London, Free Association.

Sanford, V. and Angel-Ajani, A. (2006). *Engaged Observer: Anthropology, Advocacy and Activism*. London, Rutgers University Press.

Sanjek, R. (ed.) (1990). *Fieldnotes: The Makings of Anthropology*. Ithaca, Cornell University Press.

Savage, M. (2008). *Identities and Social Change in Britain Since 1940: The Politics of Method*. Oxford, Oxford University Press.

Schensul, J. J. and LeCompte, M. D. (1999). *The Ethnographer's Toolkit*. Walnut Creek, Calif., AltaMira Press.

Schensul, J. L. (ed.) (2011). 'Building an Applied Educational Anthropology.' *A Companion to the Anthropology of Education*. B. A. Levinson and M. Pollock. Oxford, Wiley-Blackwell.

Schumaker, L. (2001). *Africanising Anthropology: Fieldwork, Networks and the Making of Cultural Knowledge in Central Africa*. Durham, Duke University Press.

Scott Jones, J. and Watt, S. (2010). *Ethnography in Social Science Practice*. London, Routledge.

Shore, C. (2008). 'Audit Culture and Illiberal Governance: Universities and the Politics of Accountability.' *Anthropological Theory* 8(3): 278–298.

Shore, C. and Wright, S. (eds.) (1997). *Anthropology of Policy: Critical Perspectives on Governance and Power*. London, Routledge.

Shore, C., Wright, S., Pero, D. (2011). *Policy Worlds: Anthropology and the Analysis of Contemporary Power*. Oxford, Berghahn.

Shostak, M. (2000). *Return to Nisa*. Cambridge, MA; London, Harvard University Press.

Shostak, M. and Nisa (1988). *Nisa: The Life and Words of a !Kung Woman*. New York, Vintage Books.

Sin, C. H. (2005). 'Seeking Informed Consent: Reflections on Research Practice.' *Sociology* 39(2): 277–294.

Smith, D. E. (2005). *Institutional Ethnography: A Sociology for People*. Walnut Creek, CA, AltaMira Press.

Spencer, D. and Davies, J. (eds.) (2010). *Anthropological Fieldwork: A Relational Process*. Cambridge Cambridge Scholars Press.

Spindler, G. and Hammond, L. (2006). *Innovations in Educational Ethnography: Theories, Methods, and Results*. New York, Routledge.

Spindler, G. and Spindler, L. (1971). *Dreamers without Power: The Menomini Indians*. New York, Holt, Rinehart and Winston.

Spindler, G. D. (1974). *Education and Cultural Process; Toward an Anthropology of Education*. New York, Holt, Rinehart and Winston.

Srivastava, P. and Hopwood, N. (2009). 'A Practical Iterative Framework for Qualitative Data Analysis.' *International Journal of Qualitative Methods* 8(1): 76–84.

Stambach, A. (2000). *Lessons from Mount Kilimanjaro: Schooling, Community, and Gender in East Africa*. New York, Routledge.

Stambach, A. (2010). *Faith in Schools: Religion, Education and American Evangelicals in East Africa*. Palo Alto, Stanford University Press.

Stenhouse, L. (1967). *Culture and Education*. London, Nelson.

Stenhouse, L. (1975). *An Introduction to Curriculum Research and Development*. London, Heinemann Educational.

Stirling, P. (1965). *Turkish Village*. London, Weidenfield and Nicholson.

Stocking, G. (1960). 'Franz Boas and the Founding of the American Anthropological Association.' *American Anthropologist* 62(1): 1–17.

Stocking, G. (1987). *Victorian Anthropology*. New York, Free Press.

Stoller, P. (1997). *Sensuous Scholarship*. Philadelphia, University of Pennsylvania Press.

Strathern, M. (1997). '"Improving Ratings": Audit in the British University System.' *European Review* 5(3): 305–321.

Strathern, M. (ed.) (2000). *Audit Cultures: Anthropological Studies in Accountability, Ethics and the Academy*. London, Routledge.

Strathern, M. (2004). *Commons and Borderlands: Working Papers on Interdisciplinarity, Accountability and the Flow of Knowledge*. Wantage, Sean Kingston Publishing.

Strauss, A. L. (1987). *Qualitative Analysis for Social Scientists*. Cambridge, Cambridge University Press.

Stubbs, M. and Delamont, S. (eds.) (1976). *Explorations in Classroom Observation*. Chichester, John Wiley and Sons.

Summerfield, P. (1985). 'Mass-Observation: Social Research or Social Movement?' *Journal of Contemporary History* 20: 439–452.

Taussig, M. (2011). *I Swear I Saw This: Drawings in Fieldwork Notebooks, Namely My Own*. Chicago, University of Chicago Press.

Taylor, S. (2002). *Ethnographic Research: A Reader*. London, Sage.

Tedlock, B. (2005). The Observation of Participation and the Emergence of Public Ethnography. *The SAGE Handbook of Qualitative Research*. N. Denzin. London, Sage: pp. 467–481.

Tett, G. (2009). *Fool's Gold: How Unrestrained Greed Corrupted a Dream, Shattered Global Markets and Unleashed a Catastrophe.* London, Abacus.

Thomas, G. and James, D. (2006). 'Reinventing Grounded Theory: Some Questions about Theory, Ground and Discovery.' *British Educational Research Journal.* 32(6): 767–795.

Thomas, W. I. and Znaniecki, F. (1918). *The Polish Peasant in Europe and America: Monograph of an Immigrant Group.* Boston, The Gorham Press.

Thomson, R. and J. Holland (2012). 'Memory Books as a Methodological Resource in Biographical Research.' *Handbook of Qualitative Research in Education.* S. Delamont. Cheltenham, Edward Elgar.

Thornton, R. (1988). 'The Rhetoric of Ethnographic Holism.' *Cultural Anthropology* 3(3): 285–303.

Tiger, L. and Fox, R. (1972). *The Imperial Animal.* London, Secker and Warburg.

Tilley, H. (2011). *Africa as a Living Laboratory: Empire, Development, and the Problem of Scientific Knowledge, 1870–1950.* Chicago; London, University of Chicago Press.

Tobin, J. (1990). 'The Human Relations Area File as Radical Text?' *Cultural Anthropology* 5(4): 473–487.

Tooley, J. (2012). *From Village School to Global Brand: Changing the World Through Education.* London, Profile.

Tuchman, G. (2009). *Wannabe U: Inside the Corporate University.* Chicago, University of Chicago Press.

Turkle, S. (1984). *The Second Self: Computers and the Human Spirit.* London, Granada.

Turkle, S. (2011). *Alone Together: Why we Expect More from Technology and Less from Each Other.* New York, Basic Books.

Van Maanen, J. (1988). *Tales of the Field: On Writing Ethnography.* Chicago, University of Chicago Press.

Walford, G. (1991). *Private Schooling: Tradition, Change, and Diversity.* London, Paul Chapman.

Walford, G. (1993). *The Private Schooling of Girls: Past and Present.* London, Woburn.

Walford, G. (1994). *Researching the Powerful in Education.* London, UCL Press.

Walford, G. (1998). *Doing Research About Education.* London, Falmer Press.

Walford, G. (2001). *Ethnography and Education Policy.* London, JAI.

Walford, G. (2003). *Investigating Educational Policy Through Ethnography.* London, JAI.

Walford, G. (ed.) (2008). 'How to do Educational Ethnography.' *Ethnography and Education.* London, Tufnell Press.

Walford, G. (2011). 'The Oxford Ethnography Conference: A Place in History?' *Ethnography and Education* 6(2): 133–145.

Waterston, A. and Vesperi, M. D. (2009). *Anthropology Off the Shelf: Anthropologists on Writing.* Chichester, Wiley-Blackwell.

Weber, M. (1948). 'Science as a Vocation.' *From Max Weber: Essays in Sociology.* H. Gerth and C. W. Mills. London, Routledge and Kegan Paul.

Weis, L. and Fine, M. (2000). *Speed Bumps: A Student-friendly Guide to Qualitative Research.* New York, Teachers College Press.

Weis, L. and Fine, M. (2004). *Working Method: Research and Social Justice.* New York; London, Routledge.

Whiting, B. and Whiting, J. (1975). *Children of Six Cultures: A Psycho-Cultural Analysis.* Cambridge, Mass, Harvard University Press.

Wilby, P. (2009). 'Intellectual guru seeks' "system redesign" of secondary education.' *The Guardian.* London. 22 September 2009.

Willis, P. (1977). *Learning to Labour: Why Working Class Kids Get Working Class Jobs.* Farnborough, Saxon House.

Willis, P. (1978). *Profane Culture.* London, Routledge and Kegan Paul.

Willis, P. (1990). *Moving Culture: An Enquiry into the Cultural Activities of Young People.* London, Gulbenkian Foundation.

Willis, P. (1996). 'TIES: Theoretically Informed Ethnographic Studies.' *Anthropology and Cultural Studies.* S. Nugent and C. Shore. London, Pluto Press.

Willis, P. (2000). *The Ethnographic Imagination.* Oxford, Polity Press.

Willis, P., Bekenn, A., Ellis, T. and Whitt, D. (1988). *The Youth Review: Social Conditions of Young People in Wolverhampton.* Aldershot, Avebury.

Wolcott, H. F. (1967). *A Kwakiutl Village and School.* London, Holt, Rinehart and Winston.

Wolcott, H. F. (1973). *The Man in the Principal's Office: An Ethnography.* Walnut Creek, CA, AltaMira.

Wolcott, H. F. (1994). *Transforming Qualitative Data: Description, Analysis and Interpretation.* London, Sage.

Wolcott, H. F. (2008). *Ethnography: A Way of Seeing.* Lanham, MD, AltaMira Press.

Woronov, T. E. (2004). 'In the Eye of the Chicken: Hierarchy and Marginality Among Beijing's Migrant Schoolchildren.' *Ethnography* 5: 289–314.

Yon, D. (2003). 'Highlights and Overview of the History of Educational Ethnography.' *Annual Review of Anthropology* 32: 411–429.

Young, M. F. D. (1971). *Knowledge and Control: New Directions for the Sociology of Education.* London, Collier Macmillan.

Young, M. W. (2004). *Malinowski: Odyssey of an Anthropologist 1884–1920.* New Haven, Yale University Press.

INDEX